Democratic Political Economy

PRINCIPLES OF ECONOMIC FREEDOM

Tonderai Chitauro

ISBN: 1499763247
ISBN 13: 978-1499763249

This book is dedicated to my wife, to my two children, and to my mother; to all who are poor, landless, enslaved, underprivileged, and oppressed; and to all such people as seek for economic freedom.

Table of Contents

Democratic Political Economy

Preface and Foreword

"Taxodus"

The song "Exodus" by Bob Marley has a question that I believe every generation should often pause and ask itself: "Are you satisfied with the life you're living? If at any time the majority are to answer that they are not satisfied, the next step should be to identify the issues that are causing the dissatisfaction and, from an eagle's viewpoint, consider what solutions can bring everyone to a better situation.

It is often the case that a total reconfiguration of systems of governance, politics and economics and philosophy is required to ensure that the new replaces the old state of things, and that process requires an honest desire to emancipate all people from their troubles.

A serious people should therefore determine the course of their escape from a system that is not working to a new system set up to bring and sustain their freedom. The call presented in this book is therefore a call to the people of the world to move to a new system of democratic political economics in which the economic systems, structures and monetary systems and governance structures are pro-people. At the heart of all current political economy issues however is the issue of taxation, namely tax systems that are in no way progressive and that are shackling most taxpayers in a cycle of poverty and slavery. The loosening of these tax chains will lead to an actual exodus of the majority of the world people from poverty and slavery into a better life.

In setting out to make the reader to understand fully the current Egypt and the future Canaan, it is necessary to go about explaining all components of political economics and with the full understanding, to then delve into the important conclusions that come from that understanding. . The book therefore sets out the background of all current oppression, seen and unseen. It calls on all and sundry to take up the fight for a better life and to make flight to a better place and time. It is a call for the captives to be freed and such a movement of tax reformation throughout the world as would cause a deliverance of exodus proportions. All countries and rulers should hear the call for a taxodus, a setting free of overtaxed citizens, a more democratic administration of the tax revenues, and equality and justice for all peoples.

I

Introduction

Tracing and Setting Out the Problems

The most pressing questions facing our world today are economic in nature, and issues such as inequality, unemployment, and poverty dominate all forms of political and economic discourse. Even though we live in an era of technological and scientific advances, involving huge leaps in knowledge and science, the world is faced with problems none of these advances seems able to solve. The recipe for economic prosperity has long been regarded as the correct political system coupled with a free market capitalist economic system with little or no government interference. This dish has been served in various forms and it has of late proved insufficient to feed all the hungry and to provide employment to all the labour and to leave enough for everyone. It's a truth held in political economy that if given the freedom, a man's life labour will be sufficient to provide for him all things that he needs, basic plus luxury, and that the same applies to a nation. So whether one finds themselves in poverty, in debt, or in any form of want, the labour of one's life offers the best chance to emancipation from such misfortune. While the world seeks to have everyone and every nation presented with opportunities to achieve their dreams, the majority of its inhabitants continue to live in a never-ending nightmare of struggle and crushed hopes. One is left with the sobering thought that it's not for a want of scientific advancement or of technological backwardness that we've such economic gloom, but that it's because of the misapplication of opportunities, time, talents, and other labour and resources. Instead of industry, unemployment has been allowed to take away the food from the table; instead of happiness, joy and gladness, there's hunger, misery and strife.

Economics and politics, the chief determinants of how resources and opportunities are allocated, don't seem to have evolved in the same direction and at the same pace. Governance has moved towards democracy, a concept that has not been fully put into practice and in its current state, democracy seems to frustrate and not fully satisfy those who've experienced it.

This book seeks to look at and to think differently on issues, using a framework built upon the ideals of equity, fairness, and democracy. The writer of this treatise is persuaded in a great way that the foundation of most of the current political and economic problems lie in the historical forms of economic and political structures that current "democratic" governments have inherited and slightly adapted to suit the present dispensation of capitalistic and pluralistic democracy. The pillars of the arguments in this book are founded on the ground that the authoritarian rule of the old kings (and queens) hasn't been corrected by democracy but has been cosmetically manicured by a system that pretends to be democratic but that retains all the trappings of kingly authority and rule. The economic policies of the former kings, centralised around the king, have also been merely made more efficient to serve our new kings.

The majority of the questions that bedevil political economy today can therefore be traced back to the formation of the current political and economic systems, and the solutions can be derived by understanding the factors that existed in the time then and how they influenced the resultant politics and economics together with the accompanying structures and legal systems. Most of the countries of the English, French and Spanish commonwealths were formed and ruled to advance the kingdoms of the respective monarchs. Even though political independence has been granted to a majority of them, the legal systems, economic policies, and practices of the former colonisers have largely remained in place. For example Roman-Dutch law remains the law of most former British colonies like South Africa, Zimbabwe, Zambia, and Malawi, to mention a few countries. The tax laws of the United Kingdom, Zimbabwe, Zambia, South Africa has remained so unchanged that case law in any of the countries has often been accepted in the other countries.

The former kings of most currently democratic nations had absolute power and control when it came to the economy and wealth of their kingdoms, their words were final and binding, and everyone paid tribute and taxes to them. The king decided the size of his government and the magnitude of expenditure to maintain his rule over the kingdom. Modern society has created new kings, a few in numbers but one in purpose and intent to rule the kingdoms. The laws of the kings have been carefully adapted to continue to benefit modern kings and their nobility. To give the new kingdoms a semblance of democracy, elections are held periodically (usually every five years) to re-elect the same kings. Kingship is no longer hereditary, but the wealth, authority and power that comes with that, is still hereditary and doesn't leave the grasp of the new kings and their new nobility.

Democratic Political Economy

The issues detailed in this book are closely related and have been separated into chapters for ease of argument and for ease of reading. The reader is requested to indulge the writer with patience while going through these sections which are required to get an understanding of the arguments. These issues include but aren't limited to the following main arguments:

- Economic systems: The current economic systems were designed and put in place in an era of kings (and subjects) and were best suited for those eras. These systems are no longer relevant in democratic societies. New economic systems suitable for democratic politics are needed.

- Economic structures: These, like the economic systems, were designed and meant to protect and serve the kings' privileges and inheritance lineages and have since become obsolete. Pro-entrepreneurship structures are required.

- The political systems: These have lagged behind and have not harnessed the scientific and technological advances to make democracy more participatory and responsive. The result has been largely autocratic governments and corporate systems that have autocratic power. Democracy shouldn't be limited to a five-year election instalment on political leadership only but should be expanded to annual participation in economic and political decisions.

- The monetary systems: These have remained archaic and steeped in central control and have led to autocratic economic decisions that have deprived the majority and benefited those with power (both financial and political). The quantity and the printing of currency can't be trusted to a government but should be a transparent democratic decision. Government borrowing and similar activities should also be limited to democratic participation.

- Inflation: Caused by excessive currency printing and unchecked government debt, it's occurred without regard to sound financial management and has ruined the savings and wealth of the poor majority. Inflation is a hidden tax by the government, and such purloining should be checked by a democratic political economy.

- Excessive taxation: The level of taxation, which for some countries can go as high as 70 per cent for working individuals. Larger tax revenues are needed for funding bloated governments and these taxes have acted to burden a yoke on the majority and to give the wealth of this majority to a few rich people (who are taxed at effective rates of less than 20 per cent). So-called "progressive" taxes are actually regressive and are the reason why a majority of educated and skilled workers have remained poor, excluded from economic freedom, and why they'll retire with miserable pensions, having slaved their lives for other masters' well-being, not their own.

- Individual taxation on gross income: Individuals have been unfairly burdened to fund the government compared to companies, and this has resulted in ever-increasing inequalities where the rich have become richer and the poorer are being made poorer. Companies are taxed a flat rate of taxation—on net profit (net profit's a very subjective figure in accounting)—while individuals, mostly workers, are taxed at increasing rates up to 45 per cent on average on gross income, not on net income.

- Corporate protection against taxation: Because of the king, nobility, and peasantry/subjects relationship in the current political economy hierarchy, governments don't pay taxes, aren't limited in size by their budget, not by any law.

Corporates and their owners are protected by many laws, structures, and tax systems that guarantee several economic advantages to them, including an effective tax discount on all their costs/expenditure (equivalent to the corporate tax rate for each country which is generally about 30 percent). The corporates pay tax not on their gross incomes, but on an amount determined after deducting all manner of expenses and after deducting generous allowances for all capital expenditure and previous losses, going back as far as five years. The other tax payers, a majority of whom are workers, are the ones who take care of the first two groups, by paying exorbitant taxes on their gross incomes, and of the remaining net salaries, they pay an effective 114 per cent (depending on rate of tax) for every expenditure they do. In total, they pay 44 per cent more for every after-tax expenditure they make than that paid by the corporates and their owners.

- Corporate funding: Jobs and employment creation are by-products of entrepreneurship, and the fascination by governments to create jobs and their pumping of currency into off-layer corporates to probe them into creating jobs is an exercise in futilities. A more geographically and demographically democratic allocation of economic infrastructure would result in more employment created than by stimulation of old dogs.

The issues in this book shouldn't be considered in isolation and should be considered together and attended to in order to achieve an economic order in which everyone has a chance to achieve his or her dreams of economic empowerment through the use of his or her God-given time, talents, opportunities, and rights. A democratic political economy is one in which there is greater public participation in economic and political decisions (such as government size, tax levels, and economic systems), and where the principles of equality and justice are upheld. Furthermore democratic political economy implies that resources and opportunities, production and capital allocation, as well as reward sharing are done in the most equitable manner to enable each economic participant equal chances of success. A worker would therefore stand the same chance of success as a company and get the same level of support, taxation and opportunities.

Political Economy

History of Political Economy

Since the creation of humankind, in one way or the other, the relationship between politics and economics has existed and has been known under a different name at each point in time. The concept of political economy has existed as long as humans have engaged in any form of control over their environments. It's a subject which has rightly engaged the interests of men and women and should continue even more, given the complexities and problems with which we've entangled ourselves as a result of how we're now affecting our environment.

Political economy is, in its basic form, what in the Holy Bible is called stewardship (e.g.,1 Corinthians 4:1) and entails a relationship of accountability on the part of the steward or manager to the one who's entrusted to him or her the role of management over a set of resources. The Old Testament description wherein Adam is commanded to be fruitful and to multiply, to have dominion over the rest of creation (Genesis 1:27), is and should be the root of all teaching on political economy. The manner and means—as well as the principles and the laws—of this accumulation of wealth constitute the subject of political economy.

Democratic Political Economy

Political economy has been shaped by the writings of about three people in recent history, the first being philosopher Adam Smith (1723 to 1790), who pioneered the "the invisible hand," theory which proposes that collectively the individuals in society, each acting in his or her own self-interest, manage to allocate resources, produce and purchase the goods and services that they as a society require and distribute. It is interesting that Smith was writing during the formative days of the theory of evolution and survival of the fittest, the Reformation of the church, and the American independence, when religious and economic freedom were well sought after and highly valued. According to Smith, the invisible hand will guide economic participants, as long as government keeps a laissez-faire attitude toward the invisible hand. The achievement would be to create the greatest wealth for the greatest number of people, and capitalism in its various forms was therefore the economic system that agreed most with Smith's theory.

The second is Karl Marx (1818 to 1883), a German economist and political scientist, whose insight into the inefficiency, instability, inequalities, and exploitative nature of capitalism led him to conclude that the resultant class struggles would ultimately destroy capitalism. He advocated for socialism to replace and overthrow capitalism. Many have argued that Marx's ideas have been proven wrong by pointing out to the failure of the socialist countries to be more efficient than their capitalist contemporaries. One of Marx's main contributions remains his ability to have long discerned the faults of capitalism and some of his insights continue to be relevant today, inspiring, and enduring.

The third economist is John Maynard Keynes (1883 to 1946), an economist who, unlike Marx, did not support the overthrow of capitalism, but, proposed a larger and active role of government in the political economy. The Great Depression, occurring in a capitalist economy convinced the devotees to capitalism to the need of a more visible guide other than the invisible hand. He proposed increased government expenditure to stimulate a consumer demand based economic revival. Most of his economic proposals are still practiced today and stimulus packages and rescue economics continue to be experimented with in various forms.

The three's main contributions to political economy was therefore related to the time period in which they lived, and they offered the best way, and manner a nation could allocate limited means among competing wants in the most efficient way. If Smith created capitalism, Marx challenged it to great effect and Keynes rescued capitalism from Marx. It is important to note at this point that while Keynes argued that government expenditure would put money into private hands; the only hands available in a capitalist economy were capitalist hands. The Keynes injections (hand-outs) tended to be delivered only to capitalists and workers were left to wait for the benefits to trickles down in wages and the questions that Marx asked about class creation, inequalities, and worker exploitation largely remain unanswered. The cyclical nature of growth in capitalism and the instability of the system are questions that need to be addressed.

Accountable Democracy

If democracy means the leaders are accountable to the masses and are in power on behalf of and by appointment from the majority, then a stewardship relationship exists between the king and his subjects, which is to say the government and its people. Such a relationship is one which should be founded on the principles whereby the government accounts to the people and the people decide on the manner of stewardship the government should employ. The relationship assumes a knowledgeable and well-informed majority who will hold to account the steward, and on the other hand, an honest and open leadership willing to be accountable to those who've bestowed the management of the kingdoms into their hands. An ignorant, removed, or oppressed majority or a leader who doesn't answer to the people violates the stewardship model and defeats the principles of accountability, fairness, justice, and equity.

Companies and other corporate entities often make decisions that affect not only their employees but also their customers, surrounding communities, and other stakeholders. Such decisions are often made by a single or a few individuals without any democratic process to enable all the people who will be affected by it to make their concerns, more so to make and be part of the decision-making. The power yielded by corporate owners and company leaders doesn't often meet the democratic standard, and these companies are often autocratic fiefdoms of their respective owners or managers.

The ideals of a democratic political economy require a perfect stewardship relationship in which the involved parties understand their roles and don't seek to usurp the power of others or to change their own roles and responsibilities. If the people are free to call on the government (either political and corporate) to render an account of its stewardship of their tax moneys, the economy, and the wealth of the nation, then the people aren't only politically free but also more economically free. An ability to hold a leader accountable on the part of the people requires a knowledgeable electorate who will participate in the democracy in a meaningful manner and make intelligent assessments of the management of the economy. An autocratic government that answers to no one and isn't accountable to the people has usurped the power reserved for the people as its own and has reversed the stewardship roles that should be in place in a democratic political economy.

Such an authority will be a law unto itself and will govern for its own sake, will judge itself on its success and failure, and won't uphold the stewardship relationship with its people, except in terms of rhetoric and propaganda. The major weapon of such an authority is withholding information and thereby perpetuating the ignorance of the electorate. A call to accountability and democracy is necessary for the government and for the corporate world, and it's the role of government and the corporate leaders to ensure that their respective electorates are economically literate and would make sound and informed decisions.

It's the goal of this book to arm every person with a basic understanding of the political economy and to enable every reader to make decisions that can emancipate him or her from economic autocracy.

Is Democracy a Harbinger of the Elixir?

The history of political economy has tended to show that whenever a people are free, their wealth has tended to multiply more drastically than when they're not free. The development of the Western nations has tended to follow this trend. During the Dark Ages, when the freedoms of the Western people were less than the post-Reformation years, the advancement and development of the people was slow, snail paced and lagging behind. In those countries where there was liberty and freedom of various kinds, even though not complete, the freedoms enabled advancement faster than in those countries that remained in the shadow of the Dark Ages.

Political democracy is said to be a form of government in which all eligible citizens participate equally in one way or another in the governance of a country. At the very least they've a chance to select and/or elect leaders and participate in the processes of constitutional law and other political activities. Democracy has generally been considered the right to exercise political self-determination freely and equally. Such rights are entrenched in the laws of a country and guarantee free social, economic, and cultural conditions that enable the citizens to establish them. Democracy may be described as people or citizen power—majority power—as opposed to kingly or autocratic power—minority power. Democracy should protect the rich as well as the majority from oppression. A democracy doesn't promote elites, favour a few, or discriminate against a class.

People have set themselves free politically and have enjoyed the fruits of political democracy and have also declared their rulers to be democratic. They've attained the right to self-determination and have emancipated themselves from their former oppressors. Wars have been fought and revolutions have come about to establish democracies in formerly undemocratic places, but it's always proved difficult and democracy remains fragile wherever it's established.

In most instances, however, political democracy hasn't resulted in full emancipation. The promises of social utopia, of economic emancipation, and of riches untold have not been fulfilled. A type of democracy exists in this world that is politically fulfilling but economically hollow. Majorities exist today that were declared to be free in name and emancipated in appearance, but they've empty stomachs, constantly grumbling, reminding them of the failure of their supposed freedom. In these cases, democracy failed to deliver its promises. The former slave, the peasant, and the worker are crying for freedom in an apparently free land. They're living in a form of democracy with the trappings but not any substance, enduring an autocracy packaged in democratic rhetoric. The rule of law in such a false democracy protects the rich elites from the poor; the laws in such a democracy hold the laws of demand and supply to be more sacred than the laws of the land. Market forces govern the working of the economy and nothing else. The democracy that people fought for constrains them to respect property rights, private property, profit maximisation, and self-interest of their former oppressors and that of their new rulers.

As a result of extolling democracy and expecting it to deliver freedom, liberation fighters may have got a poisoned chalice. Much to the chagrin of the oppressed, democracy delivered more freedom to the oppressor and less to the oppressed. Thus, political democracy exalts private property rights and the rule of law above all other rights—while it rarely considers history, equality, or equity—only seeking to maintain the status quo.

In developing nations, particularly in Africa, the advent of democracy in its various forms hasn't resulted in the expected prosperity usually attendant on such political structures. The post-liberation-war governments of Africa have grappled with democracies that have not delivered any fruits, particularly economic fruits. The liberation movements across Africa and other developing nations were generally socialist in ideology and economic thought. In achieving independence, these movements have almost all performed a chameleon feat and become capitalist upon assuming power. While clamouring for a change in the economic systems of their oppressors, the former freedom fighters have not proceeded to tear down those economic systems and structures.

These policies have, in various degrees, maintained and implemented the policies and structures that perpetuated the oppressor's dominance and control—to such a degree that it's made the liberation of the oppressed a mere pretence. The oppressor still oppresses where it matters most and where it hurts most, there in the mind and all the way to the stomach. The chains on the feet and the hands have fallen off, but the burdens are still heavy on the shoulders, the slave driver still puts loads on the back, and the mind is still shackled with brute ignorance. The cold chains of slavery upon the neck have made way for the softer silver-golden ropes tied to the hungry stomach of the labourer, which drive him and her to the factory, seeking to answer to its constant pangs.

In the period immediately after political emancipation of every oppressed people, (particularly the abolition of the slave trade and slavery in the Americas and in Europe, the achievement of independence from colonial powers by African, American and Asian nations, and the granting of equal rights to women), there's been a period of unfettered and prolonged celebration of the historic achievement, often because there's nothing meaningful done in the aftermath worth celebrating anyway. When it's dawned later of the need to do something meaningful, there's been a tendency to shy away from the radical and different, but to prolong the familiar and the normal, while offering promises as empty as the past. The reason for this is often that the oppressed are ill prepared for the freedom that they have been granted. However the main reason has often been a malicious neglect on the oppressor to prepare the oppressed for the freedom chiefly because of the underlying economic interests.

Voices—loud and quiet, distant and near—have started to question the democracy, the freedom, and the liberty that have failed to deliver on their promises. These voices clamour for a resumption of the fight for freedom, for the conclusion of the liberation struggle, for the full emancipation of the poor. The majority of the governed have continued in poverty, ignorance, and oppression. They waited for the rain, evident in the pregnant clouds of political emancipation, but a long cold and dry winter was the bargain they got.

Thinking about Them

The plight of the oppressed is often solely the concern of the poor lot, and those not in the same pot think little about the lowly sort. Only when the poverty (and its side effects) begins to affect those outside it, do those outsiders raise an eyelid to look at it. Few realise the danger of such a situation and the danger it brings on the continued existence of not just the poor but even the rich as well. In looking into a democratic political economy, it's important to study the effect of any action, not just at the few who are the subject of the action. The welfare of each individual in an economy is intricately linked in a manner that few seem to perceive. , in setting up any policy, the betterment of both the individual as well as the whole population should be the minimum objective. A majority that exploits and oppresses a minority is as bad as a minority that shackles a majority with oppression. It's a fundamental principle that the welfare of the whole and the constituent parts of the whole are inseparable.

For the preservation of the life and existence of a group, a nation or class of people, there shouldn't be a decrease in the wealth of one part of that group at the expense of the other part, even though the total wealth may have increased. Such a group or nation can't be said to be wealthier or better, wherein one of its part has been made poorer. In seeking a course to follow for increasing the wealth of a nation, the guiding principle should be one which increases the well-being of all component parts of it. Where inequalities aren't addressed and wealth accumulates in the hands of a few while the rest are reduced to poverty, the wealth of the few is at risk. The greatest risk is that the wealth of the whole will fail to increase while it remains idle in a few hands and isn't used efficiently for the nation at large.

Getting to Know Money

The greatest ills in the human pursuit of wealth have come about as a result of the majority of the people in the world not understanding the nature of wealth. Wealth, by definition, may broadly be anything useful in achieving a better state of things than prior to such effort. Usually such things will be exchangeable (for a consideration) and will be useful to the owner or possessor.

Humans have considered wealth to be something other than what it really is, and in so doing have created problems that today appear insurmountable and without solutions. They've assumed currency to be money and have made their decisions about wealth based on currency. They've mistakenly considered currency to be money and have stored their wealth in the form of currency. A correct understanding of wealth is necessary to be able to pursue it, to attain it, and to preserve it—and also to enjoy its fruits.

All Animals Are Equal

Inequality, especially of the type where the rich get increasingly richer and the poor get way poorer, has become a topical issue mainly by politicians seeking to ascend into power. It's the most widespread and most undeniable of facts, ever present and easy to identify in every society the world over. Revolutionaries have ascended to power, riding on the dissatisfaction caused but such a scenario. Perhaps the most eloquent of such arguments was the one said in the speech Nelson Mandela gave at Davos in 1992, unveiling the economic vision that he envisaged for his country and the world, and in the same speech, calling for a society based on freedom and dignity:

The ANC and I personally would like to thank the World Economic Forum most sincerely for inviting us to attend and address this important gathering. We would further like to express our profound appreciation for your decision to allocate time for discussion of the South African question. We believe that your initiative in this regard is most timely.

The impending political transformation of South Africa is part of the truly phenomenal process of renewal which our planet is experiencing. The features of this process are clear enough. They delineate a future in which the peoples, in all countries, will govern themselves under open and plural democratic systems. In our own country this means the end of white minority dictatorship and the building of a new nation of many colours, languages, and cultures, bound together by a common South African patriotism, a shared spirit of nationhood and bonds of mutual dependence.

As in other parts of the world, we, too, will establish a society based on respect for human rights, to ensure the freedom and dignity of every individual, as an inalienable condition of human existence and development.

The new world that is being born foresees the dawn of the age of peace, in which wars within nations, between countries, and among peoples will be a thing of the past.

We need to reach the point where weapons of mass destruction will themselves have been destroyed and the trade in weapons of death will have been reduced to an absolute minimum.

And yet many of these masses, who are freeing themselves from tyranny and expanding the frontiers of liberty, exercising their right to self-determination and committing their lives to the defence of peace and life itself, are themselves threatened by death from starvation. The planet they inhabit faces the awesome menace of destruction as a result of a human-made ecological catastrophe.

I am certain that it is a matter of common cause among us here that the continued impoverishment of millions of people throughout the world has become one of the great sources of global instability. Those who are deprived will inevitably act to demand a better life. The gnawing pain of persistent hunger must, in the end, lead to food riots.

In response, governing authorities that will feel threatened by the rebellion of the masses will resort to repression, to a denial of political rights and a return to a world hostile to freedom. None of us want this.

The migration of people from Central and South America and the Caribbean into the United States, a similar movement of people from Africa, the Near East and Eastern Europe into Western Europe, the phenomenon of boat people in the Far East—all serve as safety valves helping to avert the threatening food riots in the countries from which the emigrants originate.

But the question has to be posed and answered as to whether this is the best way to address the issue of poverty, which afflicts so many countries in the world. Is it in the long-term interests of these countries and humanity, as a whole, to uproot the most enterprising individuals from these communities and dump them as unskilled and semi-skilled workers on the developed economies of the world?

Nor can the reality be ignored that in response to these population flows and to the pressure of poverty, there is, certainly in various parts of Europe, a growing tendency towards the proliferation of racist and neo-Nazi ideas and the thuggery that goes with them.

I have no desire to overestimate the seriousness of this problem. But I would also like to submit that it is not one that can be ignored either. Certainly those who are immediately threatened, be they black, Arab, or Jew, cannot think this a matter to be treated with benign neglect.

The simple point we are trying to make is that the dire poverty of some is not an affliction which impacts only on those who are deprived. It reverberates across the globe and ineluctably impacts negatively on the whole of humanity, including those who live in conditions of comfort and plenty.

The inescapable conclusion from all this must surely be that our interdependence, bringing us together into a common global home, across the oceans and the continents, demands that we all combine to launch a global offensive for development, prosperity, and human survival.

We're aware of and respect the initiatives that have been undertaken in the past to address these issues, including those of the United Nations, the EEC-ACP countries, the non-aligned movement, the North-South and South-South commissions, the OAU, as well as many others.

But I am certain that none of us here can assert that there does indeed exist a real and meaningful global offensive for development, prosperity, and human survival, drawing into one concerted effort governments, the private sector, non-governmental organisations, and the people themselves.

To come closer to home and talk about the African continent, we cannot but take advantage of this occasion to reiterate the alarm that others have expressed at the continuing deterioration of conditions of life for millions of people.

There is no need for me, in front of this knowledgeable audience, to dwell at any length on the specifics of the socio-economic situation on our continent. Suffice it to remind the conference that ten years ago already, in its report entitled "Accelerate Development in sub-Saharan Africa: an Agenda for Action," the World Bank had various things to say which should have sounded the alarm bells. Here are two quotations from this report: "When, in the mid-1970s, the world economy experienced inflation and recession, nowhere did the crisis hit with greater impact than in the region of sub-Saharan Africa." And again: "For most African countries, and for a majority of the African population, the record is grim, and it is no exaggeration to talk of crisis. Slow overall economic growth, sluggish agricultural performance coupled with rapid rates of population increase, and balance of payments and fiscal crisis—these are dramatic indicators of economic trouble."

As can be expected, other issues are dealt with in the report, including deteriorating terms of trade, a continuous fall in exchange reserves, and the Dracula of an external debt which many countries can neither avoid nor afford.

With regard to the current situation, the secretary-general of the United Nations reported only last year that in the period up to 1990, "The average African continued to get poorer and to suffer a persistent fall in an already meagre standard of living."

In his report on the "UN programme of action for African economic recovery and development," the secretary-general speaks of the African continent, sinking deeper into "an unrelenting crisis of tragic proportions." He goes on to say that "overcoming this crisis represents the greatest development challenge of our time." , perhaps more than in any other part of the world, the situation in sub-Saharan Africa, which has worsened since the World Bank report we have cited was published, illustrates the importance of the global offensive for development, prosperity, and human survival for which we have called.

Quite clearly, for this project to record success, it would be necessary that a massive transfer of resources takes place from north to south. Let me hasten to state it here that we are by no means suggesting that this is an easy objective to achieve.

Nor are we suggesting that the issue be approached either as an act of charity or as an attempt to improve the lives of the "have-nots" by impoverishing the "haves." Rather we are suggesting that it is necessary that these transfers take place as a necessary condition to achieve development, prosperity, and survival for humanity as a whole.

We say this fully aware of the general shortage of capital in the world, its sensitivity to economic imperatives, and its mobility. We also say this knowing that the underdeveloped countries have to continue addressing such issues as better utilisation of resources and management of their economies, better governance, human resource development, including the upliftment and liberation of women, as well as the protection of the environment.

Among other things that the concerted global offensive would have to deal with are, of course, the debt problems, the issue of the continuous decline in the price of commodities that the poorer countries export, and access to markets for their manufactured goods.

We would like to take advantage of this opportunity to bring to your attention, as others have done before, the problems that many African and other poor countries experience as they implement structural adjustment programmes. Carried out without providing social nets to cushion their impact on those who are already gravely disadvantaged, these programmes may create more problems than they solve.

Naturally, we must also express our own unease at any developments which might result in investor attention being directed exclusively at Central and Eastern Europe to the exclusion of Africa and the rest of the Third World.

Nor would it be beneficial to allow the positive processes leading to European integration to result in a "fortress Europe" and, inter alia, the delinkage of Africa from this and other areas of the world.

My own country, South Africa, is marching on its own road to liberation and democracy. The specific process in which we are engaged, epitomised by the Convention for a Democratic South Africa, may not be irreversible.

Nevertheless, it is quite clear that there is no force that can permanently stop our advance towards the transformation of South Africa into a united, democratic, non-racial, and non-sexist country. We want to see established, as quickly as possible, a multiparty democracy, enshrined in a constitution which provides for one person, one vote, on a common voters' roll; separation of powers between the legislature, executive, and judiciary; and devolution of power to regional and local levels of government. Furthermore, we would also like to see an entrenched bill of rights, protected by an independent and representative judiciary.

Equally protected should be the rights of all our people to language, culture, and religion. Further than this, we have said in the past that we are willing to look at any proposals aimed at addressing the fears of any of our population groups, provided that this was not in furtherance of apartheid and intended to subvert the normal democratic practice of majority rule.

We need to make the point also that we are against the notion of a prolonged transitional period. We have, therefore, put forward the suggestion that this period, beginning with the establishment of an interim or transitional government around the middle of this year, should not last longer than 18months.

Thus, we are determined to end apartheid and liberate ourselves as a matter of urgency. We are as equally determined that this transformation should bring with it real changes in the material conditions of life of the people.

This is dictated both by the fact of the widespread and endemic poverty that affects millions of black people in our country and the need to guarantee the success and permanence of democratic change. This will require that all necessary measures are taken to ensure the growth of the South African economy, pulling it out of the recession and decline in which it is now enmeshed.

This will require a rapid and sustained growth in terms of capital formation or fixed investment, drawing on both domestic and external sources to finance this investment. It will also require a rapid and sustained expansion of the domestic market, as well as improved access to international markets.

Inevitably, we must address the critical question of achieving high levels of productivity for both capital and labour. At the same time, we must attend to the issue of equitable distribution of income and wealth, without which the domestic market will remain small and social stability impossible to achieve.

We visualise a mixed economy, in which the private sector would play a central and critical role to ensure the creation of wealth and jobs. Side by side with this, there will be a public sector perhaps no different from such countries as Germany, France, and Italy, where public enterprises constitute 9 per cent, 11 per cent and 15 per cent of the economy respectively, and in which the state plays an important role in such areas as education, health, and welfare.

For it to succeed to achieve such basic objectives as creating wealth and jobs, ending poverty, and creating a just and equitable society, future economic policy will also have to address such questions as security of investments and the right to repatriate earnings, realistic exchange rates, the rate of inflation, and the fiscus.

We firmly believe that the South African economy has the potential for a very bright and exciting future. It's in our interest that this economy should thrive as never before. We're equally convinced that it will also offer very good prospects for the investors present in this room, both South African and international.

We, therefore, urge you to enter into a partnership with the people of South Africa, who would like to act together with you to rebuild their country to the mutual benefit. We invite you to begin now to investigate the business possibilities in our country so that you're able to move with all due speed when the moment is opportune.

In this regard, we should once more explain that our own considered position is that remaining economic sanctions should be lifted once an interim government has been established. Furthermore, we're determined to move forward as speedily as possible to establish the political and social climate which is necessary to ensure business confidence and create the possibility for all investors to make long-term commitments to help develop the South African economy.

South Africa is also part of a region of the world which has a population of anything up to 150 million people. This region must, and will, grow and develop in an integrated manner and will thus provide a sizeable market for those investors who take advantage of the opportunities this region offers and bring in the resources necessary for its development.

We must also make the point that current developments in various parts of this region point to a common striving to reinforce the democratic process, entrench a human rights culture, end civil wars and the creation of large refugee populations.

It also seems inevitable that, sooner or later, the peoples of the region will also begin discussing such issues as regional economic cooperation and integration, a regional security system based on the reduction of armed forces and military expenditures, as well as coordinated measures for the protection of the environment.

In brief, we strongly believe that the region of southern Africa as a whole offers the possibility for us all to implement the global offensive for development, prosperity, and human survival of which we have spoken.

Needless to say, success in this great and historic venture would do wonderful things to address the concern which is common to all of us, of achieving the regeneration of African societies and the upliftment of its peoples.

Let me end with a special appeal to you all, who constitute a critical component part of the leadership of the peoples of the world. If the voices of millions have been freed to enunciate the political aspirations of the people, those voices will also surely speak loudly, proclaiming an urgent desire for an end to poverty and for a more equitable distribution of opportunities, income, and wealth within and among the nations.

We believe that those voices must be listened to and the concerns they express addressed. If the political transformations taking place across the globe are anything to go by, it would seem clear that these masses will not allow themselves to be silenced. They will not be fobbed off with polite and courteous but meaningless responses. Nor will they accept the promise of jam tomorrow if they see nothing being done today to deliver the promised jam.

Motivated by nothing other than the fact of our common humanity and informed by the realisation of the common destiny of the peoples of all continents, let us then do together what we can and must do together in the interests of all humanity, while each one of us also does what he or she must do in pursuit of their enlightened self-interest but recognizing, in the end, that no man is an island. (www.weforum.org http://forumblog.org/2013/12/nelson-mandelas-address-to-davos-1992/)

The excellent principles expounded in this speech are, in the writer's opinion, what are required in today's world as the elixir for prosperity for all. These principles can be listed as follows:

1. There is always a mutual dependence of everyone in society on each other.
2. True democracy and justice breed peace and inequalities; injustice spawns conflicts.
3. The affliction of a few should concern even those not suffering the same.
4. Political freedom should, at a minimum, also lead to economic freedom.
5. There is an urgent need to start a global offensive for development, prosperity, and human survival.
6. The same struggles for political independence will be followed by similar struggles for economic freedom.

Most former colonies of European imperialist nations, after having been able to identify the problems facing them as a people have however, failed to employ the right tools for themselves to

solve these problems, instead choosing the very same tools of oppression to try and bring prosperity to their people. In the process,
they've dismally failed and have begun to look more like the same
previous oppressors.

Castrating Bulls, Growing the Herd

The writer of this book grew up in a rural village in a poor tribal
trust land, the dwellers of which were dependent on peasant farming, where rain was always erratic and determined the amount of
harvest every year. Crop farming was done at a subsistence level
and, depending on the rainfall each year, was anything from a
few bags to a dozen tonnes of grain, and the same applied to animal husbandry, being affected by droughts and other challenges
in some years and flourishing in others.

Animals, especially cattle, were useful for ploughing the fields,
pulling the scotch carts, and as a measure of wealth. If school fees
were required for a child, one beast was sacrificed to be sold, and
the proceeds used for such emergencies. Cattle and other domestic animals are considered very valuable in these rural areas and
as such are rarely killed for meat, unless at funerals, weddings, or
similar events where feeding large numbers calls for it.

Growing the cattle herd required that one kept as many as heifers as possible to breed more calves. There was also need for steers
(castrated bulls) to yoke when ploughing the ground and other
chores. Only a single bull was required at a time, and because bulls
are difficult to rear, there was on average a single bull for the whole
village which was able to service all the village cows without a problem. The steers did all the work, were the most valuable members
of the herd, and had to be kept healthy and available all the time.
So every time a male calf was born, before it had grown into a full
bull, it was castrated. This castration enabled it to be easily tamed
into an obedient bullock which would give the farmer several years

of service on the plough before being eventually being killed for meat at the end of its useful life. Such is the lot of bullocks/steers, and it was so different to that of the bull.

The bull was mostly unmanageable; keeping it in the pen was almost impossible as it would jump out and follow the village heifers in heat at that point. We couldn't harness it to a yoke as it would be violent, untamed, and untrained. The bull was only useful for servicing the heifers, and it was considered a waste of some sort to rear a bull instead of early castrating it into a bullock for the yoke.

Bulls, Bullocks, Kings, and Similar Animals

The political economy in a kingdom where a king is the ruler is such that there has to be one bull in the whole kingdom, and that bull is the king. All others in the kingdom aren't to be bulls. Everything has to be done in the name of the king and for the king's pleasure and benefit, with the approval of the king. All the subjects are dependent on the king and are at the mercy of the king for their lives. The system of kingship is designed to ensure that the king is the most prosperous, rich, wealthy, and powerful individual in the kingdom. One such way of ensuring that the king is wealthier is to tax every individual in the kingdom, so that the tax money is for the king, to enable him to run the government of the kingdom.

The economic blueprints which are being implemented in most countries in the present day are creating a few economic bulls, and are tuned to generate a majority number of efficient bullocks to serve as workers, with limited choice to ever achieve economic freedom. An economy where individuals are limited in their choices about economic self-determination, and have no alternative other than to work for another, is no different from a slave state where work is coerced. Whether a reward is offered, or whether the individual has an option to change jobs is of little difference and it does not restore the right to entrepreneurship. Furthermore where the political economy 'machine" is tuned in such a manner that it produces inequalities among economic equals, and condemns a majority to working for the minority, the situation cannot be considered to be normal. The rest of this book considers such workers to be slaves and the wages and salaries that they receive to be slave wages.

Writing a book on political economy

This book hopes to identify and answer certain questions that have remained unanswered in our lives. As I see it, these questions can be summarised as: What are the most efficient economic systems? Which economic structures are sustainable and enduring? What is really behind rural-urban migration? In tackling these I've sought to explain the meaning of money and wealth: What is the cause of labour unemployment and poverty? What is the most equitable tax system? What are monetary and fiscal policies, and how do they drive inflation?

The book seeks nonetheless to give simple answers to these simple questions. It's not meant to be an in-depth study but a simple explanation of concepts that are common but misunderstood, issues that are familiar but remain unknown to most people both learned and otherwise. The methodology used in arriving at the solutions offered is to question and to measure everything: every idea and solution, including those things and answers that are taught as doctrine- against the ideals and within a framework of fairness, justice, and equity,

This book thus seeks to encourage the oppressed, to cheer on the pilgrim, and give hope to the heartbroken. The solutions proposed are those arrived at by a fellow struggler. The book isn't designed to criticise, as that would assume a superiority which the author doesn't possess. Neither is it meant to be prescriptive, but to be a plea for something better, as a guide for policymakers and leaders, perhaps to help them consider a bit better when they think, if they do at all, about the plight of the majority poor.

The examples used are those to which the author has been exposed to, and it's my hope that they can be seen as examples of a wider set of circumstances. I'm not a true expert in economics, taxation, or political economy. Some more astute minds may think of better solutions than those proposed here. But if experts in these fields are able to offer better solutions based on my arguments, it will be my delight to have contributed a small part. This book seeks to set in train a different thought process to enable better intellectual engagement.

This book was conceived and its questions arose when I reflected on the principle of tithing as specified in the context of religion (e.g., Leviticus 27:31). In addition, I believe—and have advised at every opportunity to many individuals—that for any enterprise a company should be formed, so that participants may enjoy the benefits offered by a company compared to the earning of an individual's wage.

I don't pretend to know everything, but respect age, wisdom, and—where they've earned it—those in authority. Being an African, I'm schooled in cultures that require deference to the elderly and those in power, even when one thinks they're wrong. Any other course encourages rebellion and lawlessness, and these can be counterproductive. I seek only to point out issues that might've been missed in our collective quest for emancipation, and I believe greater good would be achieved if the contents of this book were to be used and considered as respectful and as pleas of an inferior appealing to superiors so as to achieve the salvation of the poor, the workers, and the individuals. I aim to present a humble appeal to consciences so that solutions may be arrived at in a spirit of unity and constructiveness.

Particularly do I respect and applaud those who've given up their lives for the emancipation of the oppressed and the down-trodden and who've have fought for the emancipation of slaves, for the elevation of women, for the freedom of oppressed and colo-nised nations, and for the empowerment of the poor.

The fight for freedom isn't necessarily won in decisive battles. One thing is clear: economic freedom still eludes the majority of people in the world, most of whom also don't have political free-dom. This relationship is something we must consider.

In attempting to address the question of political economy, it's important to set it out clearly, maybe to simplify it and to define the unclear. It's important to explain previously held assumptions and to question each of them if it still holds. It's prudent to set a clear framework within which to lay the foundation of thought. By doing this I aim to provide some explanations for things common in political economies, the understanding of which may be tak-en for granted—yet with a clearer understanding, the enquiring mind may come to appreciate better the reasons for the accumu-lation of past, present, and future wealth of this world's individu-als. This appreciation will also enable an understanding of current problems and illuminate upon the right course of action to solve those problems.

The problems facing the present-day political economist are in-deed many, and the arguments I make here do generalise political economics by means of normative statements and analyses. This enables us to identify the pertinent questions and problems of our time and to seek timely answers, calling on past and recent history in arriving at solutions. I've left undisturbed generally accepted economic theories, for sake of simplicity, to enable a precise and short discourse.

In selecting the title of this book I toyed with several, to bring out the meaning and ideas discussed here. I wished to include the word "democratic" as part of the title and almost decided against it because the meaning of that word isn't clear to everyone and subject to many different definitions: Is it limited to voting rights? Does it come in different forms? And what does it achieve?—these are all questions that require answering.

This book seeks in a way to expand the meaning of democracy and to enrich that meaning. People is still understand democracy in terms of what it's achieved or failed to achieve in their lives and for most that experience it is political rather than economic also. Economics that are devoid of democracy tend to trample over the rights of the economically poor, the ignorant, and weak, in an effort to appease the powerful and wealthy.

II

Economic Systems

Introduction: Constitutional Choices, Political Participation, Elections, and Collective Action

Political economics evaluates how governments, individuals, households, businesses, and society allocate means of production—which may be scarce—how they use these to create wealth, and how the wealth obtained is distributed among competing needs and wants. All these functions can be performed in different economic systems and frameworks, and these will affect the inputs of the processes and the outputs of the economic system.

It follows that the starting point in approaching political economics is to study the important decision of which economic system is decided upon to be used as a vehicle of political economy activity. The decision of economic system is usually closely related to the decision on the political framework within which the economy will function. A democratic political system has historically meant that a free-market economic system determines the creation and distribution of wealth. An autocratic political framework doesn't generally mix well with a *laissez-faire* economic environment. In a free and just society, every individual should be free to choose how to provide for him- or herself, in creating the wealth and in distributing that wealth. The freedom to choose the type of economic system that will determine wealth creation is as important as any other freedom and people should seek it and defend it, individually and collectively.

The selected system of political economy will determine how economic resources will be allocated between competing needs and groups of individuals in the society. It will determine the allocation of economic opportunities, such as jobs or credit as well as financial resources to companies and individuals seeking these. The monetary and fiscal policies and similar interventions will be put in place in a manner determined by the dictates of the existing economic system. Taxation and other ways of distributing wealth are also largely dependent on the economic system within which they operate.

For this reason it's important that the appropriate system be well chosen, as it will influence the form of economic processes and structures and, the manner of their working within a political economic system. In a perfect democratic system of political economics, people will have not only the right to decide who their political leaders are to be, but they'll have an equally important right to determine the economic systems within which they'll live. Economic policy and decisions in such a system aren't determined by a small, influential group of economic players but should be democratically brought about through the informed participation of every member of a society.

There are various systems worth considering, which have been used in the past, and a brief look at a few of them (feudalism, capitalism, and socialism) will assist in determining the merits or otherwise of each against the other.

Feudalism

Feudalism is recognised as the political economic system that preceded most modern systems. It was—and in many places still is—a type of political economy centred on the relationships of land ownership, military security, and mutual dependency. The wealth of such a nation is obtained through the sweat of the lower classes and by plundering weaker kingdoms. The economies of the biblical patriarchs, of medieval Europe, and of the African kingdoms, among others, most nearly fit this model. The leader in a feudal economy is required to be a military leader, able to defend a particular territory from plunder by stronger kingdoms and in turn lead its subjects in the plundering of weaker kingdoms.

Such a leader guarantees personal security and the right to some private property for most subjects. The production is made in common and shared by the lord in proportion to need and contribution. Those conquered and spared become slaves. The conqueror takes over their wealth. Feudalism usually makes allowance for the poor and the bonded to attain some economic freedom by accumulating some wealth with which they may buy their freedom. Although the laws of fiefdom allow the fief to peasant to be entitled to a small part of the output, it isn't unusual for the masters to use their unfair power to deprive the peasants of their fair shares. A peasant is then allowed to decide to start a different life in a different place with another group of people of his or her choice.

Economic Elements

The feudal system doesn't allow for a lot of wealth to be accumulated because of the accompanying risk of sudden plunder resulting in loss. The wealth of a feudal lord is measured by the size of the territory ruled, by the number of movable assets within that territory, and by the size of the army and machinery available, even by their various skills. Hence, one finds wealth calculated by the number of cattle, sheep, horses, and horsemen, foot soldiers, and—in some cases—children. The land is the major economic resource, and it belongs to the king or overlord. The lord grants rights of use to land within the territory, and those using the land became subject to the lord's rule. Economic resources are granted through lesser lords or deputies, and these in turn make grants to farmers, merchants, and craftsmen. Those at the bottom of the system, namely the peasants and the serfs, work to feed those above them and also give themselves in service, military or otherwise.

Money, Capital, and Accumulation

In a feudal set-up, a wealthy nation is accounted as such when it has a long border, a greater army, many cattle, and many people. These guarantee protection, self-reliance, and the creation of more wealth. The form of government is such that it can sustain itself from its lord's treasury. The standing army is small, and the larger army is a reservist one which may be called upon in the event of war. During the farming season, the lord's subjects attend to their fields, which are the source of finance for their livelihoods and the taxes due to the lord. A huge central government isn't ideal because it would be prone to make the subjects poor. And this was especially true of historical fiefdoms, where the limitations of lacking quick communication and transportation systems didn't help the cause.

These elements of political economy generally exist, in various degrees and forms, even to this day. The feudal political economy requires that the general populace is dominated by a few lords who possess economic resources and political influence.

Wage Labour and Class Structure

Power in the feudal system rests with the lord and is passed on to a designated heir together with the accompanying wealth. Everyone else has either to work and serve the lord or to find another lord. The emancipation of the poor isn't guaranteed and is very limited, as in the absence of the right opportunities; it's not usually possible to accumulate the wherewithal to buy freedom, let alone to become wealthy. A peasant would hardly hope to become lord in the normal course of events. In the case of slavery, in contrast to poverty or bonded labour, the master uses brute force is used to oblige the slave to work. The slave isn't entitled to a wage and receives food only as would give nourishment for him or her to work again the next day and similarly is only allowed to rest enough to enable him or her to work again the next day. The slave has no rights, has no reward for labouring, and has no freedom of choice whatsoever. The slave's life belongs to the slave owner, and a slave can be sold without his consent, just as cattle would be sold.

In the feudal system, nonetheless, subjects (peasants) aren't as badly off as slaves, their chains slightly loosened to allow some leeway to make their own decisions. The greatest difference is in their being free to choose a lord for whom to work. The chains nonetheless exist. The peasant in the feudal system is hardly free politically or economically and is effectively enslaved by the poverty which forces him or her to work for the lord. Because the means of production are owned by the lord, it's only through work that the peasant may gain his or her escape from poverty. The peasant doesn't require a whip-yielding slave driver; poverty stalks by day and hunger gnaws by night, and these are enough motivation for work. The peasant is only better off than a slave in that he or she can't be bought or sold, is at liberty to choose a master, and decides every day whether to work on that day.

The peasant has to work long and hard hours to feed him- or herself and has no fixed working hours. The peasant has a few rights and is rewarded just enough to feed him- or herself and family, also just enough to make him or her remain loyal to the master. In order to supplement this income, the peasant usually requires his wife (or her husband) and able children to work in the lord's fields as well. The children of a peasant aren't expected to amount to anything other than be peasants also.

Moving Forward in Time

The feudal system is of interest in considering today's political economics because capitalist that is not practiced in some form of democratic political environment tends towards feudalism in a large way. The celebrated gains of so-called democratic capitalism have accumulated into the hands of a few individuals. The lords of the feudal system exist today in the form of a few capitalists whose economic interests and political influence reveal their essential feudal identities. The plight of labour and the poor is gradually degenerating into the equivalent of that suffered by feudal peasants and labourers.

The greatest danger facing modern societies that passed through feudal stages is the tendency to slide back into such a state, unnoticed. Although a modern government may be provided with a constitutional and political mandate for the service of everyone, the governments and the aristocratic classes of feudal lords tend to work together and become one. In most cases they control governments, influence policy, and have the means to install and remove those in power—and when they voice concerns; politicians can't but listen and obey. In most so-called democratic nations, only the rich can be elected into power, because the costs and other economic sacrifices required in entering, campaigning, are not available to ordinary aspirants. If that isn't feudalism in a modern dress, it's definitely not democracy.

The Feudal Feud

The industrial revolution refers to a period from the 18th to the 19th century when major changes in the methods (and technologies) of agriculture, manufacturing, mining and transport systems changed the political economy of Europe, and spread to the rest of the world. Political democracy started to be established itself more markedly after the same paths as the industrial revolution, and blossommed into a wave in the twentieth century because of decolonisation. The industrial revolution and the democratisation of society allowed for the participation of a larger number of people in the political economy, which initially diluted the powers of the feudal lords. Feudalism was therefore eliminated because land was no longer the only and main economic determinant. Democracy also means that sovereignty and nationalities are more stable than they were in feudalism's days. Today, however, the world faces the risk of lapsing into full feudal stagnation, caused by a few powerful individuals acquiring all the wealth, and forcing everyone to be dependent on them. The remedy may again similarly be found in the liberation of the new peasant and the new labourer.

When it subsided, feudalism didn't wholly liberate the labourer, and the lord didn't fully give up dominance. The amount of freedom granted to the labourer wasn't enough wholly to emancipate him or her, and the revolution didn't dethrone the feudal lord. In the new guise of capitalist boss, or owner of the means of production, the feudal lord is today ascending a refurbished throne, and the labourer is again enslaved in an economic fiefdom.

Example 1: A typical feudal system

> 1 Kings 9:20–23: And all the people that were left of the Amorites, Hittites, Perizzites, Hivites, and Jebusites, which were not of the children of Israel,
>
> Their children that were left after them in the land, whom the children of Israel also were not able utterly to destroy, upon those did Solomon levy a tribute of bondservice unto this day.
>
> But of the children of Israel did Solomon make no bondmen: but they were men of war, and his servants, and his princes, and his captains, and rulers of his chariots, and his horsemen. These were the chiefs of the officers that were over Solomon's work, five hundred and fifty, which bare ruled over the people that wrought in the work.
>
> 1 Kings 10:14 & 29: Now the weight of gold that came to Solomon in one year was six hundred threescore and six talents of gold.
>
> Beside that he had of the merchantmen, and of the traffic of the spice merchants, and of all the kings of Arabia, and of the governors of the country.

Feudalism was a tiered system of dependant relationships that consisted of a king at the apex and below the king was a class that enforced the king's rule over the rest of the population. In the example above, the king uses his tribesmen to be his soldiers, princes and lords over his kingdom. The interesting detail from this example of a political economy is that the king didn't make any of the children of Israel into bonded servants and did not levy a tribute. This is a very significant point and requires analysis as to why such a decision was made and what effect it had on the individual welfare of such people and of the nation as a whole.

When the children of Israel were recorded to be in Egypt and were settled in Goshen, they were cattle herders and lived a life of free enterprise and their wealth soon made them a threat to the town dwelling Egyptians. The wealth and prosperity was soon eroded when the Egyptians advised their king to make the Israelites bondmen and slaves in Egypt. The wise king in the above sited text knew better and he did not make his fellow subjects anything worse than free entrepreneurs. When one is condemned to a life of servitude to another—be it king, government, or fellow citizen—the economic welfare of that individual is at the mercy of that master. In order to guarantee the economic fortunes of the Israelites, he allowed them to be free unlike the other tribes they had conquered, from which a tribute was required. If one is free and not bonded to anyone, one is at liberty to opt for economic emancipation and have a greater chance of success than one would have under bonded servitude. As much as possible, an individual should seek to break away from bonded servitude, whether it's voluntary or entirely dictated by circumstances, and be able to enjoy economic freedom. Governments should have as a goal the freedom of its citizens from any form of servitude that hinders their economic freedom.

Capitalism

Economic Elements

Feudal political economies were generally succeeded by capitalist political economies. The change was gradual and subtle, with some of the elements and ingredients from feudal systems largely carried over into the capitalist systems. These capitalist and feudal systems aren't opposed to each other but are close cousins, the former more developed than the latter. The lord in the feudal system evolved into the capitalist, while the peasant and slave became paid labourers. The respective classes assumed different names but largely remained divided along the same lines.

Capitalism, like feudalism, is characterised by the private ownership by a relative few of the means of production in the form of capital. Individuals who own the means of production, the capitalists, can make their own decisions about the methods of production through which and the prices at which the output is distributed, subject to competition in the market. Labourers, in order to make a living, and for lack of other means of survival, offer their labour to a capitalist and are paid a wage which is determined by that capitalist, subject also to competition in the supply and demand of the labourer's skills.

While economists argue that there should be little or no interference from government in a capitalist political economy, such an argument is too sweeping and needs to be qualified. It's in practice not possible for a capitalist economy to exist without government control. The capitalists need a government in order to exist, to implement the principles of capitalism, and to guarantee the safety of the wealth created.

Feudal systems are precarious in that the right to private property, among other rights, isn't guaranteed, being subject to the risk of plunder by more powerful enemies or appropriation by an overlord. In a capitalist economy, the capitalist's desire for protection can be satisfied by the government. In turn, the capitalist works hard to influence and control the government and the government's policies that enable preservation of his or her existence. The government in a capitalist economy is there specifically to protect individual rights to private property, to enable them to engage freely in any industry, and to enforce the rights to the fruits of such enterprise. All these tend to be absent in feudal political economies.

The birth of capitalism wasn't an accident but a realisation of the stagnation that feudalism tended to and of the need for a better political economy. Capitalism greatly coincided with the industrial revolution and enabled new people, other than the hereditary kings and lords, to be able to amass great wealth and power which they could previously not have dreamed of. There was therefore a slight realignment to accommodate the new wealthy class and to protect the privileges emanating from the feudal economic system. The kings, his nobility, and the wealthy aristocracy sought to establish a system in which they'd still have the same privileges and power as before. Capitalism was their best answer. The masses work for and under the domination of the king, the upper class owns the land together with all other means of production, and the lower classes are meant to continue working for the wealthy, to be taxed and supply the needs of the haves.

In a feudal system, the lord would own the output of the farm, but had an imputed obligation to give part of it back as food and sustenance for the serf. In some way the feudal system allowed the lower class to have a residual interest in the output of their labour. Capitalism as a system does not allow for such and as long as the worker has put in the number of required hours of labour, and has been paid, what remains belongs to the capitalist lord. In feudalism the wealth and power was inherited by birth right, and the risk of a war defeat leading to loss of both wealth and birth right, was addressed by capitalism through a system of perpetual existence for any business whether the owner dies or not.

The ruling kings accepted and established capitalism to protect their privileged positions and that of the aristocracy, in that they don't have to work but obtain their wealth from the labour of the lower classes. The aristocracy became the capitalists and embraced capitalism and its privileges.

Capitalism and the government

There is always a close relationship between a capitalist and the government, whether the government pretends to be democratic or not. The capitalist has sought guarantees in statutes and in common law and has received the protection necessary to remain a capitalist. Especially structured policies and laws are necessary in order to attract capitalists and to maintain their sought-after presence. Activities that scare away the capitalist are thus prohibited or at least discouraged by the government. The capitalist is also often accorded special tax allowances and rates to enable him to operate and to invest more of his or her good capital.

Another way in which government is a requirement in a capitalist state is in providing the infrastructure and public and common goods which the capitalist needs but can't produce, because they're open and subject to free consumption by nonpayers.

The extent to which a government intervenes in a capitalist state to address the apparent shortcomings isn't in any way to be viewed as a different political economic system (mixed economy). It's just the necessary action required in a capitalist economy. It may indicate the rate and extent to which a capitalist is a good capitalist: that is, the extent to which he or she's solely profit driven and won't engage in any activity that doesn't maximise profit.

Government intervention and protection are prerequisites for capitalism to exist, because it was the government (kings) who gave birth to the system, and it's the government who currently benefits and continues to promote such an economic system. The intervention is not to address the failures of free markets or the excesses of capitalism. With less government intervention the capitalist would not have all the privileges, protection and advantages afforded him by the laws, courts and structures set up by government. The common man would be treated at the same level and be able to compete and be treated as an equal. Government intervention is the distortion necessary for the establishment of a capitalist system of inequality, monopoly, and economic oppression.

Capitalism fails to guarantee its continued existence because it fails to equitably distribute the means of production and the fruits of production and relies heavily on government support for its existence. It fails to meet the great principle of political economy, in that it doesn't consider the health of the whole economy in its allocation of resources and distribution of the wealth thus created. It concentrates wealth in too few hands and leaves the rest to become worse off. It therefore resorts to and dearly requires a strong government that enforces it and protects it.

Capitalism thus tends to be an unstable system associated with economic instability, manifesting as violent surges and depressions in economic activity. Years of plenty are followed by years of want; boom periods are followed by depression periods. The new depression is always worse than the previous one, and for these reasons capitalist systems aren't generally acceptable.

Money, Capital, and Accumulation

In a capitalist economy, the creation of wealth is considered only to be the process of making money from the means of production. Capitalism is concerned about the accumulation of more capital, over and above what was initially invested. Labourers employed in the process of accumulating this wealth are considered part of the means of production and are considered to benefit greatly from the investor, in that opportunities are created for the further employment of labour. The government in a capitalist political economy is driven to make the investing environment very favourable so as to enable more creation of employment by capitalists through such investing. A capitalist government is thus considered to have done well if it doesn't scare away investors and has created more employment for labourers; thus the wealth created by the capitalists increases.

Capital, Labour, and Financial Markets

The defining feature of capitalism, unlike in feudalism, is the existence of a market in all the three phases of political economy, which is at the resource allocation stage, production stage, and distribution stage. In the allocation of the means of production there exists a market for all the means of production, such as land, initial capital, or labour, including the investment relationships represented by an investment market. At the production stage there's competition of what is to be produced, what mix of resources is to be used, and where it's produced. On the distribution stage products compete against each other and the proceeds are shared among labour, the owners, and the government, through taxes.

In a capitalist political economy the government performs almost everything through the capitalists and in consultation with the capitalists. The allocation of capital for the creation of wealth is achieved through the financial markets. Monetary policy is also formulated with the aid of financial institutions and financial markets. When the government wants to inject capital into the economy to stimulate economic growth, usually termed "financial stimulus," it makes money available through various financial institutions, which in turn make a profit on this money by lending it (i.e., by allocating the financial means of production).

In capitalism, banks and other financial institutions lend according to the dictates of the financial markets. Generally, a big capitalist or company is considered more creditworthy than a labourer. A capitalist system will not lend to the individual labourer, whom it considers to represent a risk. It will rather lend to the well-off investor (or capitalist) who's more creditworthy. In addition, the rates prevailing in capitalist financial markets are such that more creditworthy individuals are charged lower interest rates on what they borrow, and higher rates are set for those persons considered credit risks. Thus a capitalist system allocates the means of production in a way that it reserves the capital for the creditworthy and denies the same means of production to the poor.

In the few circumstances where it extends resources to the less creditworthy, this is done at a higher cost. The system is thus doing what it's meant to do—i.e., being driven by profit. A government in a capitalist economy will in this way perpetuate the existence of capitalism. To provide public goods like road networks and other amenities, a capitalist government will also obtain these through the capitalists, who in that process will create employment for labourers.

Wage Labour and Class Structure

Capitalism hardly changes the class structure inherited from feudalism. The role of the feudal lords is assumed by the capitalists, who may not have direct political power but are very influential in governments and control their policies. The peasants in the feudal system are hired to be labourers in a capitalist structure, and their wealth hasn't noticeably improved.

It's a characteristic of capitalism that labourers receive either wage or salary, and owners receive the profits generated by the factors of production employed in the production of economic value. Labourers are seen as factors of production and don't form part of the ownership of the company. They're there solely for the salary/wage. They don't participate in the residual profits of the company.

The capitalist system has all the elements of the feudal system of lord and peasants, where the peasants were forced by poverty to work for the landlords in order to survive. Just as the landlords then benefited from the full wealth of the land, the capitalist system allows the owner to take all, and the labourer takes his or her wages.

The capitalist system has improved the plight of the slave and the peasant in a relatively substantial way, in that the capitalist has a wage to offer his or her labourer. The labourer toils a set amount of hours a day and uses the rest to be with his family. The labourer can send his children to schools to be taught to be future labourers in various trades that are available to the labour market. The reward of the labourer is sufficient to enable him to be better than the unemployed peasant. The labourer feels gratitude and indebtedness to the capitalist for giving him a job that pays. The labourer also can afford to approach financial institutions to borrow money to get assets such as cars, houses, and similar tokens of wealth. The capitalist has built good accommodation for the labourer to rent at market prices or to buy at competitive rates. He or she can now borrow for personal expenditure and pay back over time because he or she has a secure stream of income and is considered creditworthy.

The labourer in a capitalist system is afforded opportunities for self-improvement in skills that will enable him or her to be a better labourer. He or she can join trade associations, be certified, and be rewarded according to the skills acquired. The labourer can also belong to trade unions that will defend rights at the workplaces against dismissals and unfair practices and which negotiate salary and wage increases.

The capitalist system is considered to have improved the lot of the peasant and freed the former slave to be a proud, respectable, skilled, and polished labourer who renders services for a just reward determined by the market forces of the labour market.

However, it's not for the love of the labourer or due to a good heart that the capitalist has allowed the emancipation of the labourer. Being driven by the need for wealth maximisation, the polishing of the simple labourer into a skilled polished and cultured employee only goes as far as it enables the capitalist to get more wealth.

The labourer in a capitalist economy can only aim to be a better labourer. He or she remains a labourer because control of the means of production is beyond reach. The wages are agreed at the beginning of employment and are fixed until they're subjected to a negotiated percentage increase, usually a year later. They're hardly affected by "free" market forces if there's no market of active buyers and sellers available. Working harder and for more hours hardly affects the labourer's well-being in a positive way, as it disproportionately benefits and rewards the capitalist more than it improves the wealth of the labourer.

The labourer is motivated by his or her new-found comfort and the carrot of a wage. He or she often has to dig him- or herself into debt to acquire the tokens of wealth, so that he or she takes on obligations that make him or her totally dependent on his or her job. On getting a wage, the labourer often has to hand it all back to the capitalists for debt repayment in instalments, not to mention accommodation and other expenses. In this way the capitalist can made the labourer totally dependent on him or her. Whatever the labourer wants to do, he or she has to pay the capitalist for it, using earnings, be it for food, accommodation, clothing, entertainment, or travel. Capitalists have determined the layouts of cities and towns, and the labourer is obliged to live in them in order to be close to his or her workplace, and so is further at the mercy of the capitalist.

The capitalist system is a very carefully devised smokescreen. It's a way of enslaving the labourer so that it looks to everyone like a way of freeing him or her. After proclaiming to have freed the slave, it turns out that capitalism has bound the slave with a bigger and stronger invisible chain. The slave has a new respectable title and is entitled to a uniform but gets a slave wage and has rights granted only by his or her master, so that the slave's burdens are still heavy. The slave longs for freedom but can't loosen the chains. The scars a there but they're on the inside, not visible to the naked eye. The labourer doesn't know what's happened to freedom; the dream has turned into a nightmare of cyclical poverty, and the slave wonders which state was the better: unpaid slavery or wage slavery.

> In 1763, the French journalist Simon Linguet published a description of wage slavery [Marx, Karl (1969) [1863]. *Theories of Surplus Value.* Moscow: Progress Publishers.]: *The slave was precious to his master because of the money he had cost him . . . They were worth at least as much as they could be sold for in the market . . . It is the impossibility of living by any other means that compels our farm labourers to till the soil whose fruits they will not eat and our masons to construct buildings in which they will not live . . . It is want that compels them to go down on their knees to the rich man in order to get from him permission to enrich him . . . what effective gain [has] the suppression of slavery brought [him ?] He is free, you say. Ah! That is his misfortune . . . These men . . . [have] the most terrible, the most imperious of masters, that is, need. . . . They must therefore find someone to hire them, or die of hunger. Is that to be free?*

The peasant working on the lord's fields is now a professional, congregated with others in the towns or cities, free to choose who to work for in order to earn a living. A break in such employment, however, will prove disastrous, because the unemployed can't afford dwellings; the creditors will take away their cars, furniture, and other goods they may have obtained; and they'll be what they're truly worth, mere peasants, labouring in the lord's businesses, dependent on the lord for their very survival, protection, and livelihood.

Capitalism has created a class structure whereby the poor remain the poor, and they don't know why or how it came about. They know they're oppressed, but the cause of the oppression isn't visible to them. They seek a way out of the dungeon of dependency, but the door is tantalizingly unreachable. The preachers of salvation through capitalism preach a false gospel. They clamour for monetary wage increases, which within a year are insufficient again. Wages don't satisfy the wage earner; they're simply a drug to numb the pain until the next morning, and they often cause a hangover.

The capitalist system has perfected the art of slavery; it's polished peasantry to think of itself as a labour force and has managed to maintain the class structures in inherited from feudalism to its best advantage. All labourers should be seen as slaves in a capitalist system; regardless of the names their roles are given.

Can Capitalism Be Democratic?

Free-market capitalism is said to refer to an economic system where prices of the means of production and of the final goods and services are set by the forces of supply and demand and are allowed to reach their point of equilibrium without government interference. By means of government policy, the laws of supply and demand are allowed to determine prices, production, and interest rates. Such government policy typically entails support for highly competitive markets, the private ownership of productive enterprises, and the protection of property rights, among others. A democratic capitalist market is envisaged to be a capitalist economic system operating in a democratic political environment. This can only be true if democracy is narrowly defined to restrict it to a political application only, and not to economic and social spheres. Such a democracy would be limited to a few who are benefited by the system and not the rest of the people.

Democracy can't exist in a capitalist political economy because the system involves a government and a business aristocracy oppressing and suppressing the majority in economic subjugation. Free markets are an illusion created for propaganda purposes as the government is the guarantor and protector of the wealthy, through clever laws, limiting legislation, support for big business, and lower taxation for the rich, which makes it impossible for the poor majority to ever match the powerful rich. Capitalism is an economic system based on the benefit of the provider of capital and no one else. The profits of the business and the business always remains the property of the capitalist, and anyone who works for the business is only paid a salary and nothing more. It's a system of selfish and privileged exploitation of the worker and works to the benefit of the owners of capital.

Capitalism Claims
It's often implied that capitalism is characterised by freedom of enterprise (no monolithic government imposing control on decisions), free competition (everyone is free to engage in business), and private property rights (no oppression) in which the profit motive provides an invisible hand to drive economic activity efficiently (no bureaucracy limiting the smooth running of the economy) and the capitalist system eliminates poverty by creating more employment and jobs for everyone and producing higher economic output than any system.

Created by Those in Power
It has already been noted that capitalism was created for the benefit of the then-kings and the nobility and aristocracy; the system is

set by default to suppress the majority for the benefit of the ruling and the upper class. This system is designed by the rulers, for the rulers, and by creation it required a government—and a powerful one for that matter—for it to be implemented. The laws and rules that the upper class rely upon and the rulers use to establish their right to the fruits of the majority's sweat are imposed by a government. The capitalist system is a fully governmental system that relies on the power of government to exist and wouldn't itself exist without the power imposed by the laws of the governments on the lower classes. The size of the government and the amount of taxes needed to fund it, are the privilege of the government to decide and aren't left to the democratic processes.

Protected by Those in Power

Free competition isn't existent in a capitalist economic system because the barriers to entry imposed both by the government and by the capitalists are so insurmountable that it's only through a miraculous invention, or something similar, that one can hope to join the ranks of the wealthy. One would need to solicit the help of the capitalists most of the time to be able to participate in the same sphere. Capitalism allows cartels, oligopolies, and governments to limit participation by others. The systems of patents, certain property rights, and restraint of trade, among other restrictions, allow holders to exclude others from participating in certain economic activities. Capitalism makes only a few richer while the majority are made to be poorer, vulnerable, and totally dependent on the rich and the government.

Serves and Benefits Those in Power

It's a system that lends itself to the principle of survival of the fittest and the oppression and enslavement of the poor and the weak. Economic justice, fairness, and equality aren't available in this system, and where they're called for they're meant to apply only to the capitalists. The system fails to address equality and justice as they apply to the poor, the weak, and the minority. Democracy, on the other hand, is a political system based on the principles of majority consent and political equality. Under such systems, minorities and the poor are afforded fairness and equity and are accommodated rather than eliminated. A capitalist system acts in the capitalists' self-interest, wealth accumulation being the only motive that drives action. The interests of the majority are of little concern to the capitalists if they don't result in more wealth for the capitalists.

Capitalists openly finance political leaders who will in turn protect and promote a capitalist political economy. The governments in politically democratic countries with a capitalist economy are there to serve the capitalists. It's never possible in such nations for a politician without capitalist funding to gain political power, and in such nations political groupings tend to reflect capitalist interests. The political space is monopolised by the capitalists, who rule in perpetuity through whoever they put into government. It doesn't matter who's "ruling" politically, because a capitalist system is meant for the service of those in government and those of the wealthy aristocracy to benefit from the sweat of the lower classes.

Invisible Hand Directing Efficiency

Capitalism allows a few individuals to determine what has to be produced and the quantities to be produced to enable them to make a profit. Products such as luxuries are overproduced at the expense of staples and other basics that benefit the poor, because those luxuries yield higher returns. There's no invisible hand in capitalism, but there's a capitalist and a government working in partnership to preserve and prolong their long-oppressive reign on the masses by creating a system of trade that ensures a return for them in any production. Efficiency requires that no unnecessary product, service, or expense be spent. Capitalism not only has a damaging effect on the environment but also isn't self-sustaining. It's prone to cyclical periods of economic crisis and is dependent on consumerism.

Democratic Capitalism?

It's clearly difficult to arrive at a point where capitalism can be called democratic unless one is being dishonest. The freedom envisaged under democracy can't be political freedom without economic freedom. Capitalism rapidly becomes autocratic and begins to control the policies and decisions of government, working together to make economic decisions for the lower classes. Freedom can't be administered in half doses or selectively. Either a person is free, in totality, or he or she is not free at all. Economic freedom is thus a prerequisite for any democratic freedom to be complete. To be politically free to elect leaders while a minority makes decisions about economics is to be hoodwinked. Democracy and capitalism can't coexist without one being compromised. Concepts like democratic capitalism exist only in the minds of those who've allowed themselves to believe that it can exist and can never go together in reality.

A Mixed Economy

Those who propose a mixed system of political economy describe it as a largely capitalist economy where a government intervenes through macroeconomic policies intended to correct the shortcomings of a capitalist economy such as market failures, unemployment, inflation, and failure to produce any public good. However, this seems to be nothing more than a cleverly devised attempt to escape being labelled capitalist. Mixed economies are in all ways capitalist economies and the "public ownership" of the means of production is just another way in which government supports capitalism.

Capitalism, whether practised by a capitalist or by a capitalist government, remains what it is. The phrase "mixed economy" is meaningless and shouldn't have found its way into usage, because for a capitalist system to exist successfully, it needs a government to support it. A mixture of government and capitalism is required for a capitalist economy to exist and continue.

The Good in Capitalism

Economic Growth

Capitalist nations have emphasised capitalism's ability to promote economic growth as the major argument in favour of their systems. They point to measures of economic activity such as total economic output, capacity utilisation, employment rates, and the general improvements in standards of living of the general populace as a whole and argue that these are the good effects of capitalism. They maintain that letting the free market control production and price, as well as allocate resources, will make everyone better off over time.

Proponents also believe that a capitalist economy offers more opportunities for individuals to raise their income through new professions or business ventures than do other forms of economic systems. In their view, this potential is much greater than in either traditional feudal or in socialist societies.

Self-Organisation

Capitalist economists argue that capitalism has managed to organise economic activity in very large and complex economies without external guidance or centralised planning. Capitalist economies allow market forces to determine who owns the means of production, how production takes place, and also how the wealth produced is distributed. Capitalists, in order to control the means of production, the production processes, and the distribution of wealth, require that a government be in place to protect the rights of such forms of market determination to take place, as well as to the right to the wealth created. Self-organisation means that any activity that interferes with the processes leads to inefficiency and is generally frowned upon.

Capitalism has been credited with being able to organise the formerly simple processes of wealth creation by landlords into the present-day industrial operations and has managed to gather the peasants into cities and towns, providing a formidable army of labourers who must daily move to and from work. It's doubtful that another system could have achieved such a feat with similar results.

Criticism of Capitalism

Any criticism of capitalism, for it to be fair, also requires the critic to offer a better system than capitalism. It needs to be better not just in the areas where capitalism fails but must even surpass the good elements of capitalism. So far, history has shown that replacing capitalism with a different political economy results in a decrease in the overall wealth of the economy. Any system that replaces another should, for it to be considered better, result in the individual and overall wealth of that system being higher than before.

In a capitalist political economy, the capitalist owns capital, has the privilege to control employment/labour, and controls those in power. By its very nature, capitalist development leads to the concentration of wealth, capital, and power in the hands of very few, leaving the majority without these things.

Democracy and Free Markets

In a democracy, every eligible person has a right to vote and the right to choose, from a given list, who will lead them. The list is compiled by the various competing factions and interests in the political arena. The proposed and elected leaders will promote certain policies and put in certain structures which they assume will address the electorate's problems, wishes, and aspirations. In a capitalist political economy, such leaders will aim to preserve the rights of the capitalists over and above the labourers and the remainder of the population.

The allocation of the limited means of production in a capitalist political economy is determined by market forces. If one class of people happens to own the means of production, those who aspire to own the same must do so on market terms. Those who own the means of production also make the investment and production decisions. Labourers are obliged to work in order to meet their needs and wants. The government is there to protect this arrangement and to ensure that only market forces are used to determine the decisions of those who control the wealth of the nation. It's thus not possible for a capitalist political economy to be called a democratic economy.

It *is* possible, however, for those nations who've been labelled as democratic to institute capitalist political economies where democratically elected leaders implement a capitalist political economy. In capitalist thinking, political democracy should be used to decide political leaders but not the economy. To a capitalist, economic democracy means allowing those who own wealth to preserve that wealth and allowing market forces to determine economic leadership.

In reality, the one who controls the economy in turn determines the politics. The capitalist needs to protect and preserve his wealth and has to influence those in politics to enact policies that perpetuate that. It's a rarity for a political leader in a capitalist economy not to be influenced by capitalists in the making of economic policies. Political leaders may have the vote of the majority or the wind of a revolution under their wings, and they may truly have the interests of everyone at heart, but when faced with a capitalist political economy, with its laws, policies, and rights already etched in the stone by precedent and precept, they're obliged to let the market forces do the work.

Policies that bear the support of the majority but are frowned upon by the capitalist are set aside. By this means decisions that might be unpopular with the majority, but that benefit the capitalist, are supported by political leaders and are translated into law. Politicians in a capitalist economy aren't the rulers but are mere figureheads who implement the decisions of the economic lords. They're a democratic facade to sell the decisions of the capitalists to the majority by using the least offensive propaganda. They point out that the capitalists are actually creating employment for the majority and utilizing the nation's resources in a much better way than would otherwise be used, and that anything that threatens capitalism is undesirable.

Economic Freedom

The measurement of economic growth based on total output and other totals doesn't consider the effects on the distribution of income, welfare of the individual classes, and the sustainability of such outputs. There remains a deliberate propaganda to make people believe that democracy, free market, and economic freedom are synonymous with capitalism and that one needs capitalism to enjoy those values. Capitalism offers none of the three values but rather suppresses all three. Economic freedom is a privilege of the rich and wealthy only and isn't available to the majority, as they're clearly under economic burdens imposed on them by the state and the wealthy.

Capitalism leads to a significant loss of political, democratic, and economic power for a nation's majority of people, because capitalism concentrates wealth in the hands of a relatively small minority. The minority rich is able to control the majority poor by means of systems such as democratic capitalism. The wealth of the minority thus increases and that of the majority is decreased, and inequalities of wealth and income between the wealthy minority and the poorer majority of the population are worsened. The majority are only granted political freedom to choose between leaders who will be controlled and directed by the capitalists. Capitalism leads in this way to the complete destruction of economic freedom for the majority.

Capitalism has been criticised for the amount of power and influence that vested interest groups have over government policy, including the policies of regulatory agencies and influencing over political campaigns.

Socialism as an Economic System and Political Philosophy

Socialism is a form of political economy wherein the means of production are said to be owned by all the people in that economy and are managed on their behalf by the government, cooperatives, or other groups chosen by the people. The system seeks to make away with the capitalist principle of privately owning the means of production by a small minority, so that the majority is no longer condemned to work for that minority. Capitalism and socialism appear as opposites in several of their characteristics, but while socialism seeks to improve on capitalism, it imposes a planning burden on the economy that tends to choke it before any real wealth is created. Socialism engages the means of production to produce wealth, not for profit maximisation but to satisfy the needs and wants of the majority. The distribution of the wealth thus produced is distributed according to how much each individual has contributed to its production.

Criticism of Socialism

Capitalists regard private ownership of the means of production, the right to determine the manner of wealth creation, and the right to the wealth thus created—not to mention the working of market forces—as democratic rights which shouldn't be alienated from them. These are central to their concepts of freedom and liberty, and they perceive any form of government encroachment in these areas as unwarranted. Concepts such as the public ownership of the means of production or government involvement in the wealth production process and in the distribution thereof—other than through market forces—are seen as infringements upon their economic liberty.

Historically, those who've advocated for socialism have put forward government involvement in wealth production as the chief means of achieving socialism. However governments in almost all political systems aren't accountable to the people in their economic activities. Giving more control to governments who already control the bulk of economic power doesn't achieve the goals of socialism.

The ideals of socialism are most enticing, but the manner of achieving those ideals is often a grey area with various tools and various forms of economic structures, such as cooperatives, workers funds, community ownership, etc. These structures are often, in practice, less successful compared to capitalist companies and businesses because of their bureaucratic make-up and general lack of support from government.

A socialist economy is often accused of lacking the profit motive or any motive at all to increase wealth. The absence of the profit motive makes socialism as a political economy less productive in wealth creation than would be achieved under capitalism. The amount of central planning and coordination are avoided in a capitalist model, which is more efficient.

Socialism tends to rule by majority and ignore the minority. It values the well-being of the majority over and above that of the minority. For this reason it's possible in socialism to distribute the wealth of the minority to the majority, even when the total wealth of the society as a whole is lowered. It's not an efficient and equitable system in that it results in a continuous presence of such a possibility and individuals aren't motivated to engage in any greater wealth creation which they won't accumulate but be forced by the system to distribute to others.

All governments engage is socialist activities (i.e., building public infrastructure, providing free public services, etc.), and it's one of the few things they tend to do well enough in the absence of charities, religious entities, or similar philanthropic entities. All government activities in other political economic systems tend to be socialistic. Taxation has no other justification other than the socialism role of government.

Alternative to Capitalism and Socialism

The question as to which political economy system is the most suitable for a nation isn't answered by a single economic system, nor does it lie in a multiplicity or mixture of systems. Capitalism, with all its defects, is the system that dominates the world today and is built on individual enterprise, which results in high economic productivity, although the capitalist system allows the wealth to accumulate to a few individuals. Private ownership provides a necessary motive for wealth accumulation and reward for hard work. , any economic system that allows individual enterprise (i.e., a system that gives opportunities to start a business, the opportunity to work, and the liberty to reap the rewards of such labour) offers the most potent method of wealth creation and incorporates certain liberties that are important to economic freedom.

Individual enterprise is a form of democratic economic system that deals away with the autocracy of capitalism and the burden of high government taxes and also ensures economic participation of the majority through democratic decision-making, resource allocation, and rewarding systems. The advances in technology and political democracy in this day and age can easily be harnessed in disseminating economic knowledge to most people and should form the building blocks for a democratic economic system that promotes individual economic freedom.

On the Allocation of the Means of Production

The allocation of the means of production is a highly emotional issue, and rightly so. Tribes and nations have fought wars over pieces of land, oil wells, and rich mines, and water is the key resource of the future already triggering conflict. Colonised people go to war to liberate themselves and their land. Governments have nationalised land and other strategic resources to free them from the control of the few. The right to private property means that one can't be forced to lose one's property if one doesn't wish. Where an individual owns all the means of production in an economy, the rest of the players in that economy are denied their right to property. The matter is complicated further if the current holder's right to property was historically established through an unjust process such as colonisation, imperialism, oppression, or war.

A truly democratic society should be able to address this problem honestly by applying a "socialist system" to the allocation of resources, within the framework of not impoverishing one in order to make another better off. Socialism is what all governments do and should be doing, and it should be applied within a democratic system to ensure none are deprived of their wealth or made worse off. This can be achieved through equitable tax systems, fair presentation of opportunities to everyone, and participatory and democratic allocation of financial capital. Achieving these within a democratic system is the height of good governance. A good tax system will ensure that a government has got the means to distribute resources equitable among its populace without unjustly making other participants worse off.

It's important to note that both of these systems have been criticised, and particularly socialism has been painted in a bad picture, so much that the word itself has assumed a different meaning to what it should truly mean. It's used here to mean what is should always have meant: those activities of government and society (usually churches, charity organisations, and individuals) which are meant to address the shortcomings of economics.

Feudalism fails to allocate resources equitably among its participants. It leads to a society of oppressed people ruled by an overlord. Capitalism is a close cousin of feudalism, and it refines the inequalities of its cousin, although it's expanded the class structures by adding a middle class. The governments in these situations aim to address the gaps left by the feudalist and the capitalist, respectively. Governments aren't to be left unchecked and to their own whims in implementing their roles. The size of government, the extent and scope of its activities, and the budget upon which it's to preside should frequently be democratically reviewed.

On Industry and Wealth Creation

What is attributed to capitalism as resulting in economic growth is the individual enterprising that accompanies almost any economic system. Individual enterprise flourishes where everyone is given an opportunity to work out his or her own success without unfair advantage, without crushing taxes, and in a competitive environment of abundant information. Individual enterprise is the best way to make a stable and sustainable economy, based on sound industry, well distributed and not biased towards a particular class or group. Individual enterprise will create more wealth than that ever produced by capitalism, and while at it, won't provide the instability and volatility obvious in the capitalist system.

Individual enterprise should be supported by a lean and efficient government of a size that the taxes available from the people can support. Taxes that allow people to retain the bulk of their hard-earned wealth will allow even the lower classes to work up the economic ladder and to be economically free. Debt and poverty will be overcome, and those of the middle class will be able to work and save for investment in their own enterprises. It's curious to note that most educated and trained professionals in most capitalist countries aren't able to own their own businesses in the current set-up of economics, even though they're the backbones of most of those enterprises. The choice available to them is working for another and rarely is they afforded a chance to form their own businesses and actively supported by their government.

Through deliberate policies and systems, the current capitalist centred systems don't reward hard work and don't promote those who've studied and obtained specialist skills, other than to elevate them into higher level employees (slaves) for the rest of their lives. The working middle class in particular is overtaxed, hardly rewarded, and exploited. If one works hard in life to be highly skilled in a certain profession or field, he or she is entitled to the better reward than and shouldn't be taxed higher than the one who's decided not to work harder in life. Neither should he or she be considered more able to pay higher taxes than lower-level employees. Capitalism has punished this working middle class and has thus killed individual enterprise at the point at which it's most likely to flourish. Wealth creation shouldn't be made a privilege of a few rich individuals while the rest are reduced to workers and labourers.

In addition to providing equal opportunities to wealth creation, a perfect economic democratic system should enable the democratic process to make economic decisions, including national budgets and government borrowing. This doesn't mean mere consultation and public participation by an often-ignorant electorate, as in the current best cases. It requires an economically literate electorate that's well versed in the decisions at hand and allows opposite views and other alternatives to be considered before any polling. Political office polling shouldn't be used for annual decisions such as budgets and taxes because these two don't go together.

The economic democracy should also importantly be available to private company employees, customers, suppliers, and stakeholders. Customers, employees, and the community should be democratically involved in company decisions that affect them. Information should be availed to them to be able to make these decisions, and these rights should enable them to give informed input before decisions are finalised. The combination of capitalists and government forms an economic dictatorship that has led not only to less wealth creation but also to the great economic ignorance of the majority in most capitalist nations in Europe, America and the rest of the world.

The result of promoting individual enterprise in a democratic society is a more equitable society in which a just reward is paid for hard work and in which there's greater security of all economic rights, greater democracy, better economic literacy, and most importantly, greater wealth—individually and in total.

The merits of an individual-enterprise economic system can only be rightly enjoyed if the right economic structures are in place to ensure that the economic freedoms of society aren't eroded. While the production of wealth is efficient for maximizing profit, there's danger in that there might be overexploitation of labour and abuse of the environment and the economically dependent by those who control production. Unemployment and the overproduction of luxuries which don't benefit the majority are a waste of a means of production that could be used more efficiently elsewhere. Without the right structural adjustments, individual enterprise will degenerate into capitalism. Economic structures are discussed in detail in the next chapter.

On Wealth Distribution

Equity (fairness and impartiality) is a prerequisite for a system to be stable and for it to exist in perpetuity. The distribution of wealth should be fair and equitable in the sharing out of the fruits of industry and labour. Those who've made a contribution to the cake should get to eat some of it. Capitalism is inefficient in that it allocates the whole cake to the owner of the means of production and ignores the labourer who it considers a part of the means of production rather than a partner who could benefit from profits.

The best system for the distribution of wealth is a system closely linked to the allocation question of political economy. Employee participation in profit-sharing doesn't only increase the wealth created, it creates a non-toxic environment of shared goals and mutual trust between the employer and the employee. While a wage, salary, or employee-share ownership rewards the individual, a nation's wealth is also distributed through taxation, budget allocations, and other similar benefits usually managed by a government. Employees should, to the extent that they contribute to the profits of the company, be included in decision-making and also in profit-sharing. A system of taxation that is equitable, a fiscal policy that is fair and just, and a system of public expenditure that is sustainable in relation to the economy are important pillars of a democratic political economy.

III

Economic Structures

Definition Economic structure is a notion concerned with the configuration of relationships and make-up of the components of an economy and the particular way the various parts are held or put together. The way in which the components of an economy are arranged or put together to form a whole, vehicular arrangement or formation determines how the economy as an organism will operate, exist, appear, and most importantly, enable economic agents to act, make choices, and achieve their objective of creating wealth. Just like in an organism, the tissues, organs, or the way atoms in a molecule are joined to each other affect the behaviour, nature, and appearance of those, so does the pattern or system of economic beliefs, relationships, institutions, etc., in an economy affect the functioning of a nation.

Analysis of structure is an essential foundation and starting point in understanding any system or subject, and political economy is no exception. In constructing a building, the structural engineer makes sure the frame, pillars, and columns have enough strength to not only be able to hold up the weight of the building itself (dead weight), but also to withstand the additional traffic that will move into its different storeys (live weight), together with the forces exerted on it externally, such as earthquakes, wind, etc. Any structure, whether it be a bridge, a tree, or an organisation—be it simple or highly complicated—has a structure, which makes it able to maintain its systems and carry out its functions. In a similar manner the political economy of a society should have in it structures that enable the operation of its economic systems.

Legislative Behaviour and Organisation

In creating wealth, economic systems need structures place that will enable them to function. The government enacts a system of laws and rules (corporate, tax, labour, accounting, financial, property, and trade laws) that govern the relationships between people and that give effect to the creation of certain entities. Economic players make use of the available structures in an economy, to have access to economic recourses, to create wealth, and to preserve that wealth. The protection of the citizen's right to private property requires the state to have a system of recording such property and enforcing such rights. Consideration of such structures is important to fully grasp their functioning and the workings of the various political economies and will enable one to attend to the issues within these structures considered beneficial or detrimental. The government and tax structures are considered in greater detail in chapters seven and six respectively due to the magnitude of their impact on the political economy of any society.

An economy may have the best economic system, with periods of high wealth creation and productivity, but if the structures aren't designed to enable fairness, justice, and equity, the structure will act as a strangling upon the lifeline of the trampled, and the wealth will choke—rather than nourish—society. Structures are the veins and arteries, the contours and embankments that act to direct and deliver activity and nourishment to all parts of a society. They must be both well laid and designed to direct the right quantities for the good and nourishment of the whole system, or they'll act to the detriment of the system, if not well positioned and constructed.

Judicial Institutions: State/Government Protection

Any political economy system requires a state authority to enforce the rights and protect the wealth of its individual players. The feudalist required a state structure that granted the lordship over the slave, the capitalist needs protection for rights to the means of production and wealth gained, and the socialist requires a government to make all decisions for the people. The state acts as the guarantor, enforcer, and protector of such rights. In a feudalist system the state is loosely in control. The feudal lord is semi-autonomous and actively seeking to influence any laws and their implementation. The feudalist is almost self-sufficient, and the government doesn't interfere much in his or her decisions making. The capitalist society requires the state to protect its rights and to leave it to engage in laissez-faireism. The state works as an extension of the capitalist, who influences it due to the financial and economic power that accrues by virtue of his or her wealth.

Political Economics and the Law: Legal Institutions

The legal framework required for a political economy system to prevail is the most important consideration of understand political economic structures. While the right to private property is assumed in some instances, where this is challenged the law must provide recourse for the concerned parties. Statutory law and common laws are available to be utilised in this regard.

The historical development of feudalism was such that it had several disadvantages. There was a large dependence on land as the means of production. Feudalism was centralised upon a physical individual as lord, and in conditions of war, a change was likely as allegiances changed, depending on the security guaranteed by the lord. Feudalism was unstable, and continuity wasn't guaranteed as it depended on the ability of the lord to protect, tax, rule, and control his or her subjects. Feudalism created a system of classes of the rich and the poor. The rich openly exploited the poor for the system to work. The poor could hardly hope to be the lord or even to be rich at any point. It entrenched the class system and condemned the poor to poverty. The system made the minority more prosperous and the majority poorer and failed to address the welfare of the system as a whole. It was a system that set itself on the path to destruction, not addressing the political-economy aspirations of its majority players.

The capitalist system that replaced the feudalist system sought to provide remedies to the shortcomings of the feudalist system. Laws were made that created and recognised a juristic person, an entity that could be legally considered a person but which wasn't a physical person. This legal entity could do all the things that the actual person could do except that it didn't suffer from the disadvantages of the physical person. This entity was termed a company and was controlled by whoever formed the company. The company corporate couldn't die even when the owner/creator of the company died. The company was considered separate from the individual and could legally sue and be sued. The laws concerning the company are capitalism's weapons of security where the feudalist failed to provide such security. The laws of the company enabled it to be protected and also protected its owner. The company gave capitalism the legal security to private property that the feudalism failed to guarantee.

A company can be defined as an "artificial person," invisible, intangible, and immortal, created by or under law, as a separate and distinct/discrete legal entity, with a perpetual life and succession.

It's not affected by the death, insanity, or insolvency of its individual owner. The company is considered separate and distinct from its members, and it can hold property in its own name and it can sue or be sued. The invention of the corporate company was therefore the most creative invention of capitalism.

Our Politicians and Their Mistresses

History bears enough testimony of the many mistresses that politicians and other powerful people have had and of the effects these have had on the careers of the politicians and the mistresses. Power enables one to be able to break the rules that one wouldn't normally break without that power. It also enables the powerful to hide their mistresses and their affairs from their wives, and if a wife finds out, this power enables the cheating husband to suppress and muzzle his wife from doing anything that would be considered damaging to the powerful.

Society has a way of not being satisfied with calling mistresses by their formal names, since they're not formal to start with, and this infamous institution tends to get names that graphically and often more aptly match the infamy. The faithful wife often has to go through the honourable disgrace of standing by the side of her husband while his affairs are exposed. This is particularly the case in most traditional households, especially in African cultures where gender rights are limited to cultural norms.

As such one often finds that the "wife of youth," with whom a husband has been through thick and thin and to whom vows have been made for lifelong fidelity, in later life, after more power and wealth is acquired, is often cheated upon by the husband for the more dashing and "beautiful" mistress, who the wife accuses of reaping the rewards of their hard work and life savings. While these scandals are of a sour but keen interest to most people, they bear a canny and parabolic parallel to a grander and one of the most phenomenal scandals the politicians have ever pulled on their faithful electorate, and they've done this with astounding success. Political democracy is usually premised around a political representatives elected by the people to represent and implement the people's collective will. The leadership is ultimately supposed to be accountable to the people, if all goes well. The investor and business community of a nation however often makes it difficult for this relationship to work smoothly and often make the politicians accountable to them more than to anyone else, making representative democracy of no effect. The marriage relationship bears a close resemblance and the unfaithful husband being the political leaders who betray their political vows to the faithful electorate at the behest of investors and businesses in general.

The political order of most European and American nations is often one in which the leaders are chosen from the successful and powerful business people and leaders who are interested in politics and who, of course, will execute the mandate of business in their political terms before retiring and coming back to the business community. In developing nations, most of whom were under colonial powers, the throne is often reserved for those who fought in the liberation wars which ended the political grip of the imperialists. The other pretenders to the throne come from the workers organisations and similar grassroots entities which are anchored on mass support and people-oriented organisations. In all cases the politicians always pledge their undying love for all the people and swear to serve all and only all, faithfully and unswerving.

Election time often marks the only moment when leaders remember their constituencies, and they often come loaded with enough promises to make Santa Claus envious. Housing, jobs, tarred roads and other infrastructure, free social grants, you name it—they're promised as tokens of their undying love for the masses of voters. In return, all the masses have to do is reciprocate the love by voting in their number for this politician in shining shoes who's down on one knee.

Immediately after the election celebrations and its accompanying sounds and noises have subsided enough for one to make a speech, the same politicians religiously quick to issue reassuring statements and pronouncements that they're still committed to promoting businesses, that they're actually pro-business, and that they'll balance their election promises to the people with responsible actions to promote businesses. The appointment of finance ministers and similar portfolios is often the highlight of the government's commitment to business with the individuals chosen often judged by their acumen in business and their leaning towards that and being condemned if any hint of being pro-people is detected. The politician vows to the masses and the next day is telling the whole world, "It was just a necessary lie. My affections are actually with my mistress, and no one should really take those promises I made to my wife as serious. I'm going to actually do those things that will promote the interests of business."

In business the politician has found a willing mistress who doesn't hide her demands, and she has the politician on a leash. It so happens that the politician thinks the business is the solution to all the problems he has to solve. She has money to start with, creates jobs for his poor children, and is wrongly assumed to be the major contributor of taxes to the government and all other delicacies that ever made their way to the politicians. She funds his campaigns for office, and she sponsors his parades, sports events, and galas and pays for his food. In return he makes sure all her needs are catered for. He protects her business interests, allows her to engage in all other fetishes that she desires, and enacts laws to protect those rights lest the masses turn against her.

The less sophisticated housewife, not smart or elegantly dressed, is ditched for the business mistress who's more scheming and charming. Has the politician immediately broken his vows and betrayed the wife of his youth in the most hurtful of ways? Does she know about it, and does she realise what's just happened? Or does the weight of her ignorance prevent her from knowing? Does her husband manipulate her, ward her of the need for him to charm the mistress lest she run away and their children have no employment? Is she the ever-faithful wife who bears long and hopes that one day the husband will come to his senses and stop his philandering?

Since politicians have to make public statements, they've perfected the art of cheating by designing a form of double-talk addressed at the masses but directed at the mistress. What appears to the masses as a profession of love for them will turn out to be a love poem directed at the mistress, when the actions are examined.

Economic blueprints, national development plans, growth strategies, etc., are always couched in words that on the surface seem like the government has the interest of the people at heart. However a closer look at most of these shows that the implementation involves dishing out every available resource and opportunity to the mistresses. The implementation involves immediately doing something for the mistress and hoping that her abundance will result in more employment for the masses. The trickle down, slow and low, is often recorded in great detail and considered a cause for celebration. It's often contained in phrases like, "We need to grow the economy by five times its current rate by *this time* (often more than twenty years later) in order to create x million jobs, and this will reduce employment by x per cent"—a love letter to the mistress, delivered as an expression of love to the wife. To the latter, the love is to be delivered after a long time, and in some diminished quantities and only on condition of the immediate and adequate satisfaction of the mistress's desires.

The policy of delivering feasts to the businesses and hoping for some breadcrumbs to find their way to the masses is a calculated form of double-talk which is meant for the ignorant ears of the masses but which both the mistress and the politician know is propaganda, designed to keep the promise of better times ever there but never fulfilled.

The politicians have long since designed a system of apartheid economic train which has three categories. The apartheid system in South Africa up to 1994 is a perfect distillation of this machinery. Instead of segregating on racial lines, this system segregates economically. One door is for the masses, and once one enters that door, he or she is like a bull castrated, set on the yoke, and promised to be restored with his severed parts only after he's worked hard enough. This compartment is the crowded one in which all the eunuchs are racing against no one in particular but running for their lives, while the politician and his mistress enjoy popcorn and wine, watching in amusement. The other compartment is, of course, the first-class part of this train, while the third is a cockpit just at the front and occupied by none other than the politician who's the janitor of the circus.

Elections and other periodic tokens of democratic processes are reduced to mere changing of drivers and dramatisations of legitimacy. Any decisions contrary to the set configurations of the political economic system are overridden and can not work so long the system is structured to fail the majority at the expense of the powerful and rich. The new leaders have no option and no room to manoeuvre because the locomotive is not set to be changed. They become powerless figureheads of a powerful system working against their consciences and resort to propaganda to justify their powerlessness. A husband under the spell of a mistress, who enjoys the stolen pleasures; a politician under the influence of the powerful and the rich, a neglected wife and family, a jilted electorate: a structure that requires wholesale change.

The Company Economic Unit

Companies are created as legal persons by the laws and regulations of a nation. The statutory granting of corporate existence was done by way of a statute to create a specific company but came to arise from general-purpose legislation. In addition to the statutory laws, companies are subject to common law in some countries, as well various laws and regulations affecting business practices.

Historically, in a feudal system when a lord gave a piece of land to a fief to take care of, the lord expected at least an increase in wealth. He expected the one charged with looking after the land to be productive and to engage in such business as would amount to an increase in wealth for the lord. As such, if the tenant ended up in a situation where the wealth of the lord was worse than before, the lord required the tenant to make good the loss that he'd caused. The lord could take the possessions of the tenant and, if that weren't enough, could enslave the tenant or even put him or her in prison, until the loss was fully recovered. The tenant, in engaging in business on behalf of the owner of the means of production, was not spared the risk to his or her own property.

Further, when one of the parties to the stewardship contract in the feudal system changed, usually in the case of the death of the master or the tenant, the contract ended, everything was rearranged, and a new agreement with a different person was constituted. The new master or tenant wouldn't necessarily be as good as or engage in the same activities as the former. The traditional feudalist economy lacked the perpetuity of existence that was necessary to carry out wealth creation and to carry the risks of wealth creation without affecting the fortunes of the members of the system. Capitalism created the company to cater for the risks.

A company under capitalism can conduct business, and if such business results in a monumental loss to the company, the extent of that loss is only limited to the company. Only the company is in loss, in insolvency, or in bankruptcy. The owner and the directors aren't required to make good the losses by taking from their private, personal wealth. Anyone who's suffered loss against the said company can only sue the company and, beyond that won't be able to recover any loss from the individuals who formed the company and/or who operated it. The loss to the owners of the company is only to the extent that they've contributed to the company's capital.

The company, forms the most important economic unit in capitalism. Most, if not all, of the activities of the capitalist political economy are carried out through the vehicle called company. The company is able to own the means of production, is able to hire labour, is able to make decisions on investment and production of wealth, and is free to own the wealth thus created. The company can also decide to reward its owners with a dividend of the wealth it has. The company can make a loss and still continue in existence. It can borrow money from creditors and lend money to whomever it pleases. The company has at its helm directors appointed by the owners of the company. The directors make decisions on its behalf and are answerable to the owners of the company, called shareholders.

Corporate Governance, Politics and Corporate Politics

The system by which corporations are directed and controlled is referred to as corporate governance. The governance structure specifies the distribution of rights and responsibilities among different participants in the company and specifies the rules and procedures for making decisions in corporate affairs. Governance provides the structure through which corporations set and pursue their objectives, while reflecting the context of the social, regulatory, and market environments. Governance is a mechanism for monitoring the actions, policies, and decisions of corporations. Governance involves the alignment of interests among the stakeholders. The shareholders of a company put their company, in which they've invested their means of production (capital), into the hands of the directors. The board of directors is responsible for appointing managers and other labourers to perform work in the company. The directors report frequently to the shareholders. Auditors are there to verify whether what the directors have reported about the performance and the wealth position of the company are true or not true. The company pays the auditors for the work they do. Labourers in a company are considered to be internal stakeholders and aren't part of the governance structure. Customers are considered to be external stakeholders.

The internal affairs of a corporation will be governed by the company statutes and common law of the state/country in which the corporation is incorporated. The settlement of conflicts between the shareholders and directors/management, the rights of shareholders, distributions of dividends and corporate property, and the fiduciary obligations (i.e., legal obligations of one party to act in the best interest of another) of management, are all determined in accordance with the law of the state in which the company is incorporated. The external affairs of a corporation—such as labour, employment, and tax issues—are governed by the law of the state in which the company is doing business.

In deciding where to locate and incorporate the company, the shareholders of a company have to choose with the fact in mind that the location will determine which laws govern the activities of the company. They're free to choose the place that has the most favourable laws for their purpose. Laws that allow the company to freely retain wealth created and be least accountable to employees and customers, that put the least restrictions on its activities, and that impose the least amount of taxes will attract companies into that place where such laws exist. The choice has led to some nations, especially capitalist nations, to simplify their laws and make them as attractive for companies as possible, in order to attract these companies to incorporate in their jurisdictions.

Companies exist in part to shield the personal assets of shareholders from personal liability for the debts or actions of a company, and the owners will locate the companies in jurisdictions which maximise this objective.

Limited Liability

The concept of limited liability is a very important concept of the company and has major implications in the political-economic considerations of the entity that a company is. The owners in a limited liability company aren't personally liable for any of the debts of the company, and the worst that they can lose is the value of their investment in that company. If the company with limited liability is sued, then the plaintiffs are suing the company, not its owners or investors.

Although the separation of the company and the shareholder as two different legal persons may be construed to be the reason for the limitation of liability to shareholders, this isn't so. While the separation for all purposes may be important, the limitation of the liability was and remains an intentional statutory obligation. The countries and nations that practise this have enacted the limited liability concept by statute. It's an intentional and wilful protection afforded the capitalist. Limiting the shareholder's liability emanates mainly from the statutory laws by the nation and isn't a requirement for legal separation of shareholder and company.

Limited liability allows the capitalist to invest in a company without the fear that he or she will lose the rest of the wealth that isn't invested in the company. The creditor to the company who fails to recover any dues from the company can't reach beyond the company to the shareholder in order to recover such debt. An employee, who may feel undone by the company, can't approach the shareholder for settlement. The shareholder is shielded from any liability in tort for environmental or personal injuries by the company.

Corporate Shield / Corporate Veil

The corporate shield or corporate veil is a term used to describe the separation of a corporation from its owners in a limited liability company. As a separate entity, a corporation or limited liability company is set up to shield and veil the owners of the corporation from personal liability for the debts or negligence of the business. The corporate veil is the attire that the capitalist puts on in order to conduct business, create wealth, and reap the rewards, and it limits the risks that would normally arise carrying out the business in a personal capacity.

The company enables the capitalist to build a business empire, to build a big reputation and brand, to have products that are recognised across the globe, to invest in faraway lands and to have these continue in posterity even after the death of the owner.

The corporate veil is the metaphorical wall that divides the owner from the business, and protects and shields the capitalist from the risks of doing business. The capitalist can reach beyond the veil and get profits and other rewards of ownership. The owner of the company can't be held responsible for all the debts or its actions, decisions, and malpractices except in very rare circumstances, because they enjoy limited liability. The phrase "piercing the corporate veil" is used to describe the action of a court to hold corporate shareholders personally liable for the debts and liabilities of a corporation.

The history of company laws has shown that the concept of limited liability has been upheld by both common law and statute. The corporate veil has been held in sanctity since its establishment in the mercantile British Empire. The personality behind the veil, while making decisions for the company, has benefited from the veil adorned by the company. The courts have set precedent upon precedent of not being willing to unveil the capitalist behind any company exept in rare and infrequent circumstances. The separation of the personality of a company from the personalities of its shareholders has been upheld in almost all cases, and the corporate veil has thus been termed a corporate shield.

Piercing/Lifting/Rending the Corporate Veil

Piercing the corporate veil, lifting the corporate veil, or rending asunder the corporate veil, are all terms for a legal decision to treat the rights or duties of a corporation as the rights or liabilities of its shareholders. The shareholder is made responsible for the debts and obligations of the company. Only in exceptional situations have the courts "pierced" or "lifted" the corporate veil and allowed anyone to peep beyond it.

The corporate veil might be pierced by the court in the case of fraud, in which the corporation was found to be a sham (or that it was just a façade for illegal activities), set up for the purpose of carrying on fraudulent deals or for fraudulent purposes or where it's established to avoid an existing obligation.

Generally, the plaintiff has to prove that the incorporation was merely a formality and that the corporation neglected corporate formalities and protocols, such as voting to approve major corporate actions in the context of a duly authorised corporate meeting. This is quite often the case when a corporation facing legal liability transfers its assets and business to another corporation with the same management and shareholders. It also happens with single-person corporations managed in a haphazard manner. As such, the veil can be pierced in both civil cases and where regulatory proceedings are taken against a shell corporation.

Business Judgment Rule

The business judgment rule is a concept in corporate case law whereby the directors of a corporation are clothed with the presumption, which the law accords to them, of being motivated in their conduct by a bona fide regard for the interests of the corporation whose affairs the shareholders have committed to their charge.

To challenge the actions of a corporation's board of directors, one has to provide evidence that directors breached their fiduciary duty (of good faith, loyalty, or due care), or that the transaction in question constitutes waste (where the exchange was so one-sided that no business person, in his or her right mind, could've made the same decision as the directors).

The business judgment rule implies that the courts won't review the business decisions of directors who performed their duties in good faith, with the care that an ordinarily prudent person in a like position would exercise under similar circumstances, and in a manner the directors reasonably believe to be in the best interests of the corporation. The business judgment rule is very difficult to overcome, and courts won't interfere with directors unless it's clear they're guilty of fraud or misappropriation of the corporate funds, etc.

In effect, the business judgment rule creates a strong presumption (of good faith, loyalty, or due care) in favour of the directors of a corporation, freeing its members from possible liability for decisions that result in harm to the corporation. The presumption is that, in making business decisions not involving direct self-interest or self-dealing, corporate directors act on an informed basis, in good faith, and in the honest belief that their actions are in the corporation's best interest. The court won't substitute its own notions of what is or isn't sound business judgment if the directors of a corporation acted on an informed basis, in good faith, and in the honest belief that the action taken was in the best interests of the company.

The company is fortified with rules, shields, governance structures, and a legal life that all act to make it a formidable structure within the political economy. The company has higher privileges, greatly protected and endowed with numerous rights, than an ordinary citizen in a society.

Distributive Politics: Capital, Land, Labour, and Other Economic Opportunities

The second set of structures relates to economic opportunities and how they're configured and guaranteed in the political economy. Capital, land, labour ownership or availability, financial knowledge, access to markets, and technological innovations determine the economic growth of an economy. The initial and continuing configuration of these elements among players in the economy, and the manner in which the political economy structures guarantee such configuration will affect the economic prosperity of the economy. The structure prevalent among most developing countries is one where the land is owned by a few, the financial institutions and governments give money to only a few whom they consider creditworthy and risk free, and technological innovations are monopolised for long years by webs of patents to deny access to competitors. There are paradoxical policy positions in the developing world, particularly in providing economic opportunities to the populace.

There are opportunities within the control and influence of government, such as financial capital and credit provision, land rights, mineral rights, and product rights. These are granted by the governments to foreign investors through policies meant to attract foreign direct investment. They bypass their people and prefer that others from outside will come and create employment for the populace. The same people who fought colonialism to gain their land back are handing over the soul of that land to their former masters. The majority gets jobs while the opportunities are reserved for investors. The same opportunities that the settlers sought and obtained by colonialism are now handed over to them in the form of investment opportunities. The industry and other opportunities are made to pass over the people and are used to attract outside investors. The populace have to do with jobs created in the process.

Industry and businesses are the most mobile of investments, and a year or bad profits can see the business relocated to another country. The profits and earnings of the business are easily siphoned out of the country of investment. The farmer can't easily migrate as does the business. The promotion of multinational businesses and companies at the expense of developing local enterprise and without creating new entrepreneurs from the citizens is the worst economic policy one can pursue. The policies actively pursued by governments and supported by trade unions in this age of focusing on employment creation by multinationals and corporate giants, neglecting the development of the citizens, are as wise as feeding one's fat, greedy master with one's own food, expecting and hoping one's hunger will be nourished by such a course of action. The multinational companies don't create employment in the local economy other than that which is sufficient to enable them to extract minerals and other natural resources for these to be shipped and processed in their resource-hungry developed nations.

People/Labour

The relationship that the people in an economy have to the other components determines the prosperity of the economy. The

Democratic Political Economy

European colonial masters of the majority of the developing world pursued a policy of common sense regarding the native that they found in the new worlds. Instead of extermination, the native was spared in order that he may provide the rough labour required to work the land, mines, and other industries on behalf of the colonial master. The native was not made a slave, but made to work and, in return, received a weekly or monthly wage, which he was very glad to have. The wage has been the native's greatest desire and nothing more. The governments, past and present, have not sought to awaken the native from his or her love of a wage. As long as the native has a job to afford a few coins at the end of the week or the month, the native is a happy person. He or she doesn't have good understanding of money, of economics, or of any of the issues that affect him. All he or she cares about is a job that will provide a salary, month on month, year on year.

The governments of the developing world have worked hard (their frantic best) to try and create employment for their people. The policy for emancipation of individuals and people currently pursued by developing nations is to train people to be workers, labourers in the capitalist's companies. They hope by this process to empower the people. This, while being a basic requirement, falls short in achieving freedom for the poor. The effect has been to afford multinational conglomerates a pool of cheap labour which they use to maximise profits in their extractive industries. Little hope exists for these labourers to be able to be entrepreneurs one day. The stakes piled against them, and the rate of failure for any who ventures into small businesses is high. They're contended to be executives and leaders in the foreign conglomerates, and they end there.

The nations in developing countries have blinkered their education and training to produce the best workers and labourers.

The emphasis is on being employed and nothing else. Nations that have prospered in history have not done so by inviting other nationals to invest in their countries or by turning all their population into waged labourers for those investors. They have developed entrepreneurs, hardworking individuals, industrious young people who are supported by the government and given all the advantages necessary to achieve a prosperous nation. Government shouldn't be in the business of creating employment necessarily, because it's not good at that, and because employment can't be created for its sake, but is a by-product of entrepreneurship.

Reconfiguration: Redistribution, Indigenisation, and Empowerment

The structures in place to carry out wealth creation and production are seldom questioned, and they appear to be set in stone. There's a direct relationship between ownership structures and economic growth. A fairer distribution on economic opportunities and resources, working in economic structures that promote equity and fairness, will result in greater economic growth and greater wealth. The process of realigning them requires a complete review and redesign of what currently exists. Those who've attempted to correct the shortcomings of these structures have sought to introduce new participants in the same framework and structure currently in place, through such processes as empowerment, affirmative action, and indigenisation.

In particular, the governments of developing nations have engaged in indigenisation, economic empowerment, and similar such programmes, where formerly disadvantaged groups of populations are given preference in the awarding of tenders, in the employment market, and in resource allocation such as financial support. These have resulted in creating a fertile dungeon of corruption and kickbacks. The result is that cost of doing business has resulted in a lot of overcharging, to cover the costs of corruption.

Democratic Political Economy

The great principle of political economy—that in making one individual wealthier, the economy shouldn't achieve this by making another worse off—is violated by most of the current empowerment and indigenisation programmes being carried out.

These efforts have failed to address the structure problems and have sought to use the same structures with only a change in the people involved hoping to achieve a different result. Proper empowerment isn't distributing already-existing wealth that another has previously created as the result of their labours. Empowerment requires that one be given opportunities and resources at the means-of-production stage (and not at the output stage) so one can sustainably create one's own wealth. In taking from the conglomerates and the rich and dishing out these to whoever is patronage and isn't sustainable, very soon the gravy will run out, and there won't be any more wealth to redistribute.

Such empowerment tends to be selective; that is subject to manipulation. The empowerment of the political elite and the connected against the general population is no different to colonialism. Having a new capitalist, in the form of a formerly disadvantaged person replacing the old colonialist capitalist doesn't translate to economic empowerment of the poor. The crop of empowerment businesses and companies currently being incubated in developing nations can't stand on their own. They require continued connections to politicians and big business. They survive on the government and on other conglomerates, and their continued survival is by continued patronage with the powers that be. Were the umbilical cord to be cut off, they would soon fold up, dry up, and disappear.

The industrialised America, the imperialist Britain, the industrious Germany, and other nations that have at one time greatly prospered, have all achieved prosperity by engaging their people in industry, in entrepreneurial activities, and in real people empowerment.

Conclusions

Companies and individual people form the building components of the structures of an economy, and these will determine how economic opportunities and resources are utilised and distributed for employment in wealth creation. In relation to companies, the courts generally refrain from, avoid, and disdain getting involved in business matters. They don't want to meddle in the business and make decisions for businesses. They respect and uphold the structures that make up the business, and the decisions of those structures are held in sanctity. The separation of roles and duties in the structure is also held by the courts.

The state affords its support and protection of the shareholder through the unit of a company and corporate laws and rules that allow limited liability, separation existence, and perpetuity to companies. The shareholder can't be easily held liable for actions of the company, the company has the right to decide where it wants to be incorporated, and the state gets out of its way to make laws that are most favourable for the brooding of companies in its jurisdiction.

The state also affords those responsible for the day-to-day running of the company surplus protection against those who might be tempted to question their actions in running the company.

It's a fact that governments in general consider companies to be the most important economic unit, and policies and laws have been made to bring more companies into economies. Those who own companies have adequate protection b law of whatever decisions and actions they may pursue.

The company enjoys more honour, more privileges, and more protection than the individuals in a political economy. While in political democracies the individual voter has specific rights to choose leaders, the company has more rights as it can't be subjected to the rules and laws that govern individuals. It has its own separate set of rules to govern it, and the law looks at a company more favourably than an individual. The financial institutions consider the company to be more creditworthy than the individual. The state considers company prosperity more important than that of ordinary people. The workers and the lower classes are only to benefit from the residual effects and by-products of the prosperity of the company.

Solutions Proposals

The individual is the most important creator of wealth and is indispensable whether by machinery or by a juristic structure like a company. The individual worker's industry, ingenuity, and hard work are the driving hand in the company, and are the reason for the wealth being created. The company, just like capitalism, is a most important vehicle in political economy, needs to be considered with the people in mind, and should be harnessed for the benefit of the individuals in society. A full consideration in light of other important issues such as money, inflation, taxation, and fiscal policy will show that it can be a bad master or a most important servant. Just like a dog, it can be let wild to roam and hunt on its own and be vicious and a danger to many species, or it can just as well be domesticated, trained, and used for hunting, protection, companionship, and a source of joy and friendship. The company should be utilised for the benefit of the economy. It should be divested of its monopolist nature and stripped of its negative externalities. The people behind the company, namely the owners and the workers, should find a symbiotic balance of interests based on fairness, equity, and mutual justice.

The right conclusion and solutions can only be viewed in the correct light after discussions on these issues have been presented.

Suffice it, however, to point out that the sacred cow status afforded companies in the political economy is of enormous concern. The states have so far afforded the companies privileges that even dictators would be envious to have. In return, companies have become influential and have controlled political leaders and governments to such levels of puppetry best reserved for the theatre. Special interest groups by companies have supped with the governments, and the hegemony between the ruling and the business elite has left the voting lower classes at the mercy of the rulers, both corporate and political.

IV

Monetary Systems and Currency

Defining Money

Money is the wealth in the form of goods or the services that's desired by participants in an economy, and it's useful to those who acquire it. Money represents the goods or services that are exchanged when currency is used. One party exchanges its money for an equivalent amount of money in the form that it desires. If the form desired isn't easily available, a medium of exchange is put in place as a temporary store for the money until an opportunity arises to convert that store back into actual money in the form desired. Money can thus be seen as the object that is desired and so it's an exchange value, but it's the subject of exchange rather than the means of exchange. It doesn't require a government law or general acceptance to make it acceptable. It has its own intrinsic value, such that, even when stripped of any general acceptance as money or when not backed by any law, it still remains an object of desire which may be exchanged for another.

The most important functions of money are as a store of value and as a standard of deferred payment. Money has to be able to retain its value against expiration, deterioration, inflations, and obsolescence. This is what distinguishes it from all objects that have been used as currency.

Defining Currency

Currency is the medium by which goods or services are exchanged for other goods or services and is any object or record generally accepted in a given socio-economic context as payment for goods and services and repayment of debts.

A currency can be anything declared by a government to be legal tender (fiat currency) and may include plastic currency, cards, or coupons. (Fiat currency is a medium of exchange (e.g., a cheque or bank note), which is without intrinsic use value as a physical commodity. It derives its value not by the amount of material it's made of, but by the act of being declared by a government to be legal tender.)

A government enforces a currency, which can be a certain piece, a minted metal coin, or a promise written out on a certificate, to be accepted as legal tender (that which is accepted as a form of payment for all debts, public and private, within the boundaries of a specified country).

Such laws in practice cause fiat currency to acquire the value of any of the goods and services that it may be traded for within the nation that issues it. Fiat currency, without a government declaration making it legal tender, would be only as good as the paper it's composed of, nearly useless.

A currency's most important functions are as a medium of exchange and as a unit of account (that is to say it's the measure with which a people count or quantify monetary value). Any kind of object or secure, verifiable record that fulfils these functions can be considered currency but isn't necessarily money. A currency may be used to act as a temporary store of value, during the course of the transaction, to enable transactions to take place without any loss of value. A currency should not, however, be used as a means of deferred payment or store of value.

Commodity Currency and the Welfare Test of Money

Historically, currencies have evolved from commodity currency (i.e., the actual commodity with intrinsic value is used as a currency) into the present-day money systems that are based on a fiat currency system (i.e., a piece of paper is used as currency even though it has no intrinsic value of its own). Humans have tried to use almost everything as currency, with varying success: stones, candy, sea shells, metals, salt, leather strips, and hemp, among others. Cattle were and continue to be used as currency in many societies for measuring transactions such as family exchanges of a woman's labour, often known as "bride price." Cattle or other livestock perfectly fulfil the role of money as a store of value and as a standard of deferred payment. Metals also are used as currency and have the advantage of convenience and portability. Other commodities, such as salt, have the disadvantage of being difficult to store even where they carry high values, as salt's done since trade began.

Commodity currencies such as livestock and metals are useful because they're generally a good store of value. These can be measured in any place and at any time where such commodities exist. If one had a herd of ten cattle or a measure of gold and was required to account for it at a different time or place, one could easily calculate the quantity, and everyone could easily relate to the measure. No dispute over the exact amount would arise, and no loss of value would be required to determine the size between a herd of cattle there and then versus here and now. Moreover, livestock continues to grow by procreation and has other utility benefits and by-products, and all these result in greater gain for the bearer. Metals can be kept with very little loss in intrinsic value; the cost of maintenance and securing them from theft and rust are very minimal. More than this, pieces of metal can be divided into any number of parts, and those parts can easily be reunited again by addition—a quality which no other equally durable commodity possesses and which, more than any other renders, them fit to be the instruments of commerce and circulation. Metals have, the qualities of a good currency and also of good money if they're not manipulated. A shortcoming of metal is that an increase in its quantity doesn't always correspond to an increase in the welfare of its holder.

Many economies around the world developed the use of commodity currencies in various forms, depending on their economic activities. Taxes, tributes, and other obligations were originally settled by means of actual commodities like livestock, grain, and other agricultural produce—or in minerals that were considered valuable. In such economies, money and currency bear a close relationship, and an increase in the amount of currency may lead to an increase in the welfare of the people. Where a currency increases without a corresponding increase in the welfare and well-being of the people in an economy, that currency fails to be money. Whether its gold, any other precious metal, or any other form of currency, it thereby fails to be money and its use as money acts against the well-being of the economic players, particularly those who continue to accept and use it as money (i.e., as a store of wealth and as a means of deferred payment).

As measured by commodities, money manifests as the amount of currency that one needs to obtain a commodity or a basket of commodities at any given time. Money is the best measure of the well-being of a given economy at any time, expressed in a currency that best resembles money. For a commodity best to resemble money for an economy, increase in such a commodity must result in a corresponding increase in the well-being of every individual in that economy. Currency, on the other hand, represents only the medium of exchange in a given economy. Currency as such is expandable, contractible, and subject to other manipulation for the convenience of the one in control of it. It follows that a currency as close to money as possible will be more desirable than one that isn't. A currency isn't a reliable measure of wealth if it doesn't have the qualities of money and can't be used as a reliable measure of wealth and well-being.

The most ideal monetary system is a system of commodity currency whereby money is measured by the commodity currency. The currency in such a system is used only as a medium of exchange, and people aren't compelled to accept certain commodities or currencies as legal tender. They're free to determine the form of currency they'll accept, and they're free to determine its value.

A Short History of Currencies

Historically, the barter system of trade (i.e., exchanging one commodity for another) fits the commodity-money system. The use of currency to aid in the barter system was developed in economies where there was a greater complexity of transaction and higher economic activities. Such a currency was backed by money, and the currency was always convertible into money (or commodities). The currency was backed by money and not by a government declaration of legal tender.

In feudal and early capitalist economies, precious metals such as gold and silver were used as currency. This is because they have qualities closely resembling money and have the added advantage of being a convenient currency. However, because of the

need for a trader or for banks to administer trade in such currencies, banks solved the inconvenience of carrying precious metal
currency by instituting the use of representative currency. They
issued receipts to their depositors for the currency deposited
(gold, silver, etc.), and these receipts would be redeemable for
the same amount of currency at a later time. The depositor could
redeem the gold currency and make payments for commodities
at any time. However, these receipts eventually became generally
accepted as a means of payment, and they themselves came to be
used as currency.

It must be noted that the change here wasn't in the money itself, but rather in the currency. The currency was changed from
the actual metal into a paper certificate of deposit. The bank or
trader issued a receipt or certificate to the effect that he or she
holds a certain amount of currency in the bank, and whoever
holds that certificate can at any time redeem the stated amount of
currency from the bank. Over time, these certificates evolved into
paper currency or banknotes.

The "gold standard" was a currency, not a monetary system,
where the medium of exchange took the form of paper notes convertible into pre-set, fixed quantities of gold. These gold-standard
notes were made legal tender by governments, although their redemption into gold coins was usually discouraged. By the beginning of the twentieth century, almost all countries had adopted
the gold standard, backing their legal tender notes with fixed
amounts of gold.

After World War II, at the Bretton Woods Conference, most
countries adopted fiat currencies that were fixed to the United
States' dollar. The US dollar was in turn fixed to gold. However, in
1971, the US government suspended the convertibility of the US
dollar into gold. After this, many other countries depegged their

currencies from the US dollar, so that most of the world's currencies are now backed only by the governments' fiats of legal tender and the ability to convert the respective currencies into goods via payment.

It should be emphasised that fiat currency is one which the value thereof isn't derived from anything intrinsic to the currency or guarantee that it can be converted into a valuable commodity, such as gold. Instead, its value is conferred only by government order, hence the name fiat. Usually, a government declares a fiat currency in the form of notes and coins to be legal tender, making it unlawful *not* to accept the fiat currency as a means of repayment for all debts, public and private. This results in a system where a piece of paper is printed by a government and declared to be a currency in a law proclaimed by the same government. Such a law requires that the paper be accepted as legal tender for any transaction, and the paper is used as currency. Such a piece of paper is forced upon the economy as money, and people have to accept it as money in exchange for goods and services.

Fiat currency only has value if people believe it has value. If people don't believe in it, they'll be unwilling to accept it as payment, whereupon it becomes useless to possess it. This is usually the fate of the smallest denomination coins of any currency, which while still legal tender, most shops will no longer accept such copper or silver coins for payment. Those countries which have experienced long periods of hyperinflation often reached a point where the legal tender currency was no longer accepted by the population. It's important meanwhile to note that the paper currency isn't money. It fails dismally to be money in that an increase in paper money in an economy doesn't improve the well-being of the people in that economy. It's supposed to be a good store of value and a standard of deferred payment, but when this paper currency is compared with a commodity currency, it's clear that the best would be a commodity currency.

A commodity—like cattle—would constitute a better currency than printed paper, because cattle are a better store of value. A herd of fifty cattle today will be comparable to a herd of fifty cattle in fifty years' time, and will be as useful or almost as useful to the person possessing it at that time. On the other hand, a piece of paper currency today won't be comparable and can't be exchanged for the same goods or services in fifty years' time, so won't have the same usefulness to the person holding it in fifty years' time. If one was given a choice of receiving a payment in dollars or pounds currency in fifty years' time, on one hand, and on the other hand to receive the equivalent in cattle then one has to consider the value of both payment options after the said time period and whether each option has been a faithful store of value and can be easily measured at that point in time. After a period of fifty years the cattle would be more valuable, easily identifiable, comparable, and would have stored value, much better than the fixed amount of fiat currency.

Errors about Money

The gravest error one can commit in a political economy is to assume a wrong concept of money. A common error, where money's concerned, is to think that the things used as money are actual money. Most textbooks which describe money fail to define money and to state what it is. They've tended to perpetuate the error of using the functions and everyday tangible objects which are in common use as money to be the actual money.

The crisp wads of cash and the shiny metal coins that we use every day aren't money. They're just what they are: pieces of paper and nice-looking pieces of metal. They don't constitute money at all, and the correct name for them is "currency." The paper used for the currency may not even be worth the amount printed on it, and even though one may get food, clothes, etc., in exchange for that piece of paper, it doesn't mean the paper is worth the equivalent of what it can buy. It's worth that much only because a government which owns and has printed that piece of paper has decreed that it should be accepted as being worth the amount printed on it.

Money is thus not a currency, but it's the value which it's the purpose of the currency to enable exchange. These paper and coins are used to convey the value of goods and services, so that "money" can be conceived of as being the information that one needs for the purpose of exchange, but it requires to be put in a language that can be understood by both parties to the exchange. The language, "currency" in this case, enables the required ideas to be packaged and transmitted. Money needs the medium of a currency so that it may be measured and understood. A currency is the language in which money is conveniently expressed, and it's useful when measuring and accounting for money.

Functions

In literature about economics, where the distinction between money and currency is often blurred, money is generally considered to have four main functions: as a medium of exchange, a unit of account, a standard of deferred payment, and a store of value. Modern textbooks sometimes list only three functions, not considering it to be a standard of deferred payment as a distinct function, but rather subsume it in the others.

I've already shown that, in order to understand the functions clearly, money shouldn't be confused with currency. There are functions for money, and there are other functions for currency.

The Functions of a Currency

As a Medium of Exchange

Money isn't a medium of exchange; it's a currency that serves as a medium of exchange. A currency enables money to be exchanged. Money is the value which parties wish to exchange and they require a currency to transact. A currency can be anything—ranging from receipts, banknotes, promissory notes, or cheques to mere verbal promises. In prisons, cigarettes are used as a medium of exchange among inmates and are acceptable as the currency to pay for food or other goods within the prison economy.

When a currency is used to bring about the exchange of goods and services, it's performing the function of a medium of exchange. It helps to remove the inefficiencies of a barter system, by enabling the conversion of one commodity into another through an exchange of value.

A fair and just determination of value is an essential condition for the exchange of goods and services, efficient allocation of resources, and economic growth. A currency enables a monetary value to be established, and a currency is the conduit through which one commodity is exchanged for another. A currency gives parties the ability to transact an exchange. This is the most important and essential function of a currency.

To be widely acceptable as a medium of exchange, a currency should possess the following characteristics:

- It must value common assets (unit of account)
- It must have stable purchasing power (maintain value at least for the course of the transaction)
- It must maintain constant utility and divisibility (an extra amount of a currency will yield the same satisfaction as the previous equivalent amount)

- It must have a low cost of preservation, and transportation (shouldn't expire, or be cumbersome to carry around)
- It must possess a high market value in relation to volume and weight
- It must be easily recognizable and be resistant to counterfeiting

A good currency should have constant intrinsic value and a stable purchasing power. This is important because in the exchange process one gives up a commodity in exchange for a currency and holds the currency until it can be used to purchase another commodity. Over that time, the currency holder needs at least to obtain the same value at the end as was given up at the beginning. A currency that loses value or fluctuates violently wouldn't be a suitable currency for the purpose of exchange. Gold has popularly been used as a currency because as a medium of exchange and as a store of value it's convenient to move, even small amounts of gold having considerable value, and it can retain a constant value due to its special physical and chemical properties of non-corruptibility.

As a Unit of Account

Unit of account is a standard numerical unit of measurement of the market value of goods, services, and other transactions

A unit of account is often also known as a "measure" or "standard" of relative worth and deferred payment. A unit of account is a necessary prerequisite for the formulation of commercial agreements that involve debt. To function as a unit of account, whatever is being used as currency must be fungible: the quality of one unit or piece being perceived as equivalent to another. It must be divisible into smaller units without loss of value; for instance, precious metals can be minted into coins from bars or melted down into bars again without change to the value of the bars. It must also be fungible, meaning that one part of the currency can be replaced for a similar quantity, which is why works of art or real estate, for example, aren't suitable as currency. It has to have a specific weight, measure, or size so as to be verifiably countable

The Functions of Money

As a Store of Value

For individuals, money is the ultimate store of value. It consists of the objects, commodities, or whatever else is used to maintain an individual's wealth and store the gains from his economic activities. While a currency can act as a temporary store of value between transactions, money is the ultimate store of value—and in order to act as a store of value, money must be capable of being reliably saved, stored, and retrieved. Money must be able at least to maintain its value and remain stable over time. To serve as a store of value, money thus needs to have a constant inherent value of its own. By contrast, a currency which may be affected by loss of value—e.g., through inflation—can't be used as money without loss to its holder.

As a Standard of Deferred Payment

The "standard of deferred payment" is an accepted way to settle a debt and refers to the units in which debts are expressed, at the time of lending and at the time of repayment. It thus also refers to the form of payment or settlement which the lender will accept as legal tender for the amount owing. When debts are expressed in terms of money, the real value of such debts doesn't change because money should be able to maintain its value. When debts are specified in terms of currency, which may change due to inflation and deflation, the party holding the credit in a currency form may suffer loss. A worker would be better off receiving commodity money in the form of an agreed-upon "basket of goods and services" as a wage than in the form of a currency that's depleted in value.

As a Measure of Value

Money acts as a standard measure and common denomination for trade in the setting of currency prices and in the records for financial accounting systems. Money is also used as a common measure of different items and is useful when comparing the values of dissimilar objects.

While money can be used as a medium of exchange, the role of such a medium is best performed by a currency. Money is better seen as a measure of value. Once that measure is determined, a sufficient amount of currency to meet that measure is gathered and exchanged in a transaction. A currency can't be a measure of value because it doesn't usually meet the "means of deferred payment" criteria. Currencies tend to change over time and across regions, and what is a currency today will very likely be worth much less in a few years' time. A currency fails to measure value correctly and consistently, as it's always changing in various ways, and using it to measure value would require making certain adjustments to account for such changes. Using a constantly changing standard as measurement is an exercise in futility. Money, if it's true money, will maintain its value and is the best measure of value.

A market measures or sets the value of various goods and services using money as the unit (i.e., the standard or the yardstick of wealth). There's no other alternative to the mechanism used by markets to measure or determine the value of various goods and services and, , wealth. Just determination of prices is an essential condition for justice in exchange, efficient allocation of resources, and economic growth welfare and justice.

To serve as a measure of value or as a medium of exchange, money needs to have constant, inherent value of its own or it must be firmly linked to a definite "basket of goods and services."

Correcting the Currency Error

From the above definitions and functions of money and of currency it should follow that the diagnosis for most of the money problems of this day is the ignorance about money and currency festering among those who use money and currency while assuming currency is money.

The truth about money and currency must be taught by all and sundry to all its users and be used to correct not just the perceptions but also current poor practices such as setting agreements (such as salary and wage contracts and loan agreements) in currency instead of setting them in real money terms.

The world currently has too many currencies, with almost each country having its own currency. With the correct understanding of what a currency is, and after making it common knowledge that a currency is not money but a measure of money, it will be noted that a currency is nothing more than a measuring stick. A measuring tape, a thermometer, a scale for weight, or any gauge is exactly what a currency is, and it doesn't deserve the status that we've bestowed upon it. For the thermometer to measure the temperature of a patient accurately, it needs to be designed rightly and calibrated correctly. Whether the temperature is measured in degrees Celsius or in degrees Fahrenheit shouldn't matter, as with weight measured in pounds or kilograms or distance measured in miles and in kilometres. As long as the measure isn't being constantly tampered with, it'll provide a reliable measure of wealth, and conversion from one standard to the other will be fixed and predictable.

A currency as a measure of money should be as predictable as a centimetre is unchangeable. If a kilogram is set as a standard, one shouldn't be surprised that the same kilogram is now lighter and less weighty the next day or the next year. A currency should meet a similar standard. If it doesn't meet such basic requirements, it's a faulty instrument and a misleading standard of account and can never be used as a true measure of value without one party to the process being prejudiced. No one should insist on its being used as a measure. It follows also that it fails to be a store of value because it's constantly changing. No one can account in such a currency because what it was yesterday isn't what it is today, and as we speak, it's changing into something weaker and eventually useless.

The questions begging to be answered at this point are, who's responsible for this manipulation of the currency and what that individual stands to benefit. The one controlling the purse strings and the money printing machine is the government. I must point out that the printing of currency is one of those institutions which our so-called democratic rulers have enshrouded with secrecy and unaccountability.

So why, then, are governments and the powers that be insisting on a currency such as we have today, a currency which is disadvantageous to the majority, prone to inflation and depreciation? Again, I must unapologetically point out that it's the design of the system that allows those in power to benefit from such ignorance. The government has control of the currency of a country. It's able to print more currency and spend that currency without earning the value thereof. This weakens the value of other currency holders, and the government has actually stolen from holders of currency. Had these holders had real money and not currency, the purloining by government wouldn't have affected them.

That category of holders is actually the businesses, which for most the most part don't hold currency, but hold the real money in the form of capital and products (inventory stock) and services, which they adjust the prices of once the value of currency weakens. They also employ labour and fix the salaries of labour in currency terms and hence directly benefit from the loss of value in currency on such salaries and wages. The government (rulers) and their business aristocracy are the direct beneficiaries of this error by the majority, and it would be difficult to persuade observers that the perpetuation of this error isn't intentional on their part. The current monetary systems were set up in the days of the kings and queens and their aristocracy, gentry, and nobility, and the monetary system was designed for the benefit of these and their offspring and at the same time to exploit the masses and the poor in the least perceptible manner. Such exploitation has been promoted and perpetuated by those who sit on these thrones and those who inherited the riches thus obtained.

The Supply of Currency

What constitutes the money supply of a country is defined in contemporary economics as "the total of financial instruments that fulfil the functions of money." However, it's clear that this definition needs to be further refined in line with the distinction made above between money and currency. The definition of money supply should be restricted to only what is truly money. The definition of currency will also be affected and should relate only to currency and its instruments.

Money supply would represent the total amount of wealth in a given economy over a given time, while the currency supply would be the total amount of currency in circulation at any given time.

"Currency supply" refers to all currency in its various forms of banknotes and coins, "bank currency" refers to the balance held in bank accounts, and "other currency" consists solely of records. It's clear from this that a currency exists merely for the convenience of trade, as a medium of exchange, and as a temporary store of value. The amount of currency has no effect and doesn't—or at least shouldn't—affect the well-being of the participants in an economy, other than their convenience. Equally, it's a matter of similarity if one gets a thousand dollars in ten units of one-hundred-dollar notes or gets the same amount in one hundred units of ten-dollar notes.

In reality, however, policymakers tend to play around with currency. Governments are responsible for controlling the amount of currency in an economy and have the power to determine what's available. On the other hand, economic players—especially employers and employees, debtors and creditors—have erroneously set the terms of deferred payment and measured their assets in currency terms rather than in monetary terms. As a result, the majority of people in an economy may have a wrong understanding of money and hold financial instruments—such as debts, loans, cash, salary, and wage contracts, etc.—in the form of currency instead of in money form.

Fiat currency is a poor medium of exchange and store of value because, during the exchange process, the medium loses the value of the money from which it was converted and gives up less value than was put in. Fiat currency is subject to manipulation and is free floating and dependent upon its supply. The market sets a value to it that continues to change as the supply of the currency is changed with respect to the demands of the economy. If a government decides to double the amount of currency available in an economy, it means the value of money stored in the form of that currency is diminished by half.

Increasing a free-floating fiat-currency supply reduces the quantity of the basket of the goods and services to which it's linked by the market and provides it with purchasing power. Thus, currency can't be a standard measure of wealth, and its manipulation impedes the market mechanism by which just prices are determined. That leads to a situation where no value-related economic data is reliable when it's measured in terms of currency.

Money Supply and Monetary Policy

Monetary policy in present-day economics is when fiat currency is used as money and there's no form of making it standard or any link to a fixed standard such as commodity gold. This is a wrong designation, because what's being controlled here isn't money but merely the currency, and a better name would be "currency policy."

The money supply of a country consists of the items that meet the proper definition of money in an economy. It's the total of all commodities, services, and earnings that have resulted in an increase in the wealth of the country and which have been saved, stored, and preserved as "money." Once again I must emphasise that money isn't to be confused with currency.

When livestock and similar commodity items are used to measure money, the increase in the supply of these commodities actually results in an increase in the welfare of the economic players. The wealth of a nation is increased by an increase in money. There is no artificial manipulation of its supply. If one was to seek to influence the supply of true money, this would only result in greater wealth and well-being for the nation. True money should have the quality, with its increase, of increasing the well-being of a nation. Any item that may be used for money and fails to do this isn't to be regarded as money. To a user, a basket of goods today is still worth generally the same as it will be in five years' time. It can't be manipulated by artificial changes in supply, inflation, or restrictions.

When gold and silver are used as currency, such a currency supply can grow only if the supply of these metals is increased by mining or external trade. This causes inflation, as the value of gold goes down. On the other hand, if the rate of gold mining and trade can't keep up with the growth of the economy, gold becomes relatively more valuable, and prices expressed in terms of gold will drop, causing deflation.

By thinking they're controlling money rather than currency, policymakers make a very grave mistake, and it's no wonder than their policies are the greatest cause of current financial and economic problems. In such circumstances, authorities seek to control the amount of currency available in an economy and use it to control the prices and interest rates which they pretend are positively influencing the economic growth of their country. They aim, by these means, to achieve specific goals, usually listed as economic growth, price stability, maximum employment, and affordable interest rates, but they're deceiving themselves and all other economic players in their countries.

Based on the error of trying to influence money supply by manipulating the currency supply, governments, through their central banks, have used currency controls to manipulate the currency supply in their economies by the following means:

- changing the interest rate at which the central bank lends out currency to (or borrows currency from) the commercial banks
- purchasing or selling of currency
- increasing or lowering government borrowing
- increasing or lowering government spending
- manipulating of exchange rates
- raising or lowering bank-reserve requirements for a currency
- regulating or prohibiting of private currencies
- increasing taxation or offering tax breaks on imports or exports of capital into a country.

A currency is only good for facilitating transactions and for being a medium of exchange; manipulation of it in any way doesn't bring greater benefits to an economy. If a government increases the amount of paper money in its economy, it will only affect those who are bound to accept it as money and who hold it to be what it's not—i.e., money rather than currency.

Let us, in this endeavour to understand money, consider the human body—or that of any animal—and how it functions and works, and we will apply these to money. The body is the frame and structure, and within this are contained cells and nerves and many channels, veins, and routes. Processes and functions happen, and exchanges of various materials take place. A perfect transport system, sewerage system, heating, ventilation, digestion, etc., are all there. One remarkable thing about the body is the heart which pumps the fluids throughout the body and enables a perfect balance of blood in the body. A large percentage of the body can be said to be water, but this water isn't in the form of pure water, but in the different cells, fluids, and other places, where it helps in liquidating whatever is being transported, stored, or changed. Now this water is important, but increasing this water to a level of flooding or water logging the body would be harmful. On the other hand, the body surely requires the water. However, the *end* isn't the water. The water is necessary to allow the body to get nutrients and waste to the correct places, to get heat where it's required and to bring oil and healing to an ailing joint. The point of maintaining a healthy and sound body is to ensure that while it has the optimum amount of water, those other things it needs to use this water for are present. Such things are obviously food, oxygen, and other throw-ins that the body needs to nourish it. Increasing water doesn't nourish the body without including wholesome food.

The economy of the nation can be examined from this perspective, and the currency of a nation is surely the water that should be supplied in just the right amount to liquidate the body of the economy so that economic activities can take place and transactions can occur through such a medium. The currency isn't the thing that the body seeks for its own, but for the enabling of the things and the activities necessary for economics. Industries and individuals will engage in the watered valleys and misty mountains and produce the wealth that will enrich their nation and their lives.

The "New" Currency

What constitutes a currency is basically a mere record of value, and it doesn't need to be printed on paper or minted into coin. Currency in its basic form is the account of what can be commanded by an item of goods or services. The advent of cell phone banking achieves and fully illustrates this point. The cell phone company is the central record keeper and keeps all transfers of value between individuals. Goods and services can be transacted and paid for as long as that record is kept and limited to the holder of a particular number. The record is the currency in a cashless economy such as cell phone banking, and it just requires a complete acceptance of the validity of such records and the ability to get the system promulgated as legal tender. The record should obviously be of a certain standard which can't be manipulated. As mentioned in this book, the basis of this currency should be the true money, be it a basket of goods or services, an expensive metal, or the total collection of a nation's wealth.

Liquidating an economy obviously requires an unchanging standard to be set, and for this to be calibrated into smaller and higher denominations and to be backed by real money which if all the participants were to cash in they'd be satisfied with the value that they get. The scope of this book doesn't allow delving into the matter of a paperless currency, but it's the writer's desire that more thought be applied to this prospect in the right mind frame about money and currency.

Democratic Political Economy

Transformation

In most developing nations, especially in African countries, the majority of the population lives in rural or farming areas, away from the urban areas. These places often do not have easy access to financial services like banking and for one to be able to obtain such services they have to travel gruesome and long journeys to remote urban centres. Not any financial institutions are willing to invest in offices in the non-urban areas due to the lack of basic services like transport network (e.g. roads), lack of electricity, and communication networks (e.g. telephone and internet access). In addition the amount of business required to make a branch profitable would not be normally there in the non-urban areas due to low and sporadic incomes. In equal measure most of those who dwell in urban areas who are not regular income earners often find themselves excluded from banking because of the cost of banking and the need to travel to into the city every time one needs access to cash. It is these members of society who were largely ignored by traditional banking who have benefited most from paperless money through mobile money. The initial stage is to have one open an account by simply registering the cellphone number as an account and immediately one can deposit actual currency into the account and or have that amount loaded onto the cellphone number via mobile transfer. The currency becomes resident on the cellphone and one can check their balance just like they can check for an airtime balance. The amount can henceforth be spent at any time of the day by simply pressing a few buttons and transferring a certain portion of the money to the next person's cellphone and so on. The record received on each cellphone is sufficient proof that a value has been transferred and when the recipient makes a balance enquiry, the new amount is recorded in their account and at any time they can go to any agent or bank and cash out for actual currency.

A near perfect example for study is the paperless currency system in the cell phone banking in Kenya, Tanzania, Zimbabwe, the Democratic Republic of Congo, Madagascar and Nigeria. Cellphone banking in these countries works as an extension of the currency and transactions are conducted paperlessly by means of records between cell phones only for the most part. The effect has been a complete transformation and emancipation of a class previously ignored by mainstream banking, and this has also seen the entrance of new players into the banking system, in the form of mobile phone network companies. The second set of new bankers are the various businesses, usually small shop owners and companies who provide the actual banking service by accepting mobile money for payment rather than cash, and who also pay out cash to those wishing to hold hard cash. Sending money from a foreign country to a rural recipient previously involve the sender paying for an expensive postal service, incurring high wire money transfer fees or entrusting their cash to a third party to transport it and required the receiver to travel to the cities, at a high cost, and queueing in banking halls and travel back, all being at least a three day ordeal. The same can now be done in a few minutes and at less cost and in a more secure manner.

Paperless

There is therefore every possibility for actually eliminating the paper and remaining with just the record and it will work in even greater ease and with less administrative hustle. Just for argument's sake, suppose Zimbabwe's wealth is valued at ten billion British pounds as of today. The same value should then be converted back into an unchanging standard at that point, and for our argument we shall use gold because it's an easy example. So the country's wealth is measured in gold at this point in time, and then the next step is to decide how much liquidity should exist in this economy for it to function well. Suppose that 50 per cent of the wealth is desired to be in liquid form. The issue then is to introduce a currency that will ensure that enough liquidity is available for 50 per cent of that value. The Zimbabwe dollar should be determined to be a portion of this wealth.

Suppose this is calibrated into five billion Zimbabwe dollars. The value of the Zimbabwe dollar is going to be recorded against the standard of the wealth and be backed by the wealth, and any decrease in wealth in the economy will make it lose value, and more wealth will make it stronger. There's no need to print these Zimbabwe dollars on paper, although some may insist on that; however, there's no problem because these papers can still be used together with the paperless record. There's no need to change the calibration because it's the standard of measure. The paperless currency will sit in the records of the cellphone companies as the "banks" and everyone can transact and carry money on their cell phones.

The argument then leads to the consideration that currencies can be eliminated from being national symbols and can instead be measures of wealth not only for the household, but also for the region, economic block, or the world. There's no need for all these currencies that are elastic and used as devises of exploitation by the powers that be.

Money Creation and Monetary Policy

The Functions of Banks

A bank is a business set up to borrow currency from individuals, businesses, and governments and in turn to lend such currency to individuals, businesses, and governments through loans, bonds, and other forms of currency. What isn't loaned out is invested by the bank in the financial markets.

A bank's main source of income is interest (i.e., what it charges customers on the loans they've borrowed from the bank.) A bank accepts deposits made by its customers and as compensation pays them a certain rate of interest on such deposits. In turn the bank then lends this money to others customers who borrow money from the bank, and these are charged a certain amount of interest. The difference between what the banks pay out to depositors as interest, and that which it receives from those who've borrowed from it, as interest, represents the bank's net income. Some banks also gain income by charging customers a certain fee for every transaction

Fractional banking and multiplier: banks are required to keep only a fraction of their total deposits by customers in the bank. Customers are not likely all going to demand their currency all at once. So a small fraction, say 10 per cent, would suffice for daily transactions. The other 90 per cent the bank can daily loan out to those who need loans. This implies that if the bank was to receive $100, instead of keeping $10 and loaning out $90, the bank will actually keep the whole $100 in the bank, and then write out a possible amount of $900 in loans to borrowers. This way it's created $900 out of thin air and is still legally within the fractional requirements of 10 per cent. This practice of creating a huge loan book out of a small fraction of currency is called the multiplier effect and is a result of fractional banking. A small injection of currency into the banking system will result in a multiple growth.

that they perform. We must be aware that most banks are profit making, private enterprises and are there to maximise their own profits.

Most modern economic systems have elevated banks into special economic players by allocating special functions to banks in the issuing of currency and in the implementation of currency policies. Banks are used as the conduits for the implementation of currency supply and credit controls, and most importantly in currency creation, wrongly called money creation.

In economic theory, currency creation is the process by which the currency supply of a country is increased. A central bank introduces a new currency into an economy by lending such currency to financial institutions, and they in turn multiply the base currency created by the central bank through "fractional reserve banking." This expands the amount of "broad currency," consisting of cash-plus-demand (short-term) deposits in the economy. The banks are required to keep in their reserve only a small percentage of the total amount of money borrowed from the public, businesses, and governments.

Through fractional reserve banking, the modern banking system expands the currency supply of a country beyond the amount initially created by the central bank. There are two types of currency in a fractional-reserve banking system:

- Central bank currency—currency originally issued by the central bank (all currency created by the central bank regardless of its form, whether banknotes, coins, electronic currency, etc.)
- Commercial bank currency—bank deposits at commercial banks (currency created in the banking system through borrowing and lending).

When a commercial bank loan is extended, in reality a certain amount of new commercial bank currency is created, and when such a loan is repaid, that commercial bank currency disappears from existence. Since, in a normally functioning economy, loans are continually being issued, the amount of broad currency in the economy remains relatively stable. Because of this currency-creation process on the part of commercial banks, the currency supply of a country is usually larger than the currency issued by the central bank; the difference in amount is determined by the "reserve ratio" or other financial ratios—primarily the capital-adequacy ratio that limits the overall credit creation of a bank—set by the relevant banking regulators in the country concerned.

Hence if a bank receives a certain amount of currency and is required to have, say, only 10 per cent of the amount in reserve, upon receiving the currency from the central bank, and in order to maintain the reserve ratio, a bank can potentially loan out nine tenths of the amount received, so that the total amount lent out and the reserve afterwards are in line with the requirements for reserves.

The most common mechanism used to measure this increase in the currency supply is typically called "the money multiplier." The money multiplier is of fundamental importance in monetary policy: if banks lend out close to the maximum allowed, then the broad currency supply (total supply of currency including loans etc.) equals approximately the central bank currency times the multiplier and central banks may control the broad currency supply by finely controlling central bank currency, with the money multiplier linking these quantities.

Economists use the term "elastic currency," which not only implies the ability to expand but also the ability to contract a currency supply. Modern monetary policy is based partially on the theory that it's best to expand or contract the currency supply according to need as economic conditions change.

Banking institutions are in a position of power to control currency creation and are able to allocate this currency to whomsoever they wish. It's of importance to consider such allocation of currency, particularly in modern economics where currency and money are considered to be the same thing, however erroneously. If a bank awards credit to a particular individual or business, it's giving that individual financial power to do business and to use that to acquire more wealth. The allocation of such power, since it's bestowed by an economic player, requires consideration and affects the distribution of the means of production in an economy.

In this case banks are in a position that no other economic player can be in: they're involved in the allocation of economic resources. Moreover, they're in this position merely by being banks. They have the ability to create credit out of nothing and to earn interest on that credit. In this manner the state gives to a bank, which has done nothing to earn that right, a right to earn interest. Generally one would earn interest by means of an investment in or loan to another. However, in this case the bank is just handed currency, and it has the ability to create money on a multiple of the amount given.

Interest Rates and Usury

Banks determine interest rates by considering what they term the cost of money, which is determined by the rate of inflations, etc. Lending to the government is considered the most risk-free transaction, so the rate at which the general market is lending to the government is the basis for other interest rates. The bank will lend to individuals at interest rates higher than that available to government and depending on the individual applying for credit. At the bank's own discretion, higher interest rates are charged to high-risk borrowers. Lower interest rates are charged to lower-risk borrowers.

Banks also have the power to decide whom to lend to and whom not to lend to. Since banks are profit-driven, they tend to charge higher interest rates to poorer, high-risk borrowers, and lower interest rates to richer, creditworthy borrowers. Banks will generally not lend to anyone whom they consider a risk, so the poor and unemployed are generally not given any credit. "Usury" is the practice of making unethical or immoral monetary loans. A loan may be considered usurious because of excessive or abusive interest rates, but simply charging any interest at all can be considered usury.

While banks have the undeserved privilege of creating money through fractional money creation and by being the conduits for the introduction of currency into the economy, along with the luxury of being charged very low interest rates by their lenders, they have, in turn, the power to charge their borrowers exorbitant interest at varying rates. Governments have allowed banks to carry out such a practice in the name of "free market economics." While fairness, justice, and equitability would require that everyone be treated fairly and equally, banks are allowed to discriminate against individuals by means of interest rates and the selection of borrowers. They have the power to decide how much to lend, what interest rate to charge, and who may borrow.

The highest rates are levied on the poor, who least afford those rates, while lower rates are charged to the rich, who can easily afford them. There exists no justification for charging interest rates different to those determined by market rates in a free market economy. The increasing of an interest rate from that determined by the market is arbitrary and thumb sucked. The risk profiling (putting people into different risk classes) is a subjective exercise in discrimination. Curiously, if a person is charged a higher interest rate because of perceived risk but manages to repay the loan and interest within the agreed terms, the bank doesn't go back and admit it incorrectly profiled the person and should've charged a lower interest rate. There's no refund for the high interest rate charged to this person as a result of an arbitrary and subjective profiling.

In a political democracy in which people are supposed to be treated equally, it's an astonishing pity that some economic participants aren't treated as are others in similar transactions. A government has the power to control interest rates through its control of the financial systems and can decide what rate of interest will be charged on its borrowings. The banks are given the power to charge interest rates by the government which, through the central bank, gives money to banks at very low interest rates. In their turn the banks consider the government to be a good, risk-free borrower, so they tend to charge the government the lowest interest rates.

Banks also consider companies to be better borrowers than individuals and often offer lower rates to them. The rest of the economic participants, particularly the poor majority, are faced with interest rates higher than these, if they're granted loans at all. The people that can least afford the high interest rates are thus the ones which banks and the government have contrived to charge truly exorbitant interest rates.

On the other hand, there's little economic justification for charging interest rates in an economy where real money is used in setting prices and measuring transactions, as opposed to where fiat currency is used. There is even less justification for charging different interest rates to different people. If interest rates are meant to compensate for higher risk, then increasing the rate of interest where the borrower is a default risk or where has already defaulted, isn't only unjustifiable, unfair, and unreasonable, it actually will only further increase the risk of default, as the borrower now has to pay an even higher rate which he can even less afford.

Usury and Slavery in Present Day

A more creditworthy person or company in the eyes of the bank will be awarded a higher credit, which is to say a larger loan at a low interest rate, and a less creditworthy person in their estimation will be charged a higher interest rate for a much smaller loan. If risk is the consideration, then it would seem that a larger loan should command a higher interest rate and a smaller loan should command a lower interest rate. Risk should be taken into account also in determining the size of loan to be made.

The financial arrangements of the present economic systems have clearly been made to benefit the rich and oppress the poor. Credit has been advanced to the poor generally only for consumerist products and little for investment credit. When the poor who were previously denied debt are awarded loans to purchase consumer goods, many drown in debt. The capitalists have arranged for workers to have credit linked with their wages and have benefited from the business received as well at the interest rates charged.

While the practice of direct slavery is widely banned across the world, in some places "debt slavery" is still practised by financial institutions and related businesses. A debtor who's found unable to repay a loan is red listed and placed in a situation whereby his or her life and labours are directed by the lender until the debt is considered repaid. Interest rates which amount to usury are often a major instrument in imposing this slavery.

Bank Discrimination

"Bank discrimination" is the discrimination practised by banks, governments, or other lending institutions when they deny access to money opportunities (loans, working capital, banking services) to one or more groups of people—primarily on the basis of race, class colour, religion, sex, handicap, familial status, ethnic origin, or national origin. It also includes the charging of higher interest rates to one group rather than another or one individual rather than another in an effort to make borrowing by that group or individual as unattractive as possible. Governments provide finance through banks and so have directly and indirectly allowed the practice. The poor, the historically disadvantaged, and the inferior or minority people are thus often discriminated against.

As a result, the poor and other minorities find it nearly impossible to secure loans or mortgages from banks, and it can be said that there's a systematic denial of loans. Banks don't want to lend to poor people and most of those who approach banks face direct discrimination, rejection, and discouragement. Fairness in lending should require the equal treatment of applicants and equal consideration. However, few financial institutions and credit institutions will lend to anyone without a credit history or whose "credit score" is lower than a certain set score. If a person has never had any debt, that person is the least likely to receive consideration because of his absence of "credit history."

Many low-income people don't have files with credit bureaux because they don't have credit cards or any other credit history to show as evidence of creditworthiness. Banks won't lend to the unemployed or to those who've not spent a long time in employment with a single company. Discrimination motivated by historical prejudice is visible in the racial composition of neighbourhoods where loans are sought and in the race of the applicants. Banking institutions sometimes treat poor applicants differently when they seek to buy homes in affluent neighbourhoods than when they seek to buy homes in poor neighbourhoods. Banks seldom finance property in low-income residential areas but readily lend where areas are inhabited by the well-off.

Banking institutions have discriminated in three ways, namely:
- Overt, blatant, explicit, obvious, and unconcealed discrimination, where a lender blatantly discriminates on any basis (direct discrimination based on, say, gender, nationality, or race)
- Unequal, different, dissimilar, and disparate treatment, where a lender treats applicants differently based on any criterion (where the playing field isn't fair and some get preference to others)

- Discriminatory different and disparate impact, where a lender applies a practice uniformly to all applicants, but the practice has a discriminatory effect on the discriminated which isn't justified by business necessity (the discrimination is seen in the aftermath of the results; for instance the poor are given consumer loans with high interest rates and get stuck in debt)

Example 1

In order best to illustrate what money is and how it differs from currency, use shall be made of examples from the biblical story of Jacob whom we find negotiating for a wage with his employer, namely his uncle Laban.

Genesis 29:15 &18(KJV): And Laban said unto Jacob, "Because thou art my brother, shouldest thou therefore serve me for nought? Tell me, *what shall thy wages be?*...And Jacob loved Rachel and said, I will *serve* thee *seven years for* Rachel thy younger daughter." (emphasis mine)

Jacob here agrees to work for a contract period of seven years, and he will by the end of that period, by his dedicated service, have paid off the price for his wife to be. This is a good example of an employment contract, where the price is clearly stated and doesn't change and isn't subject to inflation or any manipulation.

After the seven years, Jacob goes to claim the bride that he's earned, but his uncle gives him a different payment, and he has to work another seven years for the bride he wants. There is a moral here: employers have long been in the business of shifting goal posts, and an employee should only agree to a contract that gives the wages with consistent value which should be enforceable.

After more than fourteen years of employment, Jacob decides to terminate the employment relationship, but Laban makes another offer:

Genesis 30:26–43: [Jacob says] "Give me my wives and my children, for whom I have served thee, and let me go: for thou knowest my service which I have done thee." And Laban said unto him, "I pray thee, if I have found favour in thine eyes, tarry: for I have learned by experience that the Lord hath blessed me for thy sake." And he said, "Appoint me thy wages, and I will give it." And he said unto him, "Thou knowest how I have served thee, and how thy cattle was with me. For it was little which thou hadst before I came, and it's now increased unto a multitude; and the Lord hath blessed thee since my coming: and now *when shall I provide for mine own house also?*" And he said, "What shall I give thee?" And Jacob said, "Thou shalt not give me anything: if thou wilt do this thing for me, I will again feed and keep thy flock. I will pass through all thy flock to day, removing from thence all the speckled and spotted cattle, and all the brown cattle among the sheep, and the spotted and speckled among the goats, and of such shall be my hire. So shall my righteousness answer for me in time to come, when it shall come for my hire before thy face, every one that isn't speckled and spotted among the goats, and brown among the sheep, that shall be counted stolen with me." And Laban said, "Behold, I would it might be according to thy word." And he removed that day the he goats that were ringstraked and spotted, and all the she goats that were speckled and spotted, and every one that had some white in it, and all the brown among the sheep, and gave them into the hand of his sons. And he set three days' journey betwixt himself and Jacob, and Jacob fed the rest of Laban's flocks. And Jacob took him rods of green poplar, and of the hazel and chestnut tree; and pilled white strakes in them, and made the white appear which was in the rods. And he set the rods which he had pilled before the flocks in the gutters in the watering troughs when the flocks came to drink, that they should conceive when they came to drink. And the flocks conceived before the rods, and brought forth cattle ringstraked, speckled, and spotted. And Jacob did separate the lambs, and set the faces of the flocks toward the ringstraked, and all the brown in the flock of Laban; and he put his own flocks by themselves, and put them not unto Laban's cattle. And it came to pass, whensoever the stronger cattle did conceive, that Jacob laid the rods before the eyes of the cattle in the gutters, that they might conceive among the rods. But when the cattle were feeble, he put them not in: so the feebler were Laban's, and the stronger Jacob's. And the man increased exceedingly, and had much cattle, and maidservants, and menservants, and camels, and asses.

Jacob here negotiates a wage agreement with Laban, his employer, that we can use to illustrate how a fair employment contract should be, particularly in our modern world. Firstly, he didn't choose to be paid in silver or in gold or in another form (as in the previous example, in which he'd chosen a bride as his reward and was cheated in the process). He chose livestock (cattle, sheep and goats) as his money. This is crucial because he was going to work with them and had control and influence over their increase or otherwise. He could influence his wages by working harder, more carefully, and more industriously. As his currency, he chose a particular brand of cattle, and to avoid any accounting problems, he removed, at the date of the agreement, all those that could confuse his currency with Laban's.

The currency was easy to identify, easy to account for, a good store of value, and generally acceptable (he ended up buying camels and asses for himself). The currency that he chose was able to propagate over time, giving him extra income and covering the cost of keeping and maintaining that currency. Jacob was thus able from his wages to look after himself and his family and his servants, and he was able to save for his future. A wage that allows a worker's welfare to increase is the right wage. It's a wage that not only ensures a worker's welfare but also enables that rate of increase to improve. The marginal increase in the welfare of the employee should at the least be maintained or increased.

In today's world, even when a salary increase is awarded, the increase is soon offset by inflation and taxation, and the worker may far worse off than before the increase. A wage should as far as possible generally be linked to an increase. A worker should participate in a form of profit-sharing to the extent that he's able to influence profits directly or indirectly by cost or loss containment.

Genesis 31:1–18: 1 And he heard the words of Laban's sons, saying, Jacob hath taken away all that was our father's; and of that which was our father's hath he gotten all this glory. And Jacob beheld the countenance of Laban, and, behold, it wasn't toward him as before. And Jacob sent and called Rachel and Leah to the field unto his flock, And said unto them, "I see your father's countenance, that it's not toward me as before; but the God of my father hath been with me. And ye know that with all my power I have served your father. And your father hath deceived me, and *changed my wages ten times*; but God suffered him not to hurt me. If he said thus, 'The speckled shall be thy wages,' then all the cattle bare speckled; and if he said thus, 'The ringstraked shall be thy hire,' then bare all the cattle ringstraked. Thus God hath taken away the cattle of your father and given them to me. And it came to pass at the time that the cattle conceived, that I lifted up mine eyes and saw in a dream and, behold, the rams which leaped upon the cattle were ringstraked, speckled, and grisled. And the angel of God spake unto me in a dream, saying, 'Jacob.' And I said, 'Here am I.' And he said, 'Lift up now thine eyes, and see all the rams which leap upon the cattle are ringstraked, speckled, and grisled, for I have seen all that Laban doeth unto thee. I am the God of Bethel, where thou anointedst the pillar, and where thou vowedst a vow unto me; now arise, get thee out from this land, and return unto the land of thy kindred.'" And Rachel and Leah answered and said unto him, "Is there yet any portion or inheritance for us in our father's house? Are we not counted of him strangers? For he hath sold us and hath quite devoured also our money. For all the riches which God hath taken from our father, that is ours and our children's; now then, whatsoever God hath said unto thee, do." Then Jacob rose up and set his sons and his wives upon camels. And he carried away all his cattle, and all his goods which he had gotten, the cattle of his getting, which he had gotten in Padanaram, for to go to Isaac his father in the land of Canaan.

Genesis 31:38–42: "This twenty years have I been with thee; thy ewes and thy she goats have not cast their young, and the rams of thy flock have I not eaten. That which was torn of beasts I brought not unto thee. I bare the loss of it; of my hand didst thou require it, whether stolen by day or stolen by night. Thus I was, in the day the drought consumed me, and the frost by night; and my sleep departed from mine eyes. Thus have I been twenty years in thy house; I served thee fourteen years for thy two daughters and six years for thy cattle, and thou hast *changed my wages ten times*. Except the God of my father, the God of Abraham, and the fear of Isaac had been with me, *surely thou hadst sent me away now empty*. God hath seen mine affliction and the labour of my hands and rebuked thee yesternight.

After twenty years of service, , the employee finally decided to retire from his employment, taking with him his wealth earned through his hard work and providence. The employer will always think of it instead as *his* wealth and will want to send away the employee with very little, if anything. A correctly formulated contract, a correct understanding of what money is and what currency is, and then setting wages in a money and currency form that at the least maintains its value goes a long way to improving the lot of workers. Most importantly, the wages should be set in a manner that enables a worker to realise and influence the reward. A wage that is fixed regardless of the amount of effort and work isn't only going to decrease the welfare of the worker, it won't motivate him to any effort or encourage sacrifice and exertion. As was pointed out under the chapter on economic structures, the structuring of the employment contract should consider the symbiosis of the worker and the employer and give both a chance to be successful. The optimal relationship being the one in which their wealth is maximised simultaneously.

V

Inflation Question

Understanding Inflation

When we understand money correctly, can distinguish it from currency, and have a clear understanding of the functions of money and those of a currency, it's easier to understand what inflation is, its causes, and its remedies. Money doesn't affect inflation and doesn't cause inflation. Money is the constant and stable measure of wealth that has intrinsic value and won't be affected by a sudden loss of value, whether by an increase in its supply or by any other form of manipulation. Currency, on the other hand, is the medium of exchange required to transact value as contained in money and other commodities. It's also been shown that currency acts as a transitory store of value during the transaction process, and one may hold up currency as a store of value while seeking to convert it back into real money. Also, it's important to remember that the supply of a currency is subject to manipulation by whoever has the power to introduce or withdraw it from circulation in an economy.

If cattle were the currency of a theoretical economy and the amount of cattle were to be increased by whatever means, more cattle would be available. However, they'd still be valuable for the intrinsic worth in them, and the increase in their supply would in no way diminish the value of other cattle in the economy. If one was to pay a bride price of, say, ten herd of cattle, even if the payment is delayed or prompted, the in-laws wouldn't suffer loss in the value they receive even were the supply of cattle in the economy to increase. As a form of money, the value of cattle will always be generally constant over time. However, as a currency, the cattle would suffer the disadvantages of divisibility, storage, maintenance, and transportability. Inflation wouldn't be a problem because cattle value is intrinsic and can't be manipulated easily.

If the same bride price was determined in the theoretical dollars, (one hundred theoretical dollars) and the government of Theoretical Republic has tripled the printed quantity of Theoretical dollars in circulation, the quantity of dollars required to meet the bride price changes correspondingly (three hundred theoretical dollars) because a single cow now commands a higher quantity of dollars than before. By printing and introducing more currency into the economy, the government has all but divided the currency into lower units with lower value than the nominal value. Consequently a higher quantity of the units of currency is now required to transact in the bride price in this example. Currency inflation is when the government pumps currency into an economy which lowers the buying power of the units of currency because the printing dilutes the currency.

The increasing of the quantity of a currency, where the type of currency in use isn't a close resemblance of money—e.g., paper money, fiat money, or even gold-backed money—will result in an inflated currency (and price inflation).

When carrying out economic transactions in the short term, economic participants are required to hold currency as a temporary mean of store of value and a short term means of deferred payment. A worker in a country of high inflation who's paid at the end of each month for a year will suffer greatly if the currency is being inflated because the wage is fixed in currency terms, but his or her payments are staggered over a year. He is receiving a currency that's reducing of its value as the year and months goes by.

The same applies to anyone who's fixed his or her money assets in currency terms. If the worker were to be paid in actual commodities, and his or her wages were pegged in actual money—for example the worker received a wage basket of all his or her basic needs (food, shelter, clothing, etc.)—the worker's wage (in currency terms) would be determined at each payment interval and would include sufficient currency, adequate to buy such a basket. The worker would thus be generally immune to inflation, and any attempt to manipulate the currency wouldn't affect the worker negatively. An abundance of the items in the basket will only act to benefit the worker.

Governments that engage in currency inflation by printing more fiat currency while the participants in that economy are holding currency—or financial asset instruments denominated in currency—are merely taxing or robbing such people and handing the loot over to the state, or to whomever they're channelling the printed money to. Inflating a currency in an economy in which the people consider currency to be money is a way of taxing people without their realising they're being taxed. It's a secret form of taxation where the government gives itself the power to purchase value without creating any value but by merely printing a piece of paper.

Where the currency used is backed by a certain standard—e.g., gold—the inflation will affect the economic players to the extent that the currency doesn't represent real money. The usefulness to which the people can use the currency as money or for its own value, other than as a currency, is the extent to which inflation will affect them. The use of a currency that doesn't closely meet the definition and functions of money has the chance to result in price inflation, and the currency will fail.

Inflation is the decrease in the value of a currency due to an inflated abundance of such a currency. It's the decrease in the intrinsic value and purchasing power of the currency caused by too much of the currency being in circulation in an economy. A higher quantity of the currency is now required to execute a transaction because a unit of the currency now commands a lower value than before. The general price level rises, because each unit of currency buys fewer goods and services than before. Inflation is erosion in the purchasing power of the currency, in which the value of the medium of exchange and unit of account in the economy is lost. Economists generally agree that high rates of inflation and hyperinflation are caused by excessive growth of the currency supply.

The Effects of Inflation

An increase in the general level of prices implies a decrease in the purchasing power of the currency. That is, when the general level of prices rises, each monetary unit buys fewer goods and services. The effect of inflation isn't distributed evenly in the economy, and as a consequence there are hidden costs to some and benefits to others from this decrease in the purchasing power of money.

For example, with inflation, those segments in society which own physical assets, such as property, stock, etc., benefit from the price/value of their holdings going up, while those who seek to acquire them will need to pay more for them. Their (buyers) ability to do so will depend on the degree to which their income is fixed. For example, increases in payments to workers and pensioners often lag behind inflation, and for some people income is fixed. Also, individuals or institutions with cash assets will experience a decline in the purchasing power of the cash. Increases in the price level (inflation) erode the real value of money (the functional currency) and other items with an underlying monetary nature. Debtors who have debts with a fixed nominal rate of interest will see a reduction in the "real" interest rate as the inflation rate rises.

High or unpredictable inflation rates are regarded as harmful to an overall economy. They add inefficiencies in the market and make it difficult for companies to budget or plan long term. Inflation can act as a drag on productivity as companies are forced to shift resources away from products and services in order to focus on profit and losses from currency inflation. Uncertainty about the future purchasing power of money discourages investment and saving. And inflation can impose hidden tax increases, as inflated earnings push taxpayers into higher income tax rates unless the tax brackets are indexed to inflation.

With high inflation, purchasing power is redistributed from those on fixed nominal incomes, such as some pensioners whose pensions aren't indexed to the price level, towards those with variable incomes whose earnings may better keep pace with the inflation. This redistribution of purchasing power will also occur between international trading partners. Where fixed exchange rates are imposed, higher inflation in one economy than another will cause the first economy's exports to become more expensive and affect the balance of trade. There can also be negative impacts to trade from an increased instability in currency exchange prices caused by unpredictable inflation.

According to the famous monetarist-economist Milton Friedman, "Inflation is always and everywhere a monetary phenomenon." Any change in the amount of money in a system will change the price level, and the primary driver of the change in the general price level is changes in the quantity of money.

Impact of Inflation

Inflation has the greatest effects on those participants in the economy who are at the mercy of others for their survival. The government itself is immune to inflation because it controls the currency supply and the interest rates, it controls taxes, and it's able to borrow and spend beyond its means. The government is in all cases the one causing currency inflation, has the fore-knowledge of the effects of inflation, and will be affected by inflation minimally.

Companies and other businesses are in a position to also immunise and shield themselves from the effects of inflation because they're able to control the means of production and the prices of their goods and services as well as the majority of their costs. Companies are in most cases holding little or no currency; instead they're holding assets, stocks of commodities, and products. They're holding in their hands capital assets used in production of goods and services. These assets and stock items aren't subject to loss of value in inflationary times and automatically adjust in price in line with inflation. The company is able to change the price of its assets, including the goods and services, in a manner that will compensate it for any change in the value of the currency. If the price isn't right, the company will simply hold on to its product. Because the commodity has intrinsic value, it protects the companies against inflation.

Companies also have access to finance, and in most cases they benefit from inflation by having to pay off loans using weaker units of currency than when they borrowed. Companies who employ a large amount of labour also have the advantage of not adjusting their salaries frequently, in line with inflation (in a similar way as they would with prices). A company has the luxury not to increase wages until a new agreement is made with workers.

The remaining economic participants are the majority poor who depend on salaries and wages. Wages which are pegged in a currency have a tendency to be sticky. They're not determined by market forces as are prices of goods and services. They're determined by a tedious and protracted method of negotiation and are generally lagging behind inflation. The majority aren't only able to quickly adjust their earnings but are faced with prices for goods and services that are changing faster than their earnings.

The consumer price index, which measures the general price increase based on a basket of goods and services, is a far-too-artificial measure which doesn't take into account the uneven effects of inflation on the poor majority who are the victims of inflation. It's, , the poor majority who bear the brunt of inflation. It's clear that a government that engages in currency inflation is merely robbing the poor and sharing their earnings between itself and the companies and businesses in its jurisdiction.

Inflation Tax: Inflation Is a Hidden Tax

When a government spends more than its income (revenue from taxes and other sources), it's required to finance the extra expenditure by borrowing. These amounts borrowed will be repaid using future tax revenue. Most governments have tended to spend beyond their incomes and haven't, in subsequent years, collected more to cover for the deficits. Instead they've accumulated large amounts of deficit and have financed these by creating public debt. These borrowings have been manipulated by the governments by controlling both the interest rates charged to them and the payment terms. The interest rates are set by the government at artificially low rates to avoid accruing higher interest charges. The repayments have been postponed to future generations by issuing new debt to itself whenever older debt becomes due.

The effect is that governments have borrowed out the life of their subjects to a level where they can't get out of the debt dungeon. The amount of taxes required in repaying the debt plus the interest thereon isn't even possible to tax from the people. The government has to then print money and finance its debts and current expenditure. The effect of printing money is that the buying power of a currency is weakened in proportion to the quantity of currency printed.

The effect of this weakening of the buying power of a currency by the government is an act of taxation on its subjects. This is a hidden tax because inflation rate, unlike the tax rates and interest rates and other rates are known and publicly determined and clear. The government engaging in inflationary activities is secretly robbing its citizens through a form of taxation hidden in its nature. The inflation, just like all taxes, falls heavily on the vulnerable of a society. The sapping effect of this hidden taxation by the government is most felt by its poorer subjects, particularly workers and pensioners who receive wages, salaries, and pensions fixed in currency terms and who keep currency as a form of money.

Businesses are able to avoid the effects of both inflation and taxation to a greater degree, but workers, consumers, and the poor majority, whose salaries and wages are measured in currencies, the quantity of which is fixed for them by an employment contract, a wage agreement, etc. The effect of inflation is also to widen the gap between the rich and the poor. It's a form of surreptitious taxation that takes from the poor and vulnerable and gives to the powerful, rich, and well-off.

Financial Repression

Government policies such as interest-rate manipulation, monetisation of debts, putting limits on interest rates on government debt, and other kindred financial exercises on currency result in the debts of the poor and the interest rates they pay being high, while the government enjoys low interest rates. The government passes the cost of its interest rates as higher inflation to the poor who aren't hedged against inflation. The effect is that the poor are constantly in economic repression from which then can hardly escape.

In high-inflation economies, the rich get richer and the poor are condemned to greater poverty at an increasing rate.

Conclusions

Economic policies that allow for some inflation promote inequalities that emanate from the effects of inflation. Inflation shouldn't be tolerated, especially in an economy with high numbers of taxpayers who are receiving money in fixed amounts of currency.

The effects of inflation on the poor and the wage earners can be corrected to some degree by adjusting the basket for calculating inflation and providing for the provision of these baskets to these people, in the place of currency-denominated wages. A wage based on a basket of goods that affect those vulnerable to inflation would protect them from inflation to the extent that the baskets reflect their expenditure.

VI

Taxation

Taxation is a process whereby the government takes part of the income of an individual for its own use. That "own use" includes government running expenses, public infrastructure, and other such activities, necessary or otherwise. These activities by the government usually benefit the taxpayers in an indirect manner and in a general manner. Taxation is a way of taking away individual wealth and using it for the maintenance of government and its activities.

Tax as a verb describes the economic activities where the government takes money and allocates it to itself. As a noun, taxation refers to the structure of tax the government has set up to harvest wealth from individuals to itself. Taxation hasn't always existed in some countries and was historically usually imposed by the king or queen in war times in order to help fund wars. Taxation is now usually backed and implemented by means of enacted laws, case laws, and other legal instruments, all of which are set up by politicians and enforced by government in order to extract maximum amounts from taxpayers. It's a powerful tool mostly wielded by the kings and the government, and it's rarely subjected to any democratic processes such as voting, participation, and debate.

Taxation is a tool for economic management because it allows an opportunity for the ruler to take wealth from one group and to leave it with another group. Taxation is a distribution activity and structure that affects the configuration of economic wealth among the economic participants from whom tax is being wrung. Taxation varies for each of the economic participants: the labourers/people are taxed at higher rates than companies, while the government doesn't tax itself. The government is both the setter of the rate of taxation and the beneficiary, with little or no oversight, nor accountability to the taxpayer.

A tax is a financial charge, any contribution, or other levy imposed by the government, state, or the functional equivalent of a state enforced by legislative authority upon a taxpayer (an individual or legal entity), and failure to pay is punishable by law. It can be in the form of a tax, a rate, a levy, a toll, a tribute, a tallage, a gabel, an impost, a duty, a custom, an excise, a subsidy, an aid, a supply, or another name. A tax is a non-penal, compulsory transfer of resources from the private individual or company to the government, levied on taxpayers without receiving any specific benefit.

Since taxation is a form of distributing the wealth and money which are produced in a nation, the objective of taxation should be to maximise economic welfare through taxation, or in other words, to minimise its negative effects on wealth and wealth creation.

Types of Taxes

Income Tax

Income tax refers to tax the income of individuals and business entities, including companies. Rates of tax may vary or be constant (flat) by income level. Many systems allow individuals certain personal allowances and other non-business reductions to taxable income.

Personal income tax is often collected on a pay-as-you-earn basis, with small corrections made soon after the end of the tax year. These corrections take one of two forms: 1) payments to the government, for taxpayers who've not paid enough during the tax year 2) and tax refunds from the government for those who've overpaid. Income tax systems will often have deductions available that lessen the total tax liability by reducing total taxable income. They may allow losses from one type of income to be counted against another. For example, a loss on the stock market may be deducted against taxes paid on wages. Other tax systems may isolate the loss, such that business losses can only be deducted against business tax by carrying forward the loss to later tax years.

Individual Income Tax

In South Africa, tax tables for wage income range from 18 per cent (for income below 160,000 Rands) to 40 per cent (for amounts over 617,000 Rands), although the tax threshold of 63,556 Rands (for persons below age sixty-five) means that anyone earning less than this amount pays no income tax.

South Africa Income Tax Table (2012/2013)

Taxable Income (in Rands)	Rate of Tax on Taxable Income
0–160,000	18%
160,001–250,000	R 28,800 + 25% of amount above R 160,000
250,001–346,000	R 51,300 + 30% of amount above R 250,000
346,001–484,000	R 80,100 + 35% of amount above R 346,000
484,001–617,000	R 128,400 + 38% of amount above R 484,000
617,001 and above	R 178,940 + 40% of amount above R 617,000

Individual personal income taxation is calculated on gross wage and salary income, plus any allowances received that are subject to tax. The tax rate per the sliding scales is then applied to the gross taxable income thus calculated.

This system of having different taxes for different income categories is prevalent in most countries in the world and is applied similarly, only the tables vary slightly per country in line with the currency and the salary levels. There is no justification for imposing a higher tax burden on hard working individual who have worked hard in their past to achieve a high earning career and earn a living out of their talents, skills and trade, while charging a lesser tax on those who have for various reasons attained to lower income jobs. 18per cent is considered by this write to be too high a tax for any individual and if this was levied as a flat tax on everyone in the above table, it would be still too much tax. At a flat rate of tax for everyone, the individuals earning higher amounts of gross income would still pay more tax than those earning lower income because the actual amount of tax on a higher figure is always more than that on a lower figure of gross income.

The logic of charging a higher tax rate on higher gross incomes is based on misunderstanding the fact that even at a flat rate higher income earners already pay more taxes in terms of the actual amount. Increasing the rate of tax for higher individuals means that they are sacrificing more on tax than everyone else. The tax levied in this manner is an inefficient and unfair tax that pretends to achieve equity when in it actually does the exact opposite. Taxation should be charged on an equal sacrifice basis. By merely applying a percentage, high earners are automatically paying more than those who earn less. Adjusting the percentage is unfair, arbitrary, and unjustifiable.

In most cases, those who end up falling in these brackets aren't rich and are mere workers who've worked hard and have reached the upper echelons of the corporate ladder. The rich people, the ones who sign these worker's paycheques, aren't even earning salaries and wages as they tend to own companies and pay themselves through dividends rather than through a salary. The truth and reality is usually that the rich don't pay taxes. They have the flexibility and power to avoid taxes. They utilise loopholes and provision in the tax laws to avoid tax. They relocate to places and states where there's lower tax. They stash their earnings in trusts and other forms of entities which are tax proof, and they pass the wealth to their offspring, untaxed.

The higher percentages for taxation for high salary income earners are discriminatory, and they do segregate people in that they bundle up individuals into thumb-sucked categories and tax them at different rates. The circumstances of individuals are never the same just because they've reached a common wage level. The thresholds are arbitrary and unjustifiable, not meaning anything. The principles of equal sacrifice aren't present in these percentages, and they discourage the wage earners who excel in their careers by imposing a punitive burden on them.

The tax tables make the system of calculating and understanding tax very complicated and difficult to understand. It's a system that allows tax authorities for those countries who use tax tables to pretend they've adjusted the tax threshold to give back money to taxpayers by the token of slight adjustments to the thresholds, when the actual effective tax rate has hardly changed. Fidgeting and fiddling with the tax bands annually creates an illusion of benevolence by the taxman which is in reality non-existent.

A worker is taxed on his or her gross income. From the after-tax net income, the worker will then make a budget and allocate all his or her expenditures accordingly—such expenditure as food, shelter, travel, entertainment, telephone costs, clothes, personal capital expenditure, etc.

In addition to that, individuals are also responsible to pay VAT or sales tax. All consumers/individuals pay this tax and are faced with it every time they make purchases which have VAT levied on it. This means that after the worker receives his or her net salary (so named because tax has already been deducted, he or she has to spend it on items on which another tax is payable), and this adds to the individual's tax burden.

Tax Status of an Individual

An individual is taxed on gross income at higher percentages than companies. The individual then has to face all other expenditures using money that has already been taxed. Expenses such as accommodation, travel, food, entertainment, clothing, telephone costs, the cost of education, buying capital assets, electricity, and water costs are all paid using money that's already been depleted by tax. This after-tax currency is spent on expenditure on which the taxpayer will be subjected to further taxes, such as VAT, property tax, toll fees, fuel levies, and other taxes. The individual taxpayer ends up having paid much more than the percentage charged for income tax.

If we add VAT at 14 per cent and property rates, fuel levy, and toll fees, the effective tax rate for an individual will be over 50 per cent for most countries in the world. It means that for six months in a twelve-month year, the individual is contributing his or her full salary towards taxes.

Individual taxpayers are at the bottom of the tax pyramid, in that they're the main contributors of tax both in the amount that they sacrifice out of their total income and also in the privileges they have in terms of the tax laws. The tax falls heaviest at these bottom dwellers and lightens as we go up the pyramid. Individual taxpayers are the majority of the people in a society and include mainly workers, who are generally the poorest in society and on whom many other people depend (they're mainly breadwinners).

Company Income Tax

It's often that one hears a prominent business person brag, somehow assertively, that he or she is one of the people paying the highest tax because of his or her company paying taxes. Business owners often think that everyone else is paying very little taxes and their companies are making a lot of taxes for the government, and they're owed some praise or gratitude by the nation. Business owners often consider the taxes that they collect on behalf of the government from employee earnings as being their own contribution and not of the employee.

The tax that the company pays refers only to that part of tax which is calculated on the company's taxable income, which roughly equals its net profit before tax and which is calculated at the end of the financial year. The taxation of companies is very different from that of individuals. Companies are taxed on net profit, after making minor adjustments for a few immaterial accounting treatment differences, to arrive at taxable income.

The rate of tax for a company is substantially lower than for individuals, and it's a single-fixed rate, unlike for individuals. Generally the tax is imposed on net profits from business, net gains, and other income. Computation of income subject to tax may be determined under accounting principles used in the jurisdiction, which may be modified or replaced by tax law principles in the jurisdiction. In South Africa, the company income tax rate is levied at 28 per cent of the taxable income of the company. Certain companies qualify as small business corporations, where tax is levied at 10 per cent for taxable income above 59,750 Rands, up to a limit of 300,000 Rands and 28 per cent on taxable income above 300,000 Rands. Employment companies pay a tax of 33 per cent. Dividends are subject to an additional tax called the Secondary Tax on Companies, which is 10 per cent of declared dividends.

In 2009 to 2012 tax periods the company tax revenue statistics as shown in the table below reveal the startling fact that an average of 27per cent percent of all the companies who are eligible to pay taxes ended up paying any taxes at all. On average a total of 73per cent of all company taxpayers in South Africa claimed that they did not have any tax to pay and did not pay any noticeable tax at all. So a majority three quarters of all company tax payers were either declaring that they have tax losses or they are at zero tax (their tax income matches their tax expenses). It must be noted that these companies declared a tax loss or a zero tax after applying the tax laws and they are legally permitted by these tax laws to do that. They employ experts to ensure that their tax revenue is less than, or equal to the total of allowable expenses and tax allowances available to companies.

Table A3.3.1: Companies: Taxable income and tax assessed by taxable income group, 2009 – 2012 Source:http://www.sars.gov.za/About/SATaxSystem/Pages/Tax-Statistics.aspx

Tax year	2009		2010		2011		2012	
Taxable income group	Number of taxpayers	Tax assessed (R million)	Number of taxpayers	Tax assessed (R million)	Number of taxpayers	Tax assessed (R million)	Number of taxpayers	Tax assessed (R million)
Total	**664,399**	**129,653**	**647,857**	**126,275**	**600,526**	**139,355**	**440,550**	**84,955**
Total < 0 taxable income	222,997	987	220,402	876	199,705	548	148,660	42
Total = 0 taxable income	260,168	55	255,387	43	234,969	10	156,197	5
Total > 0 taxable income	181,234	128,611	172,068	125,355	165,852	138,796	135,693	84,908
Total	**664,399**	**129,653**	**647,857**	**126,275**	**600,526**	**139,355**	**440,550**	**84,955**

Democratic Political Economy

Percentage				
Total < 0 taxable income	33.6%	34.0%	33.3%	33.7%
Total = 0 taxable income	39.2%	39.4%	39.1%	35.5%
Total > 0 taxable income	27.3%	26.6%	27.6%	30.8%
Total	**# 100.0%**	**100.0% #**	**100.0%**	**100.0%**

Tax Status of Companies

Throughout the whole world, the taxation of companies is very different from that of individuals in that companies are allowed to deduct any expenses that they incur as companies (except expenses incurred in the breaking of a law—e.g., a traffic fine won't be allowed). A company calculates its gross profit/earnings, and from that amount it deducts all its expenses. These include, but aren't limited to, salaries and wages of employees, accommodation, travel (local and foreign), food, entertainment, clothing, telephone costs, the cost of education/training, electricity and water costs, property rates/taxes, fuel, cleaning, advertising, marketing, heating and lighting, stock losses, recreation, and legal fees. In addition to the expenditures listed, for all capital assets that the company acquires, it's allowed to deduct, over three years, the total cost of these assets from the taxable profit, just like expenses. The taxman also allows businesses that have a tax loss to carry these losses from year to year and deduct them against taxable profits in future years.

The company then calculates the tax on the remaining amount, and this is only what they're required to pay. It should be noted again that companies are effectively incurring the above listed expenditures without all the other taxes such as VAT, toll fees etc., because the fact that they're able to deduct these in computing tax implies mathematically that they only pay 72 per cent of the costs, and that is the calculated net of VAT. The company is thus able to avoid VAT and pays for its expenses tax free. The benefit the company is receiving is 28 per cent of its expenditure.

A comparison of individual taxation and company taxation

Company	Individual
Taxed only on net profit after a long list of deductions	Taxed on gross income after very few, insignificant deductions
Tax rate percentage is single and lower.	Tax rates are high and increase per income bracket.
Doesn't face VAT on its expenditure	Bears the brunt of VAT in full
All and any expenditure is deductible. T, total tax benefit is total expenditure allowed, times the tax rate.	No personal expenditure is allowed and pays out using after tax income.
Capital deductions are allowed and accelerated allowances.	No capital allowances on capital assets
Losses incurred and assessed in previous years are cumulatively deductible against taxable profit.	No special deductions on losses
Tax is easy and simple to determine.	A complicated system to determine actual tax.
Pays tax in one or three payments spread in a year.	Tax is withheld at source and deducted monthly.
Can deduct other taxes such as property rates, tolls, fuel levy, customs duty, etc., as part of its expenses.	Can't escape any other taxes.
Incurring more expenditure results in greater tax saving.	Incurring more expenditure results in greater taxation.
The marginal tax (tax per extra dollar earned) always is decreasing.	The marginal tax per extra income always increases with income.

The table below illustrates the manner of taxation faced by an individual and that faced by a company based on the tax rates applicable to South Africa for the 2013 tax year. The table is a general illustration and is meant to illustrate the effect on income and also on cash flow for both. Gross income for a company is considered here to be the gross profit after removing all direct or prime costs.

When an individual receives income, the taxman immediately takes more than a third of it. The individual then takes the remaining portion and starts to incur expenditure, all on which he or she pays further taxes. A higher tax-to-income proportion exists for the individual while it is much lower for companies. If a company was to receive similar income as the individual, the current tax laws in our so-called democratic societies would allow the company to deduct as many indirect costs as he can be able to from the income. Whatever remains, after the spending spree, the government then taxes that portion, at lower rates than that of the individual. In all the expenditure that the company incurs, the government will actually refund the company any tax, such as VAT, that the company can prove to have paid.

	Individual			Company		
	Tax expense (benefit)				Tax expense (benefit)	
Gross Annual Income	1,000,000.00			1,000,000.00		
Allowances	100,000.00			100,000.00		
Interest received	10,000.00			10,000.00		
Dividends received	1,000.00			1,000.00		
Gross income	1,111,000.00			1,111,000.00		
Tax		-376,540.00	34%		0	0%
	734,460.00			1,111,000.00		
			VAT			
travel	100000	14000	14%	100000	-28000	28%
Accommodation	100000	14000	14%	100000	-28000	28%
Food	200000	28000	14%	200000	-56000	28%
Holiday	50000	7000	14%	50000	-14000	28%
Entertainlent	40000	5600	14%	40000	-11200	28%
Housing	70000	9800	14%	70000	-19600	28%
telephone	25000	3500	14%	25000	-7000	28%
education	50000	7000	14%	50000	-14000	28%
electricity water	40000	5600	14%	40000	-11200	28%
	675000	94500		675000	-189000	
Total expenditure	769500			486000		
Capital expenditure	200000	28000		200000	-200000	100%
Previous years' loss	0	0		250000	-250000	100%
	200000	28000		450000		
	228000	0		450000		
	997500	0		36000		
Company tax					10080	28%
Totals	-263,040.00	499,040.00		225,920.00	-628920	

Gross advantage

If an individual were to receive an equal amount of gross income as a company, immediately on receipt, assuming he or she would be falling into the highest bracket of tax, they would be taxed at a percentage (40per cent on gross) that is higher than for companies (28per cent on Profit Before Tax). The company isn't taxed on gross income because the tax law doesn't require it to pay any tax on gross income, but rather allows the company to incur any expenditure that it can imagine and deduct this from the gross income. Then the company will be taxed on the little amount remaining after deduction all those expenses.

Net-off advantage

Furthermore, the individual pays his or her expenses inclusive of VAT or sales tax (14 per cent in the illustration), but the company doesn't pay VAT or sales tax on its expenditure. It's able to net-off VAT on any of its expenses against its VAT on sales and on the difference it can claim a refund if VAT that it paid on its expenses exceeds that which it has received on its sales.

Tax-formula advantage

A company deducts all its expenses in full from its gross income before it calculates its taxes, unlike an individual who has to pay on the higher gross figure. The tax benefit of this is illustrated in the table to be the rate of company tax multiplied by the expense. The company hasn't only avoided VAT on its expenditure but has the luxury of a benefit on each and every expenditure that it incurs. In this case, the company tax rate is 28 per cent, implying that the company gets a 28 per cent relief for every form of tax claimable expenditure it incurs. The difference between the amount the individual is paying and what the company pays for any expenditure is the sum of VAT and that of the company tax rate.

The individual in every expenditure pays 42 per cent (14 per cent VAT and 28 per cent company tax benefit on expenditure) more that the company. The individual's expenditure above is a total of 769,500 Rands, but a company paying the exact amount of expenditure would at the end of the day pay only 486,000 Rands. The total difference is 283,500 Rands.

If we consider this at an economy level, the total expenditure for individual is 42 per cent more expensive than for companies. Individuals pay at least 42 per cent more on every expenditure than do companies. The individual can't avoid taxes such as VAT sales tax and other taxes such as property tax, tolls, duties, and excise.

Capital expenditure and tax losses advantage

After deducting expenditure, a company can claim the full cost of any expenditure on fixed assets such as cars, properties, machinery, computers, houses, and any other capital expenditure. The company is allowed to remove from its income the cost of such assets before being taxed. The company also can remove in full the assessed tax losses from previous tax years. The tax laws usually go as far as five years looking for losses that the company can deduct from its income just to reduce its tax burden.

No such reliefs are available to any individual. The individual taxpayer not only faces the cost of his or her capital assets in full (plus other taxes such as VAT) but isn't allowed to carry deficits and losses from history into the current tax calculation. In percentage terms, the difference for individuals and companies for capital expenditure is at least 42 per cent (for capital expenditure) and 100 per cent for losses. The individual pays 42 per cent more for houses, cars, computers, property, etc., than is paid by the company. For any losses that the company incurs, it's allowed a tax break for it in future.

The tax eventually paid by the individual in the above illustration is the total of both the VAT and the income tax amounting to 499,040 Rands. The individual has paid fifty per cent taxation on his or her income. He or she has worked half a year for the benefit of the taxman. The other half is for him or her to face expenditure, both capital and non-capital.

The individual illustrated above ends up in a negative cash position, which has to be financed by borrowing, since surely there can't be any savings from the previous year in such a situation. On the other hand, the total tax paid by the company in this illustration is a mere 10,080 Rands. The company has lawfully complied with the tax laws and still has a bank balance of 225,920 Rands from its income.

Discretion advantage

Currently companies are encouraged by the tax laws to pump up expenditure and to increase losses as much as to enable them to pay as little tax as possible. Companies are being used to incur expenses such as advertising, fuel, holiday travel, telephone, entertainment, teas and refreshments, allowances, tuition fees, training, legal fees, consulting fees, medical fees, interest charges, directors fees, etc., that don't relate to the income-making activities of the company. There's no motivation to reduce these costs as doing so would result in higher taxes. Capital expenditures are being claimed on costs such as expensive furnishings and fittings, cars, aeroplanes, yachts, holiday houses, paintings, state-of-the-art offices—costs that aren't justifiable for deduction but still pass under the current tax system.

Paying taxes for companies is actually an optional choice. The company can decide to always match its expenditure and capital allowances to match the taxable income every year. Companies can legally avoid paying taxes year on year by a clever mix of expenses and capital expenditure to claim allowances that eliminate taxes altogether.

To further illustrate this inequality, let's suppose for one moment that the individual was to be awarded and taxed in the same fashion as the company and at the same rates as the company. That would mean that from the total income, the individual would be allowed to deduct any and all expenses that he or she incurred in the process of trying to obtain that income. All travel expenses to and from work, food and drink used during the working hours, accommodation, fuel, entertainment costs, telephone costs, medical costs, insurance costs, general expenses, etc. would all generally qualify for tax as deductions. Additionally, all capital expenditure such as property, motor vehicles, and furniture would be allowed as capital deductions, including instalment payments on finance arrangements. It goes without saying that the remaining income after all these "discretionary" expenditures would leave the taxable profit very small, and the tax on that would be very low.

The majority wouldn't be taxed at all because if one's tax expenses exceed one's tax income, the deficit could be claimed against taxable income in subsequent years. Individuals would ensure that their tax incomes were always exceeded by their tax expenses. This just goes to illustrate the tax utopia that companies currently live in, in which incurring any expenditures gives them tax advantages, and making losses every year is rewarded by a tax advantage which is actually an asset they can deduct for the future.

Table A3.3.1: Companies: Taxable income and tax assessed by taxable income group, 2009 – 2010 for South Africa

Tax year	2009			2010		
Taxable income group	Number of taxpayers	Taxable income (R million)	Tax assessed (R million)	Number of taxpayers	Taxable income (R million)	Tax assessed (R million)
A: < -10 000 000	3,632	-264,377	949	4,034	-309,737	847
B: -5 000 001 to -10 000 000	3,107	-21,719	1	3,315	-23,050	10
C: -1 000 001 to -5 000 000	20,098	-41,940	35	21,937	-45,873	2
D: -500 001 to -1 000 000	19,619	-13,799	1	20,789	-14,649	16
E: -250 001 to -500 000	27,269	-9,693	0	27,869	-9,947	1
F: -100 001 to -250 000	39,887	-6,553	0	39,707	-6,532	0
G: -1 to -100 000	109,385	-3,321	0	102,751	-3,133	0
H: = 0	260,168	–	55	255,387	–	43

167

Table A3.3.1: Companies: Taxable income and tax assessed by taxable income group, 2011 – 2012

Tax year	2011			2012		
Taxable income group	Number of taxpayers	Taxable income (R million)	Tax assessed (R million)	Number of taxpayers	Taxable income (R million)	Tax assessed (R million)
A: < -10 000 000	4,001	-321,810	544	2,569	-174,268	40
B: -5 000 001 to -10 000 000	3,389	-23,541	0	2,568	-17,775	0
C: -1 000 001 to -5 000 000	21,881	-45,741	1	17,117	-35,709	1
D: -500 001 to -1 000 000	20,054	-14,168	1	15,746	-11,105	0
E: -250 001 to -500 000	25,715	-9,185	2	19,449	-6,961	0
F: -100 001 to -250 000	35,181	-5,803	0	26,039	-4,300	0
G: -1 to -100 000	89,484	-2,745	0	65,172	-2,021	0
H: = 0	234,969	–	10	156,197	–	5

Such is the great injustice of the current tax systems in most countries in the world. The company is the sacred cow in terms of taxation. It's a system set up intentionally by the kings and the nobility for the capitalist aristocracy to benefit from the tax web. The company was meant as a vehicle for wealth creation for the rich and powerful and was not burdened with taxes—and it's still not.

Immunity advantage

In light of this it's interesting to note that if the company tax rate was reduced to a rate of, say, 5 per cent on net profit, the tax difference between companies and individuals would actually reduce (the tax inequality would be lower) and companies would effectively be paying only 19 per cent less (currently as high as 42 per cent less) than individuals for every expenditure they incur.

In addition, one will be intrigued even more to note that the effect on total taxes paid by companies due to an increase or decrease in the tax rate is always insignificant as long as the tax on companies is calculated on the bottom line after deducting all expenses and allowances already alluded to. The tax system and companies were designed to allow minimum effect, maximum cushion, and lavish discretion on amount paid and comes with a whole lot of doors and loopholes that afford the company to dodge the taxes.

It's a result of these advantages that the national revenue receipts of most countries, including the three countries as shown in the pie charts above, had very little receipt coming from corporate tax. The tax on companies is levied in a more lenient way than on individuals and the individuals are almost directly funding the profits of the companies. Governments intentionally let companies retain profits, and proceed to tax individuals more, in the process creating a tax subsidy for companies funded by individuals. The excuse proffered is that companies create employment, and in order to attract companies to an economy, tax breaks and the most lenient tax rates and systems are required, so as to have as many companies as possible.

It's surprising that, given the leniency of the tax laws relating to companies, in the present times one finds there are companies engaged in tax avoidance and tax manipulation. The profit motive and the selfishness that accompanies the profit-maximisation capitalist economies currently existing in the world economies have left governments overtaxing their citizens and casting a blind eye on companies. If the tax laws are to be equitable and fair—and just surely a basis fairer—more equal sacrifice is an urgent need.

Long term sustainability problem

The current system of taxation for individuals and companies isn't tax efficient. For individuals, it's overtaxing. The individual is bearing the majority of the tax burden, while the company is hardly carrying any tax burden. The individual tax isn't sustainable at the current rates.

On the other hand, the company isn't only undertaxed but is also taxed on the wrong basis. Taxing a company on the bottom line amounts, after expenses, is an untenable anomaly. The amount and type of expenditure is left at the discretion of the company, and any expenditure goes and is allowable for tax purposes. Companies who don't control their expenditure and incur too many costs are rewarded for such an effort by a higher amount of tax relief. A company that's managed to keep its costs low will get a smaller tax relief. Also a company that makes more losses is able to carry them into the future, while the one that makes a profit faces more taxes. It's a bad form of reward system that tends to reward wastefulness and poor performance.

Companies currently enjoy the most generous tax regiment and are privileged to pay tax after having subtracted from their gross income all expenditure they incur, (distribution, marketing, administrative costs, general expenses), and also after further subtracting from that any capital allowances (i.e., the cost of motor vehicles, buildings, furniture, and any such type of expenditure). The company is at liberty again to further subtract from the balance any losses incurred from previous years (five years usually) until they're netted off against any future taxable profits. This allows a loss-making company to regard such a loss as a tax asset, claimable against any future profits, as the company will be able to reduce its tax bill.

Individual tax on Gross Income

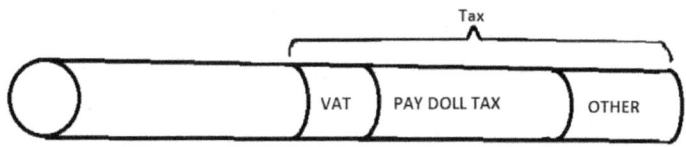

Company tax on Gross Income/Profit

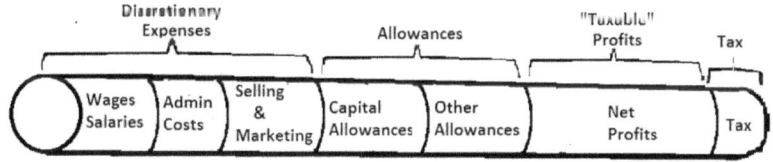

Tax Discount on Expenditure

A basic consideration of the current company tax, especially on expenditure treatment will show that in reality any tax rate charged is basically the size of the "tax discount" on such expenditure. If one company has expenditure totalling 100,000 dollars at the end of the tax year, and the tax rate is 30 per cent on companies, it means they're allowed to deduct this whole expenditure from income before applying the tax rate to the remaining amount. Applying the rate to the expenditure means that after tax the company has benefited to the value of 30,000 dollars. , in after-tax terms, the company only incurred expenditure of 70,000 dollars. The tax has the effect to offer the company a discount on each and every expenditure it makes, and the size of that discount is the tax rate charged on companies.

The logical end of this analysis is that increasing company tax rate means the company has a higher tax discount, and reducing the tax rate reduces the tax discount. In a regime of high taxes, the company avoids taxes by matching expenditure and allowances to its taxable income. In a regime of low taxes, the same applies, and the only difference is that the motivation to do so is reduced. It's a truth that increasing or decreasing the company tax rate doesn't make any significant difference to most companies in the current tax system as they're still able to legally avoid taxes by adjusting their expenditure mixes.

A tax system that will make the tax on the individual and the tax on the company equal, that will make companies minimise cost and maximise income, that will result in equitable (equal-sacrifice) contributions to the national pie by both individuals and companies, that isn't skewed or inefficient, that eliminates manipulation, and that doesn't reward failure with bigger tax deductions is surely a desirable system.

Taxes on Goods and Services

Value Added Tax (Goods and Services Tax) and Sales Taxes

A value added tax (VAT), also known as goods and services tax (GST), single business tax, or turnover tax in some countries, applies the equivalent of a sales tax to every operation that creates value. Sales taxes are levied when a commodity is sold to its final consumer. VAT is charged and remitted at every value-adding stage of a product. The business incurs and passes on the higher amount to the consumer. The last VAT amount is paid by the eventual retail customer, who can't recover any of the previously paid VAT nor can claim to the tax authorities for a refund. For a VAT and sales tax of identical rates, the total tax paid is the same, but it's paid at differing points in the process.

VAT and sales tax aren't good taxes, and they're not equitable because they're not based on the equal-sacrifice principle. The manner in which these taxes are levied doesn't result in equal sacrifice among those who eventually pay VAT or sales tax. The rate of tax is a percentage of the product price. A customer buying a product—e.g., a house, a car, or a litre of fuel—will suffer the tax regardless of the amount of income he or she has. A poor person, living on donations; a widow, living on government grants; a student, without any form of income—all face this tax despite their circumstances.

Companies, on the other hand, have been made immune to this tax and are allowed to pass it on to the poor consumer. The poor spend most of their income on goods and services, and the amount of VAT or sales tax relative to their income is proportionally higher than what the rich pay relative to their income. This is a skewed type of tax because it falls only on one set of economic participants, namely consumers.

The companies/businesses and the government don't pay VAT but simply collect it on behalf of the government, by charging it on every product and handing it over to the tax authorities. They don't have an expense on their financial statements called VAT or sales tax, as they're mere conduits for it and don't face such taxes. Only in a few exceptional circumstances, some particular expenditure is disallowed by the taxman, but they're still able to claim it as a deduction for normal income tax purposes.

It's because VAT was set up to benefit the ruling class and the business aristocracy that it works in the current fashion, which allows the government departments and entities to claim back all VAT payments and expenditure made from the tax authorities for their own use. VAT, just like company income tax, is set up to make the company able to subtract the VAT on expenditure (both operating expenses and capital expenditure) from the VAT on its income and revenue. The government is allowed by the VAT legislation to claim all VAT even where it has no revenue from value addition. Everyone else in the political economy isn't afforded these special privileges.

Little justification exists for VAT or sales tax, and those who add value or who benefit from the sale don't bear the tax. It's a tax that exists only to increase the gap between the rich and the poor. The rich don't pay VAT or sales tax because they're the owners of companies and businesses. They incur all their expenditure in companies and in trusts. The rich organise their affairs such that they pay as little tax as possible. The expenditure isn't incurred in a personal capacity but is incurred by the company on behalf of the rich individual. The rich man or woman goes to holiday under the company name, he or she drives a car bought by his or her company and which is fuelled daily by the company, and the car and insurance are paid by the company. The rich have their medical bills paid for by their companies, they have their wives, husbands, and children as directors, and these also claim the same benefits. The companies in turn don't pay the VAT or sales tax at all; they simply claim it back from the government. Only the poor majority among the people pay VAT and sales tax and aren't able to claim it from the government.

It's common for the taxman to exempt food, utilities, and other necessities from VAT or sales taxes, since poor people spend a higher proportion of their incomes on these commodities. This is another form of illusion meant to disguise an unfair and bad tax. If you remove the tax on basic commodities, it's the rich who benefit most because they've always spent a higher proportion of their income on these commodities, by virtue of being able to afford more of them. They'll get a bigger size of benefit than the poor.

In any case, this doesn't narrow the gap between the rich and the poor because less tax is being collected, and it has to come from other sources anyway. Giving a tax break on certain basic commodities is segregating the poor from the rich based on arbitrary product selection and perceived consumption trends that aren't realistic, as individual consumption always varies. Expenditure patterns are always different from individuals, and not all money is always spent on the few goods which have been made tax free. A widow on a social grant is likely to pay more VAT than a business owner, and relative to their incomes, the poor widow faces more VAT than the rich business person who can easily avoid VAT altogether.

If VAT or sales tax is to be levied at all it should only restricted to luxury and elitist products and services and only to people or companies who consume such products. Such products as jewellery, tourism, fashion, entertainment, air travel, hotel services, and kindred dainties and luxuries. The VAT or sales taxes should be levied only to the extent that it lightens the tax burden on the majority of the people in an economy. A country with a large number of tourists, travelling traffic passing through its borders, could justifiably charge such taxes if they resulted in reduced tax pressures on individual tax for its citizens.

For a business to be able to charge VAT or Sales Tax, and for it to be able to claim back all VAT paid on what it buys, the tax authorities require all businesses to be registered for such tax and they will give an identifying number as proof of registration. Such a number is quoted every time a business issues an invoice. If a business isn't registered for VAT, it has to foot the VAT amount as an expense, and can't claim it back, means that every business should aspire to be registered for VAT so that it join the gravy train and start claiming back any VAT paid. The tax authorities always set a qualifying threshold for one to qualify to register for VAT. This is one of the unfair ways in which capitalists have sought to suppress the emergence and make hard the survival of small, start-up businesses. Surely as long as one is adding "value," he or she's entitled to claim the VAT. Small businesses struggle with tax bills, cash flow, and other problems because they've not been admitted into the exclusive club where they can claim back their tax expenses as far as VAT is concerned. If VAT registration is to be equal, fair, and equitable, every business, particularly small businesses should be allowed to register for VAT to benefit from its advantages to the company.

Fuel Levy

The fuel levy in South Africa represents a tax paid at the pump on fuel, predominantly processed fossils fuels like petrol and diesel. In 2013 this tax represented about 29.6 per cent of the price of 93-octane petrol and 30.3 per cent of the price of diesel.

Five per cent of the total fuel price paid at the pump in South Africa goes to the Road Accident Fund, a state insurer that provides insurance cover to all drivers of motor vehicles in South Africa in respect of liability incurred or damage caused as a result of a traffic collision.

Analysis of fuel tax in South Africa for 2013.

	petrol 95 ULP	petrol 93 ULP	Diesel
	Rand	Rand	Rand
Basic fuel price	7.7917	7.7617	8.0003
wholesale price	12.238	12.008	12.1967
Fuel levy	2.125	2.125	1.975
RAF levy	0.96	0.96	0.96
Customs and excise duty	0.04	0.04	0.04
	3.125	3.13	2.98
VAT	1.71	1.68	1.71
Total tax on fuel	4.84	4.81	4.68
Fuel levy as a percentage of basic fuel price	27.27%	27.38%	24.69%
Total levies as a percentage of basic fuel price	40.11%	40.26%	37.19%
Total levies as a percentage of wholesale fuel price	25.54%	26.02%	24.39%
Total tax levied on fuel as a percentage of wholesale fuel price	39.54%	40.02%	38.39%

From the figures presented in the table above it seems the government is collecting 40 per cent of the basic cost for itself. For every litre of fuel that one buys, the government is adding a markup of 40 per cent on the cost. If one was to consider the mark up the fuel retailers are putting on fuel, it's likely the government is making more (about double) from the sale of fuel than the actual fuel retailers. The consumer, for every litre of fuel purchased, pays 25 per cent to the government for taxes.

Fuel costs are pervasive for the whole economy and are the main cost drivers for a large number of goods, products, and services. They result in the cost of a lot of goods, both for the poor and for the rich, increasing. While I've shown already that companies are able to avoid VAT, it's also a fact that companies get to deduct the costs of their fuel as part of the tax calculation. The effect for companies is to lessen the impact of direct taxes on goods or services.

The effect of the taxes on fuel costs is to add a 40-per-cent burden on consumers, particularly the poor majority, who are most affected by fuel costs as they tend to affect every aspect of their lives, including transport costs, food costs, and almost every other cost.

A tax that has a fixed amount, no matter the change in circumstance of the taxed individual, is a regressive tax. Those with lower income must use a higher percentage of their income to fund it than those with higher income. The effect is most felt by the lower income and is felt less by those earning a higher income. Just like VAT or sales tax, a tax such as fuel levy increases the gap between the rich and the poor and isn't justifiable, regardless of the use to which it's put.

A tax isn't and shouldn't be justified by the use to which it shall be used, but should be able to be justified on its own. Shall the government rob, steal, and plunder for a good cause? A tax levied to attend a good cause, but which is levied from a single disadvantaged group and worsens their welfare, can't be a good tax.

A Good Tax

A tax can be considered a good tax (if a tax can ever be good) if it's fair, equitable, and efficient. A fair tax means that it's reasonable, justifiable, and impartial without any bias. Equitable taxation is an even-handed taxation which doesn't discriminate one class from the other or one person to the other (legal person or actual individual). An efficient tax is a tax that isn't only easy to determine and calculate, but it's a tax that achieves the goal of taxation. It's sufficient to fund the government and leaves sufficient money in the hands of the taxpayer to be able continue industry. It's a tax that doesn't exhaust the worker to a point of discouragement, nor does it harvest the fruit tree so much as to leave it unable to bear more fruits. Taxation should be sustainable for both the taxpayer and the one collecting it.

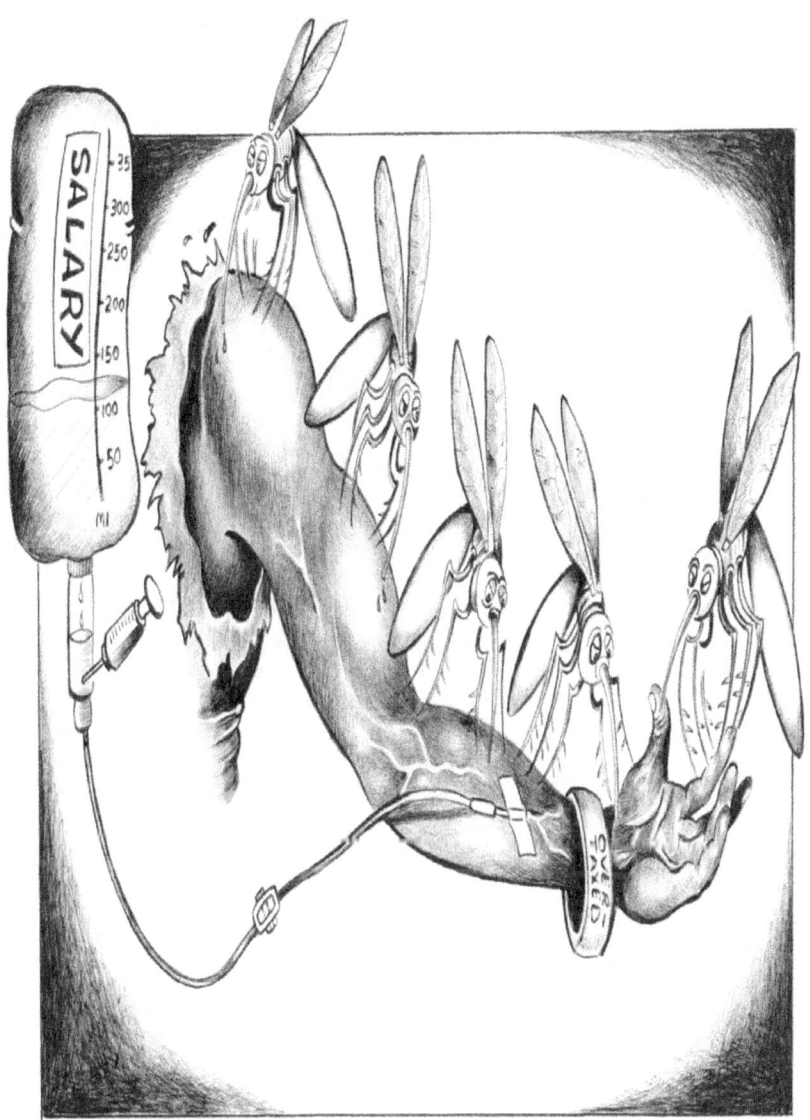

A Progressive Tax

A progressive tax is defined as a tax system that takes a larger percentage from the income of high-income earners than it does from low-income individuals. Individuals earning higher salaries are taxed at higher rates, and those at low salaries pay taxes at lower rates. Taxpayers are broken down into categories based on taxable income; the more one earns, the more taxes he or she will have to pay after crossing the benchmark cut-off points between the different tax-bracket levels.

It's worth noting that the word "progressive" is quite an ambiguous one, especially regarding taxation. This type of taxation isn't only regressive, it's the worst example of taxation. Individual workers earning high salaries are never the highest earners in society; rather, companies, making millions or more, are the high earners. Tax should give equal burden to all taxpayers, not some thumb-sucked tax bands discriminating and categorising workers into different classes.

Most national governments claim to have a system of "progressive" income taxation system which is based on the premise that the wealthy should contribute a greater proportion towards supporting the state than the poor. This, they say, means that the more a person earns the higher percentage tax they pay. The individual tax is withheld by employers using tax tables with variable rates that increase as the quantity of wages increases.

If those who support this type of taxation were to be consistent they would then also charge different tax rates to companies who earn different profits. They should be charging higher tax rates to the more profitable companies and lower tax rates to smaller, less profitable companies. This tax system is regressive in that it punishes employees who've worked hard to achieve higher-paying jobs through various sacrifices. Why such people should bear the brunt of a dictatorial tax system and be taxed at higher rates, and how that can be called progressive, is a mystery of cunning proportions.

The current so called "progressive" tax systems are devoid of most qualities of a good tax system. There's a false notion that the government attempting to tax higher income at higher rates will result in equity, fairness, or something "progressive."

A tax system should require equal sacrifice from taxpayers in particular and all economic players in general. Equal sacrifice requires that those who earn less income sacrifice equally with those that earn higher. The quantity will automatically be different, but the extent of tax per income will be the same. Any tax that doesn't encourage and ensure equal sacrifice is neither efficient nor fair or equitable, and it can't be termed progressive.

The progressive tax proponents also ignore the ethics of such tax on the fruits of labour. The root cause of wealth differentials is at the distribution of the means to wealth. To be most progressive, attention should be aimed at addressing the differences on the means of production, and not wait until the worker has earned his or her wages or until the wealthy have engaged in business and at the point of profit/income distribution, then try to plead the progressive cause.

When the government has collected the tax revenue, they have at their disposal the ability to distribute the tax to benefit those that are not wealthy in as progressive a manner as they think.

Tax Incidence and Wealth Creation

The current payroll tax systems common in most countries in the world—where those employees who earn high salaries are made to bear a greater tax burden than any other taxpayer, with the tax rates going as high as 45 per cent in some countries—isn't only painfully comical, but it's regressive in economic terms. This band includes and will net those professionals, artisans, and industry captains who've worked hard and have obtained academic and professional qualifications to be where they are and form part of the economic engine that drive an economy and its wealth creation. These are the people to whom a nation should be endowing all opportunities to develop industries and companies and wealth. Doctors, accountants engineers, electricians, managers, you name it—they all fall into this bracket.

Taxing these people up to their neck makes them unable to save for investment or for any other risky venture they would've easily saved for because of their skills. These are the only people who would stand a chance to establish and sustain a company that would compete against the big businesses. Taxing them at higher rates makes them unable to start their own businesses or to engage in any other business other than their employment. This makes them faithful workers who'll spend the best of their lives working and slaving for the big companies, creating more wealth for the big capitalists. Through taxation, these once fertile, able men and women have been castrated by the tax system into malleable steers and bullocks that will spend their most productive years of life pulling the yoke for the capitalist.

In a bid to be "progressive," the very people from which economic emancipation would be easy have been robbed by a regressive tax regime that will milk out all their energies until they're discarded at retirement and offered a meagre pension.

The Tax Spider Web

Tax collectors in biblical times were detested individuals, seen as assisting an exploitative system. They were even considered chief sinners and were excluded from the society of pious men. The modern taxman is considerably smarter and more sophisticated, but doubtfully less guilty. The taxman is the enforcer of the oppressive rules that hold the majority in tax slavery.

Tax collection is today performed centrally by a government agency usually called Internal Revenue Service or Revenue

Authority. However, the revenue services use a network of tax collectors who've cast a web of the tax net across the various spheres of the economy. These are the foot soldiers that perform most of the duties of tax collections, usually for free to the government.

Employers are required to deduct from workers' earnings a set percentage as tax, and businesses and shop owners are required to levy a set rate of sales tax, value added tax, or carbon and fuel levies when selling fuel, and these are all paid into the revenue service account. The payment of taxes for the majority of the economic participants is at the point of expenditure or even before receipt. Employees are taxed before they get the paycheque. The employer pays the employees their salaries and wages as a net amount after having already deducted the tax thereof, and businesses such as shops are required to charge prices that are tax (VAT(value added tax) or sales tax) inclusive on the products. In both cases they promptly remit these to the tax authority.

However, these same businesses and companies are allowed the luxury to pay their own taxes (company tax) annually or quarterly in a year, and there's a cash flow benefit in the process for companies which isn't available to individual taxpayers. When taxes aren't fully paid, civil penalties (such as fines, penalty charges, interest, and forfeiture) or criminal penalties (such as imprisonment) may be imposed on the non-paying entity or individual.

The cost of collecting revenue is often calculated as the operating costs of the tax collector compared to the total tax revenue. The cost to the businesses and similar entities used as conduits for tax collection is not taken into account. In order to account for the taxes, employers and retailers need adequate payroll and accounting systems for recording all taxes at their own cost and at no commission.

Table: Cost of revenue collections, 2008/09 – 2012/13 for South Africa (Source- SARS)

#R million	Tax revenue collected	Operating cost[1]	Cost of collection[2]
2008/09	625,100	6,511	1.04%
2009/10	598,705	7,032	1.17%
2010/11	674,183	7,426	1.10%
2011/12	742,650	8,221	1.11%
2012/13	813,826	8,679	1.07%

1. *Operating cost as disclosed in the Statement of Financial Performance for the controlling entity in the SARS: Own Accounts Annual Financial Statements.*

2. *Operating cost as a percentage of tax revenue.*

The aim for collecting taxes is to be able to fund expenditure that benefits the taxpayers directly or indirectly. The true cost of tax collection should therefore be based on not only the operating costs of the tax collector. It should be a comparison of what was collected, and what was eventually distributed in various forms, back to the general population. The costs of collection and distributing the tax reflect the total cost of collecting taxes. The actual cost of collecting taxes it therefore always higher than what is admitted due to the inefficiencies of bureaucracy and other leakages. The most efficient way therefore to leave the tax in the hands of the taxpayers as much as possible is not to tax it in the first place.

A tax system based on every individual reaching a certain threshold being registered (just like national registrations) and all businesses being registered on a similar basis, and ensuring that income and expenditure that qualifies for tax is captured at every turn, is the most wide tax that can be set up. The cost of such a system would be very low because it would be individually driven, with all income being recorded to the individual, and all expenditure being allowed to be deducted against income. Value added tax would be the net of actual individual value added, less expenditures in the value addition.

Additionally a system that allows payments directly to tax beneficiaries would be more useful and reflective. Local companies and individuals should be allowed to pay taxes directly to local tax beneficiaries. What should be centralised are administration and records etc., but the processes around payments, etc. can be more efficiently executed locally. Only top-ups and excesses would be rendered to a central pool. A local road network being constructed out of direct tax payments to a contractor would not only enhance citizen participation and accountability, it would also change the nature of taxation from an inefficient mammoth that it is in most countries, into a localised necessity that directly impacts the taxpayers.

The democratic impact of such a system will ensure that everyone is accountable and there is greater transparency of the revenue and the expenditure sides of taxes. Revenue flows should not fly directly to a central pool without watering the streams that lead there. A localised system that does not ignore the less watered areas, and that does not run dry the springs, should be more efficient. Only a portion of the local revenue should be forwarded to the central authority. It follows that while the central tax pool will be still larger, it will have less pressure on it, and it will be easier to manage. Damming up all the tax into one vault and to soon after be tunnelling it out to the source area, is an exercise in futility and leakages and evaporation are bound to happen along the process.

Democratic Political Economy

The democratic effects of the tax methodology is best compared to the financial structures of churches, which are of interesting significance to the way they tend to follow the governance model used in the church governance. A church under the bishopric of a central figure and that is dependent mainly upon that central authority, tends to have all tithes and offerings swept into one central bag from which life support will be finger administered, drop by drop to different needs. There is also those churches which have financial and governance autonomy at local level, with the power to appoint a local pastor and leaders whom they pay from their tithes and offerings. These tend to work best where there is enough quality membership from which adequate funds meet the local expenses. The independence and objectivity of the pastor tends to be more threatened by those who contribute the most to the offerings and tithes. There are those churches which offer some autonomy to local churches but still give support to the central administration by cascading a fixed percentage of their income via a regional structure who also take their portion. The added ability to decide on a larger portion of the funds while also aware of the importance of the bigger organisation makes decision making and finances more transparent at all levels of this structure. Members have some say in what their money is used for and the decisions are generally democratic.

The tax collection and expenditure and the governance structures should be made to reflect each other and be useful in strengthening accountability. While the giving of tithes and offerings in churches is mostly a voluntary act, it is a system that, where properly administered, reflects the use of the funds with efficiency, in a manner that closely estimates the wishes of the giver. A democracy should afford every taxpayer an explanation of the costs that come to meet their tax contribution. That cost is not a narrow accounting calculation, but should be a measure of the amount in every dollar of tax that is usefully used to give value to society.

Tax collection targets are set every year, and the revenue services find pride in exceeding these targets every year. Quality-based targets—such as expanding and growing the tax base, the quality of taxes collected, and the tax efficiency—would be better targets than a quantity-based target that promotes a self-serving application of the law.

Local authorities at the local government level, such as municipalities and metropolitans, collect their taxes (called rates, levies, etc.) through a system of monthly invoicing. Failure to pay property rates usually results in termination of other not-tax services such as electricity, water, etc.

Purposes and Effects

Money provided by taxation has been used by states and their functional equivalents throughout history to carry out many functions. Some of these include expenditures on war, the enforcement of law and public order, protection of property, economic infrastructure (roads, legal tender, enforcement of contracts, etc.), public works, social engineering, subsidies, and the operation of government itself. Governments also use taxes to fund welfare and public services. A portion of taxes also goes to pay off the state's debt and the interest this debt accumulates. These services can include education systems, health-care systems, and pensions for the elderly, unemployment benefits, and public transportation. Energy, water, and waste management systems are also common public utilities.

Governments use different kinds of taxes and vary the tax rates. This is done to distribute the tax burden among individuals or classes of the population involved in taxable activities, such as business, or to redistribute resources between individuals or classes in the population. Historically, the nobility were supported by taxes on the poor; modern social security systems are intended to support the poor, the disabled, or the retired by taxes on those who are still working. In addition, taxes are applied to fund foreign aid and military ventures, to influence the macroeconomic performance of the economy (the government's strategy for doing this is called its fiscal policy), or to modify patterns of consumption or employment within an economy, by making some classes of transaction more or less attractive. A nation's tax system is often a reflection of its communal values or/and the values of those in power. To create a system of taxation, a nation must make choices regarding the distribution of the tax burden—who will pay taxes and how much they'll pay—and how the taxes collected will be spent. In democratic nations where the public elects those in charge of establishing the tax system, these choices reflect the type of community that the public wishes to create. In countries where the public doesn't have a significant amount of influence over the system of taxation, that system may be more of a reflection on the values of those in power.

Tax Pie

National and local governments raise revenue in various ways, and their tax revenue make-ups tend to differ. However, the constitution of such revenue is important for consideration in political economy.

At the local government level, property taxes (called property rates in most English speaking countries) form the highest percentage of the revenue pie for the local authority's revenues. Property taxes/rates aren't calculated based on any consumption or services offered but are determined by applying the local tax rate to the assessed value of an individual's property. This calculation means that localities that have low property values will have a much smaller tax base to draw revenues than a more wealthy area. Property taxes are levied as a percentage of the estimated value of land and structures and are paid by the property owners.

At the national level, the highest percentage of the revenue pie for government revenue from tax comes from personal income tax for most countries in the world. Personal income tax has an appearance of fairness and purports to be equitable, because of the inclusion of deductions and exemptions in calculating individual personal and because of the sliding scales applied in its calculations.

A smaller source of revenue comes from corporate income tax which taxes each corporation based on its profit, similar to an income tax on an individual.

The second major revenue source for state funding for most countries in the world is generally sales tax, (also similar to its alternative form called value added tax or VAT). Sales taxes are levied as a percentage of the total amount spent at retail stores. VAT is almost the same as sales tax, except that VAT is calculated and determined at every stage in the value chain until at retail point.

Duties, excise, and other customs charges form the third form of revenue for most governments, and the contribution to national revenue increases with trade with other countries.

Finally, both at the national and local government levels, tax revenue is made up of taxes collected on specific goods such as on alcohol, on tobacco, and so on, and other smaller taxes. These types of taxes are a small portion of total tax revenue and are usually implemented to discourage participation in a particular activity.

The contributions made by each major player towards the national tax pie are of importance in answering issues of political economy. I've already shown that the biggest and most important players in the political economy are government and businesses, mainly in the form of companies. Governments' estimation, and acknowledgment of the important role of companies, is attested by the many laws and policies in favour of companies and the way the government gets out of the way to create the best environment for companies and businesses. The other players are the workers, small business owners, and their kindred.

The contributions of individuals and of companies to the national pie are considered below for three countries. It's also important to note that the government contributes close to nothing in the revenue of any of these countries and is there to consume and distribute what is brought in by the other players.

The figure below shows estimates of the federal receipts for the United States for the fiscal year 2014. Payroll taxes (34 per cent) and individual taxes (46 per cent) constitute the bulk (80 per cent) of the receipts. Corporate income tax from companies and businesses amounts to a curiously small amount of 11 per cent. Recent news has been dominated by stories of large corporations who've avoided paying taxes legally by locating their activities, incomes, and profits in tax-haven places such as Ireland, the Cayman Islands, and similar places.

The relatively small contributions of companies to the national pie are definitely an anomaly and go on to show that the tax burden of the national budget is borne largely by individuals only. The major players in the economy aren't sharing the yoke of taxation in financing the expenditures of government.

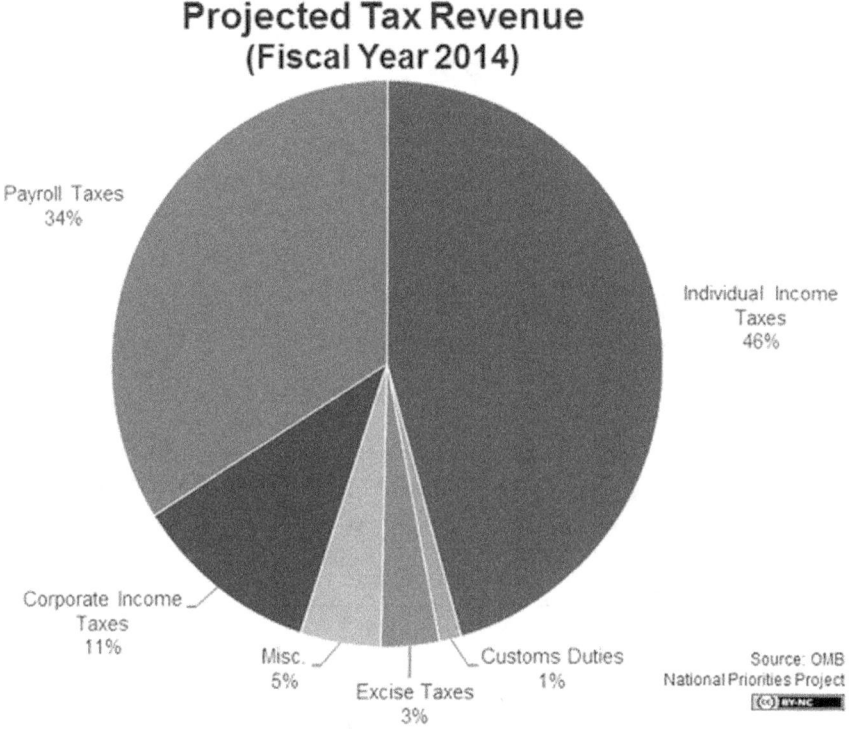

**Projected Tax Revenue
(Fiscal Year 2014)**

Payroll Taxes
34%

Individual Income
Taxes
46%

Corporate Income
Taxes
11%

Misc.
5%

Excise Taxes
3%

Customs Duties
1%

Source: OMB
National Priorities Project

The next two charts relate to the United Kingdom's tax receipts for the 2010-2011 and 2011-2012 tax years respectively. The same trend is evident where income tax of individuals amounts to 30 per cent, national insurance being 19 per cent, and VAT being 17 per cent. These three taxes form the majority of the contributors to the pie. All three are taxes that fall on the individual mostly. Companies make a feeble 8-per-cent contribution to the pie. The question that needs to be answered is, with all the importance and the dedication that governments and the state give to companies, what do they bring to the table as their contribution to the tax pie?

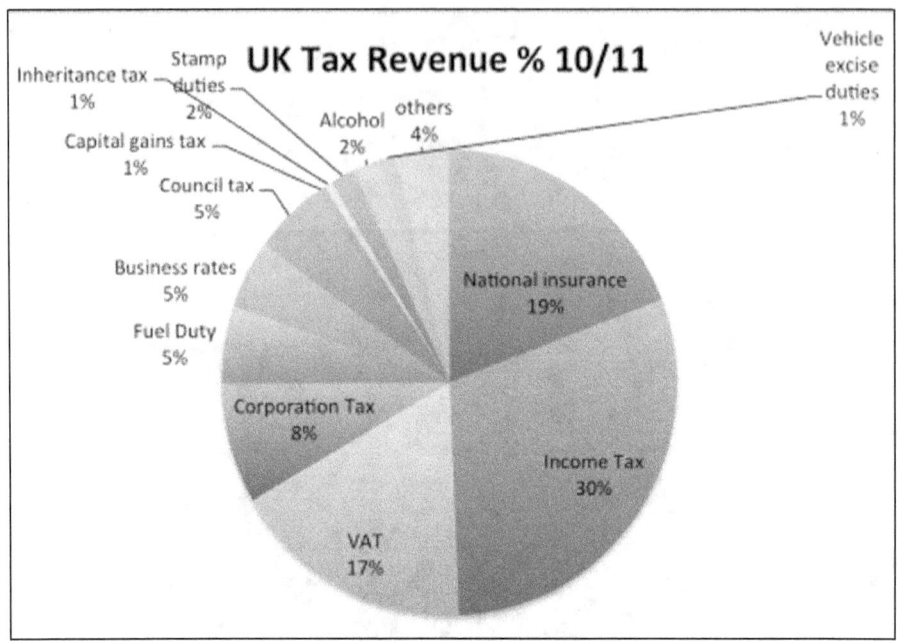

UK Tax Revenue % 10/11

Inheritance tax 1%
Stamp duties 2%
Capital gains tax 1%
Council tax 5%
Business rates 5%
Fuel Duty 5%
Corporation Tax 8%
VAT 17%
Income Tax 30%
National insurance 19%
Alcohol 2%
others 4%
Vehicle excise duties 1%

Chart 2: Government receipts 2011-12

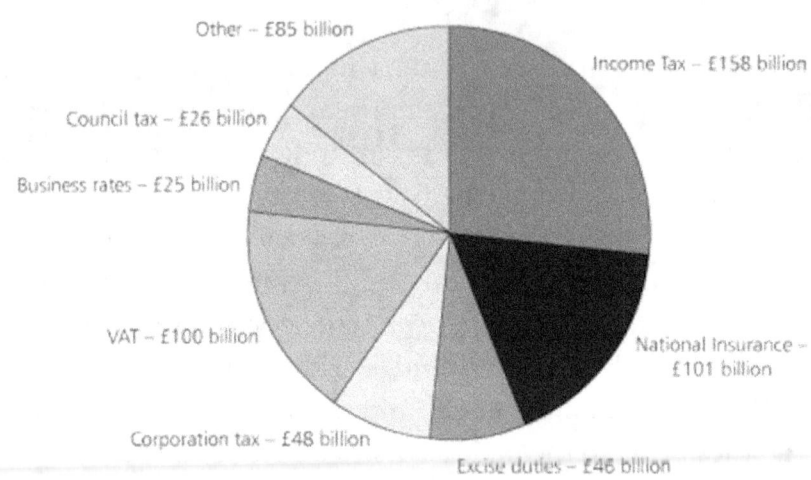

Other – £85 billion
Council tax – £26 billion
Business rates – £25 billion
VAT – £100 billion
Corporation tax – £48 billion
Excise duties – £46 billion
National Insurance – £101 billion
Income Tax – £158 billion

Source: Office for Budget Responsibility, 2011-12 estimates. Other receipts include capital taxes, stamp duties, vehicle excise duties and some other tax and non-tax receipts – for example, interest and dividends. Figures may not sum due to rounding.

The fourth and final illustration of the public pie is for the taxation revenue in South Africa. Government revenues come primarily from income tax, VAT, corporation tax, and fuel levy. In the 2010–11 fiscal year, the tax authorities, SARS, collected 674.2 billion Rands in tax revenue; 75.6 billion Rands (or 12.6 per cent) more than the previous fiscal year. Of the total pie, the major contributors are once again the individuals through income tax, VAT, and fuel levy.

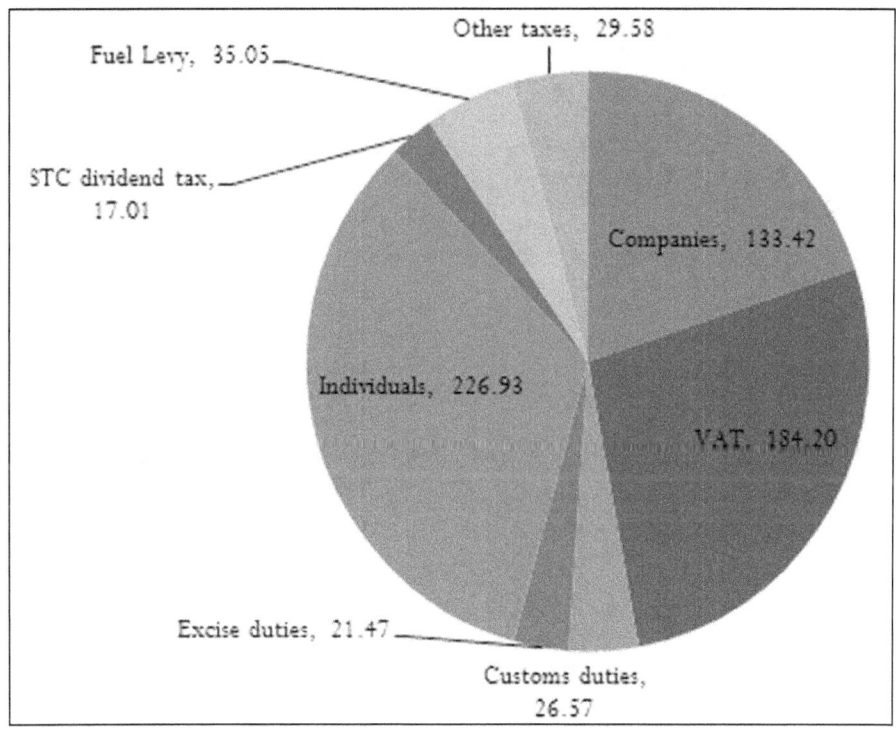

In the above four pie charts, ranging from different years in the past five years, in three different countries, they are a good illustration of the normal contributions to the national income by different role players in the economy and the pattern is consistent over the years and are a good peak at the common trend in most countries in the world. Only a few nations who are fortunate to be endowed with natural resources such as crude oil, or natural gas, are the excerption, as they tend to get the majority of their national income revenue from taxes on those resources.

The table below shows the revenue trends over a period of six years for the revenue collected from different taxes in South Africa. The majority of the total receipts are clearly shown to be coming from individuals by way of VAT and income tax, while the contributions of companies are decreasing. No account is made in these figures of local government property taxes, of tolls, and other direct levies or of other transfers to government.

Table 5: Breakdown of revenue collected and contribution to tax revenue – 2006/07 to 2011/12

Year	PIT	CIT	STC	VAT	Fuel levy	Customs duties	Other	Total tax revenue	GDP*
	R million	R million	R million	R million	R million	R million	R million	R million	R million
2006/07	141 397	120 112	15 291	134 463	21 845	23 697	38 744	495 549	1 832 761
2007/08	169 539	141 635	20 585	150 443	23 741	26 470	40 401	572 815	2 075 695
2008/09	196 068	167 202	20 018	154 343	24 884	22 751	39 834	625 100	2 303 553
2009/10	206 484	136 978	15 468	147 941	28 833	19 577	43 425	598 705	2 440 164
2010/11	228 096	134 635	17 178	183 571	34 418	26 637	49 647	674 183	2 752 119
2011/12	251 339	153 272	21 965	191 020	36 602	34 198	54 253	742 650	3 017 939
	%	%	%	%	%	%	%	%	%
2006/07	28.5%	24.2%	3.1%	27.1%	4.4%	4.8%	7.8%	100.0%	27.0%
2007/08	29.6%	24.7%	3.6%	26.3%	4.1%	4.6%	7.1%	100.0%	27.6%
2008/09	31.4%	26.7%	3.2%	24.7%	4.0%	3.6%	6.4%	100.0%	27.1%
2009/10	34.5%	22.9%	2.6%	24.7%	4.8%	3.3%	7.3%	100.0%	24.5%
2010/11	33.8%	20.0%	2.5%	27.2%	5.1%	4.0%	7.4%	100.0%	24.5%
2011/12	33.8%	20.6%	3.0%	25.7%	4.9%	4.6%	7.3%	100.0%	24.6%

Source: * Q1-2012 GDP, Statistics SA.

The chart shows the tax contributions with personal income tax (PIT) being the highest, followed by value added tax and it has already been mentioned that these two taxes are directly levied on individuals the majority of whom are the low income majority.

The personal income taxes have increased over the six year period shown while company income taxes have actually gone down over the same period. A fair tax system shouldn't be marked by such distortions as are illustrated above. Excessive inequality, especially where the major players do little and the weaker and less powerful bear the burden, will eventually lead the whole system to collapse, as it's not sustainable. While individuals have their taxes withheld at source, companies have the luxury to settle them after a year, and they have several means available to avoid the taxes.

Current Problems in Taxation

Outdated Tax Structures

The principles of taxation and the manner of calculating taxes are generally uniform worldwide. The manner of computing company taxes is generally similar with only the rate being different from country to country. Payroll taxes also have a lot of similarities with a few variances which are not materially different. The sales tax, value added tax, or similar taxes on sale of goods and services are also universally similar in most countries. The perfect case of new wine in old bottles applies to the current tax structures of the world. Copied from the former colonial masters of the world, the tax codes haven't moved with time and haven't adapted to the needs of the economies to which they apply. For lack of advocacy, the tax codes have remained hardly unchanged at the expense of the taxpayer. The uniformity in almost all worldwide tax codes in structure and pattern isn't only reflective of the way it's remained rigid despite the need for change, but it also shows that the changes have been cosmetic and were obviously influenced by power. Those stakeholders who are powerful in the tax equation have managed to accommodate themselves in the shadow of the corporate rates while the weak and the poor are exposed to toil in the heat of the higher rates for wage earners.

The capitalist nature of most world economies means these structures go unchallenged and are considered virtuous and fool proof. It's considered a desirable practice for one to minimise the corporate tax burden as much as possible, through any means lawful, even though this results in the least contribution to society by such entities. There is moral justification afforded to entities who evade taxes by transfer pricing, use of tax havens, or similar tax gimmicks. A capitalist mind does not consider a fair share of tax contributions to be virtuous, and gives no consideration to making a fair contribution to the economy and society in which the business operates.

Accounting rules and principles have a huge influence on the way taxation is calculated. The accounting standards of the world are highly uniform, and the accounting for tax has influenced the amount of taxation paid by companies. The practice has been to find the best accounting and tax law practitioner who will minimise taxation by utilising every loophole available. Declaring the source of income to be in a country or place where there are lower taxes, transfer pricing, and the types of expenditure that are allowable for tax purposes have affected the amounts of taxation paid by companies.

Developing countries are affected by their fear to upset investors from developed countries, so they've tended to adopt a tax regime similar in many aspects to those of the more developed Western economies. In this regard, economists and accountants have conspired to maintain a clearly unfair tax structure on companies and individuals. The reason for this being mainly that these two groups of professionals are paid by companies, and those who pay the piper have always called the tune.

Policing the Whole Tax Base

In many countries, there's too much government and government expenditure, which requires higher taxes on a shrinking tax base. It's always easiest to tax workers and most formal businesses. Workers are easy targets because the tax is deducted at the source, determined and withheld by the employer. Businesses on the other hand are allowed to determine their own taxes and report and pay them as such. Some businesses aren't taxed at all, and the determination of taxable income is left in the hand of the business taxpayer who manipulates it to his or her benefit. The National Football League (NFL) is one such example which represents a multi-billion dollar business in an economy but because they elected to register as a "not for profit" entity, the NFL does not pay any taxes. Most economies, particularly in the developing world, have a large informal sector which constitutes a large percentage of the economic transactions of an economy. Most transactions taking place in this sector are not recorded and the tax effect of these is lost. The informal sector is usually the result of a failure of the formal sector to function efficiently. An informal sector then mushrooms up and is usually fertilised by players in the formal sector who seek to by-pass the inefficiencies that are throttling the formal sector. Taxing the informal sector is usually difficult and may not be efficiently achieved using the current tax systems that a centred on formally employed taxpayers and the companies employing them.

Tax Evasion by Multinational Companies

Multinational companies are making news headlines about avoiding tax in almost all the countries in which they make their profit from. Through the use of tax havens and transfer pricing, they only declare their income as emanating from low tax regions and the effect is to make the total tax bill of these multinationals very small and insignificant. Through the use of tax expert advisors and clever lawyers and due to the influence held by these multinationals, they're considered "hard to tax," as they evade taxes legally.

Tax Holidays

Most developing countries dish out tax incentives in their growth-point areas, where the infrastructure and utilities aren't to the liking of companies. This is in order to attract investors and help develop these areas. It's often the case that these countries are desperate negotiators, they give in too much ground, and ending the incentives to attract investment results in a higher loss of tax than is necessary. Tax for companies is generally a small, insignificant amount to significantly change the mind of an investor, also given that they have evasion techniques at their disposal, were the taxes to be too high for their pockets.

Thomas Jefferson, United States

Although Thomas Jefferson (1743–1826) led the United States as president from 1801–1809 and is considered one of its founding fathers, he died with immense amounts of debt. Regarding the interaction between social classes, he wrote:

I am convinced that those societies (as the Indians) which live without government enjoy in their general mass an infinitely greater degree of happiness than those who live under the European governments. Among the former, public opinion is in the place of law and restrains morals as powerfully as laws ever did anywhere. Among the latter, *under pretence of governing they have divided their nations into two classes, wolves and sheep. I do not exaggerate. This is a true picture of Europe.* Cherish therefore the spirit of our people, and keep alive their attention. Do not be

> too severe upon their errors, but reclaim them by
> enlightening them. If once they become inattentive
> to the public affairs, you and I, and Congress and
> Assemblies, judges and governors shall all become
> wolves. It seems to be the law of our general nature,
> in spite of individual exceptions; and *experience de-*
> *clares that man is the only animal which devours his own*
> *kind, for I can apply no milder term to the governments of*
> *Europe, and to the general prey of the rich on the poor.*
> —Thomas Jefferson, *Letter to Edward Carrington,*
> *January 16, 1787 (emphasis mine)*

Setting an Equitable System of Taxation

In a democracy, because the government is the party performing
the act of imposing taxes, society as a whole should decide how the
tax system should be organised. The payment of taxation is justified as part of the general obligations of citizens to obey the law
and support established institutions. Anyone who earns an income
and from whom the tax can be efficiently and profitably collected
from should be made to contribute his or her potion of tax, a fair
share in all cases. A company or individual carrying out economic activity should be taxed and made to bear an 'equal sacrifice'
share of the tax burden. No activity should be excused from taxation on the basis that the activity resulted in a loss to the company.
Allowing losses to be claimed as tax benefits and accepting these
as excuses for not paying taxes allows economic inefficiency to be
rewarded.

The government's capacity to tax income from all economic
participants, and all economic activity, particularly on companies,
would lessen the current tax burden borne by the workers and

would be an advance in democracy where equality, participation, and fairness are achieved. Businesses engage in commercial activity by using publicly established and maintained economic infrastructure, and it's a fair thing that they should equally be taxed.

Tax Size

Taxes should be affordable to the taxpayer and should be reasonable. A worker generally uses his income for five things, namely for 1) personal upkeep and sustenance, 2) for going to and from work, 3) for food and drink, 4) for his or her household and family upkeep, and 5) for maintaining his or her family and him- or herself. On average therefore each of these five would form a fifth of the total expenditure one has to meet and would require a fifth of income to be dedicated to them. Reducing the disposable income of a taxpayer through taxation means they have to sacrifice in one of these areas. If a taxpayer has to pay 50 per cent of his or her earnings to the government, he or she can't afford to save, to attend to personal and family wants, and invest for the future.

A month's earnings in a year should be enough tax, and two months' earnings should be too much tax. The maximum that a government should take of one's income shouldn't exceed 10 per cent of one's earnings, to encourage industry and hard work and to provide motivation.

The current rate of taxation motivates tax avoidance. A rate of 10 per cent is high enough to be felt as a sacrifice towards to cost of government and low enough to enable the taxpayer to continue to engage in industry. Such a rate encourages everyone to play his or her part and isn't only reasonable but is consistent with normal income trends. Those who engage in businesses and in work don't charge mark ups or margins in the region of 50 per cent. A business usually makes a profit of up to 25 per cent on a product, just like a worker would charge 10 per cent for his or her labour on a task or job card. Taking away 50 per cent or more of that isn't only robbery, it's unfair, unjust, and can't be sustainable. Neither the worker nor the business wants to work for someone else to take away the income. They want to enjoy the fruits of their labour.

Companies should be charged taxation at the same rate of 10 per cent although the base should be changed from the current 'net' basis to a broader gross basis, to ensure equality between companies and actual individual tax payers. All economic increases should be taxed at a low enough rate to ensure good reward as well as reduced motivation for evading taxes.

The tax collector, it seems, is always hovering upon every taxpayer for potential taxability at every turn in life. When one is employed, is changing employment, is emigrating or immigrating; when one marries or divorces or decides to retire; when one finally decides to die or is fortunate to receive a gift, donation, or inheritance, the taxman will always participate in any income that accompanies the event.

The following song written by George Harrison captures this notion perfectly, and the song writer correctly perceived the high tax rates that the taxman has collected from individuals (95 per cent tax rate in the songwriter's case, and the taxpayer remains with only 5 per cent of his or her income, or tax of nineteen parts out of twenty). Cars for those who drive and feet of the humble walker are taxed, streets are tolled, houses (seats) are levied, heat (energy and fuel) aren't spared, and any activity, be it wiping of feet or something similar, has a taxman's hand in it. The songwriter concludes that the taxpayer is actually working for the taxman, which is to say that the taxpayer works to give the whole salary over to the taxman. While the dead are dying, the taxman is taxing them into the grave and beyond. The dead man has to pay his taxes otherwise the taxman will dig up the dead to tax him for his tax sins.

Taxman
Songwriter: Harrison, George

Let me tell you how it will be.
There's one for you, nineteen for me.
'Cause I'm the taxman.
Yeah, I'm the taxman.

Should five per cent appear too small,
Be thankful I don't take it all.
'Cause I'm the taxman.
Yeah, I'm the taxman.

(If you drive a car car) I'll tax the street.
(If you try to sit sit) I'll tax your seat.
(If you get too cold cold) I'll tax the heat.
(If you take a walk walk) I'll tax your feet.

Taxman!
'Cause I'm the taxman.
Yeah, I'm the taxman.

Don't ask me what I want it for,
(ah, ah, Mr. major)
If you don't want to pay some more.
(ah, ah, Mr. [..])
'Cause I'm the taxman.
Yeah, I'm the taxman.

If I reduce it, can you sleep?
(ah, ah, Boris Yeltzin)
Get back [..] v.a.t.
(ah, ah, Mr. Bush)
'Cause I'm the taxman.
Yeah, I'm the taxman.

If you get a hat hat, I'll tax your hat.
If you get a cat cat, I'll tax your cat.
If you wipe your feet feet, I'll tax your mat.
If you walk away away, I'll tax your [..]

Now my advise to those who die:
(Taxman!)
Declare the pennies on your eyes.
(Taxman!)
'Cause I'm the taxman.
Yeah, I'm the taxman.

And you're working for no one but me.
(Taxman!)

Yes, I'm the taxman.
Yeah, I'm the taxman.
Taxman lyrics © Sony/ATV Music Publishing LLC

The tax multiplier

If the current system of taxation was to be changed to one where the rates were a tenth of the income or less for all tax payers including companies, more taxpayers would participate in taxation, greater enterprise would be wrought, more economic activity would ensure, and the government would end up with greater tax revenue than they currently get from a narrow tax base. The current tax rate which hoover around the 50 percent regions for the majority of countries in the world, have the effect to stifle growth and to reduce taxpayers into debt ridden strugglers who can hardly afford the life they live. Any favourable change in taxes rates or in their income in general is hardly enough to extricate them out of their current situation.

The multiplier concept as explained elsewhere in this book is an economics mathematical concept that illustrates the exponential benefits that a small change in one economic variable has on the economic output. In monetary policy terms, if the fiscal authorities want to increase the total "money" available for economic activities, they only give a small amount of cash into the system. Financial institutions, because of fractional lending, only have to keep a small percentage in cash in the till and the rest they will lend out to interest bearing loans. The overall effect is that the smaller the fraction, the greater the multiplier, while the opposite is true.

In terms of taxation, if the government skimmed off most of the income from individuals and companies and leaves income only enough for their expenses, they will not be any multiplier effects on the economy. However if economic participants are allowed to retain most of their income, they will create more economic activity and more income and ultimately by extension, the tax will be more.

Most countries that have practiced this have higher standards of living than those that have punitive tax systems.

Table of countries with relatively low tax rates:

Country/Region	Corporate tax	Individual (max)	Payroll tax	VAT / GST / Sales
Albania	15%	10%		20%
Andorra	10%	10%	N/A	4.5% or 1%
Bulgaria	10%	10%		20%
Kazakhstan	17.5%,	10%	11%	12%
Macedonia	10%	10%		18% or 5%
Mongolia	10%	10%		10%
Paraguay	10%	10%		10%
Guatemala	31% of Net Income or 5% of Revenue	7%	17.5%	12%
Bosnia and Herzegovina	10%	5% FBiH, 0–15% RS	33.76% FBiH, 42–57% RS	17% FBiH and RS
Afghanistan	20%			2% to 5%
Bahamas	0%	0%	10%	0%
Bahrain	0%	0%	0%	
Bermuda	0%			

Country/Region	Corporate tax	Individual (max)	Payroll tax	VAT / GST / Sales
British Virgin Islands	0%	0%	10%–14%	N/A
Brunei	20%	0%	8.5%	N/A
Cape Verde	25%			15%
Kuwait	10%, 0% on dividends	0%		16%
Macau	12%			
Maldives	8%–15%			6%
Marshall Islands	0%			
Monaco	6%.		Social Security between 28%–40%	19.6%–5.5%
Oman	12%	0%		0%
Qatar	10%	0%	0%	0%

Country/Region	Corporate tax	Individual (max)	Payroll tax	VAT / GST / Sales
Saudi Arabia	0% if 100% Saudi owned, 85% for oil and gas companies, 20%all other companies	0%	11% Social security	0%
Turks and Caicos Islands	0%			
United Arab Emirates	0%	0%		N/A

Setting an Equal Tax for Everyone and Uniform Treatment of Taxpayers

A flat tax rate to all taxpayers, regardless of their personal incomes, would ensure an equal sacrifice from all taxpayers. The rich would pay a higher quantity of tax, and the less rich pay a smaller quantity of tax, but the amount of sacrifice would be the same. The taxpayers would thus be equal before the law. No preference would be given to the rich or the less rich. Everyone would pay according to his or her ability. Everyone would bear to tax yoke evenly and pull as much as his or her strength can allow. No one group would be crushed under the weight of an unbearable tax system.

Every extra dollar that one earns pays the same amount of tax as everyone else's extra dollar. A flat tax is easy to administer and has no deadweight loss, since. Tax rate variations on income can't be used to achieve redistribution because income isn't the tree but is merely the fruits of labour and industry. Taxes on the fruits should be limited to a small percentage.

Fiscal incidence, which is within the control of the government, is the right tool to address imbalances, and will achieve distributive equity in the most progressive manner. Addressing imbalances in the distribution of the means of production is obviously the most progressive method of addressing income imbalances. Waiting until the individual or company has earned the fruits of their labour and then attempting to apply any so called progressive tax rates is unethical.

Companies can decide the size of their taxes in the current state of things by taking advantage of the many instruments available to them. Increasing capital expenditure, increasing operating expenses, and increasing losses, are some of the many ways of avoiding tax for companies.

Treatment of "Income" for Individuals and Corporates/ Companies, just like individuals, should be taxed on gross income. This will allow optimal economic decisions and efficient expenditure because no benefit will arise from incurring higher expenditure. Companies that minimise their costs and maximise their income will be rewarded for their labours. Tax on gross income will also result in equitable taxation among individuals and companies.

Companies should face taxation at the point where the increase in income is made, this point being the gross profit or prime profit, determined as being the increase in income after deducting prime costs identifiable with a product or service. A tax rate, not exceeding 10 per cent, should be levied on gross income. Other administrative costs, advertising and similar marketing costs, legal costs, entertainment costs, etc., shouldn't be allowed to influence the income tax on companies.

Treatment of Expenses

What constitute expenses for the individual should be equal to what constitutes expenditure for the company. An expenditure that isn't allowable as a deduction for an individual should equally be not allowed as a deduction for a company.

Companies should be taxed at the same point for income and for expenditure as individuals. No preferential deductions should exist for companies that won't be available to individuals. Where a company buys a house or machinery, it should be treated the same for tax purposes as it would for individuals. The same expense for a company should have the same tax treatment as for individuals. It the tax authorities feel strongly that they should allow certain expenditures for tax, there shouldn't be distinction between individuals and companies. Capital allowances should either be available to both individual and companies or unavailable to both. No justification exists to deny individuals but to allow companies to enjoy such benefits.

The current status of allowing all and any expenses for companies as being deductible and the same expenses not being deductible for individuals allows companies to pay only 72 per cent of the cost (assuming a 28-per-cent tax on companies) while individuals face a 100-per-cent cost. Inequality is therefore systematic in the tax system and individuals are destined to be economic servants of companies. The benefits of the companies are obviously subsidised by individuals.

Treatment of VAT/Sales Tax

The current situation of allowing companies to claim back, in its entirety, any VAT it's paid on purchases and expenses isn't fair to other VAT payers as it doesn't let the company shoulder its fair share of the tax. The actual VAT is only charged on the cost of goods sold, not on entire organisational expenses. A company should be allowed to claim back VAT only on actual value added, which is on prime costs. On all other expenditure, the company, just like the individual, shouldn't be allowed to claim such VAT back. Such a situation will allow the company to engage in efficient decision-making as unnecessary expenditure isn't subsidised by VAT claims. Neither should the cost be passed on to the consumer.

Additionally, all VAT should be for value added and nothing more, especially for those entities which are allowed to claim and charge VAT for expenses and for incomes on which they've not added any value. In most countries companies and government entities such as municipalities, trading companies are allowed to claim a VAT refund on all expenditure regardless of whether that expenditure is related to value addition or not. Even if the expenditure is judged to be wasteful, fruitless, and in vain, there's no prohibition for such expenditure to be claimed for VAT purposes. VAT is being used as a way of punishing the end users who can't claim the VAT from the government and is benefiting businesses and government, who've made themselves immune to the VAT system.

Individual consumers who add value should be allowed to also claim VAT on all expenditure that companies are allowed to claim and be allowed to charge VAT on their products and services for the system to be fair on such taxpayer consumers like workers. Uniform treatment of VAT status would mean the worker will charge the employers a VAT portion on his or her salary and be able to claim all the VAT on expenditure that they incur.

For the situation to be fair, individuals should also be allowed to claim back VAT on all expenditure and on the same footing as the company for the expenditure they engage in. An individual who works is surely engaged in value addition and should have a deemed input and actual output tax. The individual should also be able to use this deemed VAT to make a VAT claim after considering the amount of estimated expenditure, both capital expenditure and non-capital normal expenditure.

Currently companies don't face any obligation for all VAT/sales tax as they're allowed to claim it back every month for all expenditure on which they're charged VAT whether it be operational, capital, or any other expenditure. The effect of this is that companies are paying less for the same services and goods as individuals. A company essentially passes in full all sales sax to the customers/consumers. The economic effect is that the individual pays 14 per cent more for every expenditure (assuming a 14 per cent VAT/sales tax rate) than companies. The company is being allowed to live in a tax-free position, while the consumer, the worker, and the individual are paying more than their fair share of taxes.

The company enjoys these advantages for both operational expenditure and capital expenditure. The individual has no such relief both for operational expenses and for capital expenses. No justification for this discrepancy exists, and either the same treatment should be received or the whole tax should be done away with as it results in unfair taxation of most individuals and gives others an unfair tax advantage.

The same definition of what constitutes income and expenditure should be used for companies and individuals. Common law on tax has adequately defined what constitutes income being gains, profits, and income derived from salaries, wages, or compensation for personal service of any kind and paid in any form, or emanating from any trade, business, or dealing or from interest, rent, dividends, or securities derived from any source whatever. However, what constitutes expenses hasn't been clearly defined, and it's been left to the statutory laws to determine what expense will be deductible and which won't be deductible.

Employees of a company add value to the company and its products or services. The company is able to claim VAT on materials, machinery, and other inputs because they come with a VAT charge when they're acquired. However, labour comes free of VAT and the value added by labour isn't accounted in the hands of labourers, but in the hands of the company. In order to solve this discrepancy and to correct differences where labour-intensive entities are taxed more than those that are less labour intensive, all labour should have a deemed VAT, and the tax should be accounted in the hands of the employee and be used as a tax credit by the company.

The proposal to treat all taxpayers equally will open scope for the common law to guide on what's allowable expenditure for tax purposes and what isn't allowable. The determination of what constitutes direct costs, and what is allowable as a deduction for tax purposes, should be determined in similar fashion as has been done to the definition of income by common law.

Treatment of Allowances

The allowances, particularly capital allowances, should be the same for individuals and for companies. Currently companies are allowed to deduct in full, from their taxable income, the costs of capital expenditures such as machinery, buildings, furniture, equipment, etc. (all capital expenditure). Individual taxpayers aren't afforded such a luxury. No capital tax allowances are made for individuals. I've already shown that no justification for such an unfair practice can be put forward.

Companies are also allowed to deduct from taxable profits any tax losses that may have been incurred in any previous year for the last five tax years. This means that a company that makes the wrong decisions and operates at a loss, after deduction any of its expenditures and after deducting all capital allowances and still has a tax loss can carry forward that loss to the subsequent years. The tax loss is used to reduce any taxable income that may arise in future years. Unbelievable as it may be, it's the current practice of almost all tax systems. Companies are rewarded for failing to contain their costs within the limits of their incomes. The effect is that companies which match their expenses with their income every year or have their income exceeding their expenditures will continue not have to pay any taxes as long as that situation continues. After they manage to keep costs within their income, they'll still be able to use the previous losses to avoid paying any taxes until they've made good such losses by not paying any taxes.

Any individual whose expenditures are higher than his or her income will be taxed on his or her salaries and wages. After that the individual has to find a way to borrow to fund his or her deficit. The privileged position enjoyed by companies in our current tax systems is in stark contrast to the perilous economy of the individual who's taxed thin and dry while the company is allowed every indulgence by the taxman.

The company's privileges are as many as the individual's disadvantages. The current tax systems of the world afford so much leniency to the company that it's an act worth marvelling at when a company pays tax altogether. It's only a few companies that prefer to be seen to be good corporate citizens who pay taxes.

Tolls

Suppose a government imposes a toll system on its freeways in big cities and towns in order to finance the construction of wider roads in an effort to reduce traffic jams during peak hours. Assuming the government had no other option than to impose this toll fee, a bad toll fee would be a flat toll that doesn't change no matter how much one used such a road. A good toll fee would be one that adjusts with the time one passes through the toll.

Most roads aren't congested at night. It's not a good practice to charge tolls even when the road isn't congested. The toll fees should kick in when there's traffic. Immediately when the traffic ends, they should lower the fees or no toll fees should be charges. Users would accordingly arrange their affairs so that they'd travel through the tolls during non-peak hours. The government would in this case have achieved raising funds for the roads financing, as well as controlled congestion by encouraging travel during non-peak times.

Microeconomic Perspective of a Good Tax

A eunuch is a male person who, by birth, misfortune, or by choice in life, has been castrated and lacks the means to procreate offspring. Eunuchs are mentioned in several verses in the Holy Bible, and Ethiopia seems to be one of the places which had a good supply of them. The eunuch was a faithful servant, useful in the treasuries, harems, and household chores of the king, and the king had no fear of losing his wife or daughters to the eunuch. The eunuch didn't have familial links (wife, children, in-laws, etc.) and was free of influences that would affect his judgement. Dedication to work was maximum and undivided.

The modern political economy system has sought to make every worker a eunuch and has achieved that in a large way. The eunuchs dedicate their full lives (eight hours daily) in dedicated service to the capitalist ruling class and get paid a fixed allowance called a salary. But before they get it about half is given over to the government. It benefits the government more to get the majority of its population to be workers (not entrepreneurs) and thus to be taxed at higher rates for the benefit of government.

Eunuchs' social standing was considered low, and they could be easily rid of through death, dismissal, etc., without any consequences or repercussions to their masters. The same status attends the modern eunuchs who the government and their partners in crime have exploited and can as easily replace with other, more productive and profitable eunuchs, or with machinery and other technology.

Men and women trained and skilled in various trades, at their youthful prime, are pawned by the government to industrialists who will harness them in employment at the least possible salaries for their class and put other eunuchs in charge of them. The salary is low enough and the tax is high enough to make the eunuchs just able to look after themselves and their limited offspring. They can hardly afford a lot of offspring and can hardly spend a few hours with family and loved ones. Their time, affections, and energies are mostly spent in serving their masters.

Macroeconomic Perspective and Results of Good Taxes

A system of taxation that is unfair and that treats some taxpayers more favourably than others isn't desirable. It chokes the majority of taxpayers and rewards only a small portion of the taxpayers with a lot of advantages. The effect is to make poorer the overtaxed individuals and to allow the favoured taxpayers to gain unequal advantage over the overtaxed. The macroeconomic effects of a fair and equitable tax are too many to enumerate. However, the good-will that would come as a result of setting an equitable and fair tax system also can't be adequately estimated. A fair tax is easy to administer and isn't too prone to avoidance and evasion.

The savings of individuals and the demand potential of individuals paying fair taxes would both be sufficient to drive economic activity and spur growth in any given economy without the government resorting to failed monetary policy tricks and similar gimmicks. It is an accepted dogma that economic activity in an economy is spurred from demand by individuals. The aim of all tax policy should be therefore to make the individual as economically viable as possible.

High and unfair taxes stifle hard work and industry among individuals. A fairer tax system for individual taxpayers would leave individuals motivated to work, to engage in entrepreneurial activities, knowing that the rewards of such efforts would benefit them more than other economic players.

A tax system for companies based on prime costs rather than net profit would enable the most economic decisions on incurring operating costs and on incurring losses. No expenditure would be incurred that wouldn't be justifiable. Taxing companies at the gross profit would enable companies to rationalise their costs and to determine which costs are unnecessary. All costs would be kept at a minimum, and the determination of costs would be a function actively scrutinised by these companies as they answered to their shareholders, government, and the taxman. All expenditure that is unnecessary to bring the taxable income of the company would be to the account of the company, without any tax advantages and loss allowances. The companies would begin to make the same rational decisions that individuals have been making in keeping their costs to the minimum. Again, the savings and resultant profits should be sufficient to spur economic activity and growth for the economy.

All economic activity such as financial and all other intermediary activities that are based on economic inefficiencies such as the lack of perfect information to all economic players, or certain advantages, will be reduced by a tax directly on gross profit. Sellers will seek to improve margins by eliminating middlemen and distribution chains will be shortened. The middlemen who add their own costs and charge their own mark ups would be hard pressed by a tax that charges the gross profit rather than the net profit. There would be no economic sense for such activities and they will be eliminated where they are not necessary. No tax benefits should exist for setting up intricate and long distribution systems with high costs. The elimination of tax benefits for incurring any cost should result in reduced distribution and related costs.

Example 2: Establishing a fair and equitable tax in Egypt

Genesis 41:14–57: 14 Then Pharaoh sent and called Joseph, and they brought him hastily out of the dungeon, and he shaved himself and changed his raiment and came in unto Pharaoh. And Pharaoh said unto Joseph, "I have dreamed a dream, and there is none that can interpret it: and I have heard say of thee, that thou canst understand a dream to interpret it." And Joseph answered Pharaoh, saying, "It is not in me; God shall give Pharaoh an answer of peace." And

Pharaoh said unto Joseph, "In my dream, behold, I stood upon the bank of the river. And, behold, there came up out of the river seven kine, fat fleshed and well favoured; and they fed in a meadow. And, behold, seven other kine came up after them, poor and very ill favoured and lean fleshed, such as I never saw in all the land of Egypt for badness And the lean and the ill-favoured kine did eat up the first seven fat kine. And when they had eaten them up, it could not be known that they had eaten them; but they were still ill favoured, as at the beginning. So I awoke. And I saw in my dream, and, behold, seven ears came up in one stalk, full and good. And, behold, seven ears, withered, thin, and blasted with the east wind, sprung up after them. And the thin ears devoured the seven good ears, and I told this unto the magicians; but there was none that could declare it to me."

And Joseph said unto Pharaoh, "The dream of Pharaoh is one: God hath shewed Pharaoh what he is about to do. The seven good kine are seven years; and the seven good ears are seven years: the dream is one. And the seven thin and ill-favoured kine that came up after them are seven years; and the seven empty ears blasted with the east wind shall be seven years of famine.

This is the thing which I have spoken unto Pharaoh: What God is about to do he sheweth unto Pharaoh. Behold, there come seven years of great plenty throughout all the land of Egypt. And there shall arise after them seven years of famine; and all the plenty shall be forgotten in the land of Egypt; and the famine shall consume the land; And the plenty shall not be known in the land by reason of that famine following; for it shall be very grievous. And for that the dream was doubled unto Pharaoh twice; it is because the thing is established by God, and God will shortly bring it to pass.

Now therefore let Pharaoh look out a man discreet and wise and set him over the land of Egypt. Let Pharaoh do this, and let him appoint officers over the land, and take up the fifth part of the land of Egypt in the seven plenteous years. And let them gather all the food of those good years that come, and lay up corn under the hand of Pharaoh, and let them keep food in the cities. And that food shall be for store to the land against the seven years of famine, which shall be in the land of Egypt; that the land perish not through the famine."

And the thing was good in the eyes of Pharaoh, and in the eyes of all his servants. And Pharaoh said unto his servants, "Can we find such a one as this is, a man in whom the Spirit of God is?" And Pharaoh said unto Joseph, "Forasmuch as God hath shewed thee all this, there is none so discreet and wise as thou art. Thou shalt be over my house, and according unto thy word shall all my people be ruled, only in the throne will I be greater than thou."

And Pharaoh said unto Joseph, "See, I have set thee over all the land of Egypt." And Pharaoh took off his ring from his hand, and put it upon Joseph's hand, and arrayed him in vestures of fine linen, and put a gold chain about his neck; And he made him to ride in the second chariot which he had; and they cried before him. Bow the knee, and he made him ruler over all the land of Egypt. And Pharaoh said unto Joseph, "I am Pharaoh, and without thee shall no man lift up his hand or foot in all the land of Egypt." And Pharaoh called Joseph's name Zaphnathpaaneah; and he gave him to wife Asenath the daughter of Potipherah priest of On. And Joseph went out over all the land of Egypt.

And Joseph was thirty years old when he stood before Pharaoh king of Egypt. And Joseph went out from the presence of Pharaoh, and went throughout all the land of Egypt. And in the seven plenteous years the earth brought forth by handfuls. And he gathered up all the food of the seven years, which were in the land of Egypt, and laid up the food in the cities: the food of the field, which was round about every city, laid he up in the same. And Joseph gathered corn as the sand of the sea, very much, until he left numbering; for it was without number. And the seven years of plenteousness, that was in the land of Egypt, were ended. And the seven years of dearth began to come, according as Joseph had said, and the dearth was in all lands; but in all the land of Egypt there was bread. And when all the land of Egypt was famished, the people cried to Pharaoh for bread, and Pharaoh said unto all the Egyptians, "Go unto Joseph; what he saith to you, do." And the famine was over all the face of the earth. And Joseph opened all the storehouses, and sold unto the Egyptians; and the famine waxed sore in the land of Egypt. And all countries came into Egypt to Joseph for to buy corn; because that the famine was so sore in all lands. And there was no bread in all the land; for the famine was very sore, so that the land of Egypt and all the land of Canaan fainted by reason of the famine. And Joseph gathered up all the money that was found in the land of Egypt and in the land of Canaan, for the corn which they bought; and Joseph brought the money into Pharaoh's house.

And when money failed in the land of Egypt, and in the land of Canaan, all the Egyptians came unto Joseph and said, "Give us bread; for why should we die in thy presence?" for the money faileth And Joseph said, "Give your cattle; and I will give you for your cattle, if money fail." And they brought their cattle unto Joseph, and Joseph gave them bread in exchange for horses, and for the flocks, and for the cattle of the herds, and for the asses; and he fed them with bread for all their cattle for that year.

When that year was ended, they came unto him the second year, and said unto him, "We will not hide it from my lord, how that our money is spent; my lord also hath our herds of cattle; there is not ought left in the sight of my lord, but our bodies and our lands

Wherefore shall we die before thine eyes, both we and our land? buy us and our land for bread, and we and our land will be servants unto Pharaoh; and give us seed, that we may live and not die, that the land be not desolate." And Joseph bought all the land of Egypt for Pharaoh; for the Egyptians sold every man his field, because the famine prevailed over them: so the land became Pharaoh's. And as for the people, he removed them to cities from one end of the borders of Egypt even to the other end thereof. Only the land of the priests bought he not; for the priests had a portion assigned them of Pharaoh and did eat their portion which Pharaoh gave them; wherefore they sold not their lands.

Then Joseph said unto the people, "Behold, I have bought you this day and your land for Pharaoh; lo, here is seed for you, and ye shall sow the land.

And it shall come to pass in the increase that ye shall give the fifth part unto Pharaoh, and four parts shall be your own, for seed of the field, and for your food, and for them of your households, and for food for your little ones." And they said, "Thou hast saved our lives; let us find grace in the sight of my lord, and we will be Pharaoh's servants." And Joseph made it a law over the land of Egypt unto this day, that Pharaoh should have the fifth part; except the land of the priests only, which became not Pharaoh's.

Equitable Corporate Tax

Companies were previously a preserve of the nobility and aristocracy who were the hands of the king, and these tax indulgences weren't means to create jobs or employment in the kingdom, neither were they meant to attract investment, but were made chiefly as a class privilege for the aristocracy engaging in the commercial expansion of the kingdom.

How, then, should corporate tax be set, and what part of income should be taxed without burdening these economic citizens?

The taxation should be based on the gross sales made from a product or service, which is the gross income of the company. The amount that the company invoices out to its customers, is the one that should be used to determine corporate tax. The turnover, sales, gross income or total revenue, or whatever names it is given. This is the most objective figure with the least susceptibility to manipulation, and is the same basis on which other taxpayers are being taxed.

A nearer basis would be to tax the company on a gross profit basis, after removing cost of sales, or prime costs, these being costs directly attributable to the product or service. Production efficiencies and savings would however be masked by such a basis. The fault would again be that those entities that are less efficient and are able to pump up their prime costs end up benefiting from tax by reducing their profits, while those that are efficient and can lower their production costs are taxed on the higher gross profit achieved. Such a tax basis would therefore reward inefficiencies and is not an improvement to the current tax system.

Capital allowances:

Allowing companies to deduct capital expenditure such things as buildings, motor vehicles, and machinery from their incomes is a luxury only afforded to companies, is unreasonable, and isn't necessary. Such a luxury isn't afforded to individuals and this is unfair. A company buying a car can deduct the cost of buying it over three years for tax purposes An individual taxpayer can't do so for the cars that they buy. Rich company owners are able to use their companies to buy cars for themselves so they can recover the tax advantage, a privilege not available to individuals.

Losses:

Accumulated tax losses from previous years shouldn't be used to reduce tax liability for a company. A company that still makes losses after all the current advantages available to corporates should surely be allowed to sink or swim on its own.

Setting a rate:

Because of the many advantages and because of their ability to dodge taxes, companies have hitherto not been at the forefront of complaining about the high tax rate. If the tax field is levelled and all the inequalities are eliminated for individuals and for companies, it would be necessary to then consider the best tax rate for collecting tax. The rate of corporate tax (average 30 per cent of net profit), just like individual tax (average 45 per cent of gross income), is currently too high for the good of the economy or for the good of the taxpayer. A rate of 10 per cent or below would best serve to allow enough money to remain in the hands of entrepreneurs and at the same time ensure a fair and simple tax system.

It's interesting (just for academic purposes of argument), to note that while individual tax on salaries and other income is considered progressive when a higher percentage is levied on those earning above a certain arbitrary set of bands, there are actually no such bandings and such progressive branding for corporate tax. Companies that make more profit are allowed to be taxed at the same rate as even the smallest company with a small profit. If the "progressive" propaganda were true and credible it would've been long applied to companies as well. But like I've already mentioned, it's an argument of academic importance only because the companies we're talking about are for the aristocracy who rule together with the royalty (government), and no one dares be progressive with those, not anybody.

It's the height of naughtiness for companies, particularly the multinational monster spiders that have been allowed to network their webs on our lee side, after being showered with all these royalty level tax breaks and indulgences, to try and evade taxes by hook and crook. The political establishment will make the customary noises about it and seek to be seen doing something about it, but don't be fooled for a moment to think a thief who himself had his hands in the public tills, stealing from the masses, is going to catch his fellow partner in crime for a similar offence.

The only basis that appears fair is a basis that equates both individuals and companies. A tax based on gross sales for companies, is equivalent in all respects to a tax on gross income for individuals.

Equal taxes based on turnover (R million) for South Africa					
Year	Taxes on Individuals	Individual Taxes to GDP	Taxes on companies	Company taxes to GDP	GDP
2004/05	111,697	8%	71,629	5%	1,449,021
2005/06	126,416	8%	87,327	5%	1,613,812
2006/07	141,397	8%	120,111	7%	1,832,761
2007/08	169,539	8%	141,635	7%	2,075,413
2008/09	196,068	9%	167,202	7%	2,296,571
2009/10	206,484	8%	36,978	6%	2,452,538
2010/11	228,096	8%	134,635	5%	2,735,274
2011/12	251,339	8%	153,272	5%	2,973,287
2012/13	276,679	9%	60,896	5%	3,213,433

In analysing the table above, one has to consider that the salaries are at most only a third of the total revenue of a company. The 8 per cent of GDP means that if an equitable system of taxation is applied for corporates to the turnover of companies, just as to the gross incomes of individuals and to all other gross amounts, then the tax on companies should be three times more in percentage terms relative to GDP. The corporate contribution to the tax revenue, compared to the personal contribution would thus be between double and treble. The implication of this is that double the current revenues could be achieved by merely applying the equal flat tax on gross income, which at current rates, the tax rate that can be levied at current GDP figures is 14 per cent. Considering that the GDP is a largely understated figure of all the economic output of the economy, the rate required to achieve the current levels of revenue will definitely be lower than the average above of 14 per cent.

RETURNS OF ACTIVE CORPORATIONS: USA

Table 5--Selected Income Statement, and Tax Items. Source: http://www.irs.gov/uac/SOI-Tax-Stats-Table-5-Returns-of-Active-Corporations

Tax Year 2011

(All figures are estimates based on samples--money amounts are in thousands of dollars and size of business receipts is in whole dollars)

All Industries	Total returns of active corporations	
Number of returns...	5,823,126	
Total receipts...	28,335,600,572	100%
Compensation of officers............................	453,807,361	2%
Salaries and wages....................................	2,636,757,330	9%
Taxes paid...	519,383,532	
Income subject to tax...............................	994,393,494	4%
Total income tax before credits		
(35% of $994,393, 494)...........................	349,347,851	
Income tax..	345,414,746	
Alternative minimum tax.............................	3,440,855	
Foreign tax credit.......................................	107,103,753	
General business credit..............................	19,364,739	
Prior year minimum tax credit.....................	1,559,010	
Total income tax after credits..................	220,894,314	1%

To further make clear the above argument, the table above allows us to consider the tax profiles of United States companies that contribute taxes for the 2011 tax year, their total gross revenue receipts being the figure marked 100% in the table. The current situation is that only 1 per cent of revenue ends up as tax for corporates, and this is because only 4 per cent of the gross revenue is subjected to tax, and thanks to generous tax credits on that already small amount. Interestingly, for the same tax year the total income tax for individuals amounted to 1,045,510,793.

If corporates were taxed on a flat rate before they subtracted all the discretionary costs and other costs from the gross revenue (at a rate of say 10 per cent), the total tax revenue would be $2,833,560,057 which is more than twice the combined tax revenue from both individuals and corporates for that year. In other words, for the year 2011, the same tax revenues could be achieved in the USA, had a flat tax rate of only 4 per cent been applied to all gross income equally.

Equitable Individual Tax

The individual taxpayer currently contributes an average of 75 per cent of the tax income to the government, chiefly through tax on salaries, wages, and other income, and secondarily through the value added tax. It's sufficient to note that companies contribute on average about 22 per cent of the tax pie.

South Africa: Composition of main sources of tax revenue, 2008/09 – 2012/13

	Personal Income Tax	VAT	Fuel levy	Customs	Specific excise duties	Other	Total	Company Income Tax
2008/09	31.4%	24.7%	4.0%	3.6%	3.2%	6.3%	73.3%	26.7%
2009/10	34.5%	24.7%	4.8%	3.3%	3.6%	6.3%	77.1%	22.9%
2010/11	33.8%	27.2%	5.1%	4.0%	3.4%	6.5%	80.0%	20.0%
2011/12	33.8%	25.7%	4.9%	4.6%	3.4%	6.8%	79.4%	20.6%
2012/13	34.0%	26.4%	5.0%	4.8%	3.5%	6.6%	80.2%	19.8%
Average							78.0%	22.0%

The tithe system used in religious systems to finance the priesthood and the church administration is almost a perfect example of an equitable system in which even the poorest widows are bid to make an equal sacrifice according to their meagre income for the cause of the church, without any exclusion. And the rich also are equally burdened and indeed make a similar sacrifice. There can never be a tither that is higher than the other because it measures the sacrifice. Even though the rich will pay a greater quantity of currency as tithe, and the poor will pay a measly penny as tithe, they've made a similar sacrifice. So the rich can't disdain the poor's penny, neither should any congratulate the rich for his generosity. Indeed, it's the poor who deserve praise because they've not given out of much abundance, but rather out of their little means. They have more justification to be unfaithful than the rich.

It's rather unreasonable that recent world events have seen the undertaxed multinational conglomerates making the headlines for their sterling efforts in evading taxes. The same principle of equal sacrifice applied by God is applicable to those things that belong to Caesar. A flat tax rate on individual income is the only option available. Anything else is apartheid.

Mar 12:41-44 And Jesus sat over against the treasury, and beheld how the people cast money into the treasury: and many that were rich cast in much. And there came a certain poor widow, and she threw in two mites, which make a farthing. And he called unto him his disciples, and saith unto them, Verily I say unto you, That this poor widow hath cast more in, than all they which have cast into the treasury: For all they did cast in of their abundance; but she of her want did cast in all that she had, even all her living.

Equitable Government Tax

In basic democratic political economics, the role of government is to administer the taxes of the people in the activities (usually public benefit goods and services, which may be defence, law and order, transport infrastructure, etc.) which they (the people) have decided are necessary for their common well-being. They have set up a common fund to meet such expenditure, and these are to be managed within the limits of the common fund and any savings are reserved for future expenditure. The government is tasked with collecting the funds (taxation) and administers it in the intended purposes. However, in the current state of things, in the so-called democratic economies, a government is a king unto the people and determines its own taxes, its own size, its own borrowing levels, and more so what to do with the taxes.

A typical government in this day has borrowed too much on behalf of the people (the people have to pay back the borrowed money, not the government). The government doesn't live within its means, even though it requires other economic players to abide by such principles.

Should a government be taxed, and what would be the purpose of such a tax? The household, if well managed, is a good example of how a company or a government should be run. The individual and household are required to live within their means, and if they've borrowed, to make sure they make sacrifices and adjustments to their needs in order to recover and pay back the borrowings. Governments should likewise be made to live within their means and more so to repay government borrowings through savings from their allocated means.

A tax on government income should be one of the means with which such borrowings are settled. This would ensure that not one single generation is saddled with debt, and none borrows too much for the next generation to pay. Some third-world countries' taxpayers are still paying for the government debt that was created by their former colonial masters when they were under those governments.

Tax Reformation

Many countries have come up with committees for tax reform, and learned men and women have been tasked to come up with tax systems that will result in maximum tax revenue and also greater tax bases and equality. These tax review committees are almost always set up by the government and report to the government, and their recommendations are subject to approval and implementation by the government. Mostly these are mere extensions of government and, other than window-dressing issues, they result in the implementation of only those recommendations that favour government and business. The rest of the recommendations are conveniently ignored. The following example is one such committee that was set up to review a national tax system:

Example 3: Tax review committee

---

1 Kings 11:1–4:

1 But king Solomon loved many strange women, together with the daughter of Pharaoh, women of the Moabites, Ammonites, Edomites, Zidonians, and Hittites;

2 Of the nations concerning which the Lord said unto the children of Israel, Ye shall not go in to them, neither shall they come in unto you; for surely they will turn away your heart after their god.: Solomon clave unto these in love.

3 And he had seven hundred wives and princesses, and three hundred concubines; and his wives turned away his heart.

---

4 For it came to pass, when Solomon was old, that his wives turned away his heart after other gods, and his heart was not perfect with the Lord his God, as was the heart of David his father.

1Kings 12:1–20: 1 And Rehoboam went to Shechem; for all Israel were come to Shechem to make him king.2 And it came to pass, when Jeroboam the son of Nebat, who was yet in Egypt, heard of it, (for he was fled from the presence of king Solomon, and Jeroboam dwelt in Egypt),

3 That they sent and called him. And Jeroboam and all the congregation of Israel came and spake unto Rehoboam, saying,

4 "Thy father made our yoke grievous; now therefore make thou the grievous service of thy father, and his heavy yoke which he put upon us, lighter, and we will serve thee."

5 And he said unto them, "Depart yet for three days, then come again to me." And the people departed.

6 And king Rehoboam consulted with the old men that stood before Solomon his father while he yet lived and said, "How do ye advise that I may answer this people?"

7 And they spake unto him, saying, "If thou wilt be a servant unto this people this day, and wilt serve them, and answer them, and speak good words to them, then they will be thy servants for ever."

8 But he forsook the counsel of the old men, which they had given him, and consulted with the young men that were grown up with him, and which stood before him.

9 And he said unto them, "What counsel give ye that we may answer this people, who have spoken to me, saying, 'Make the yoke which thy father did put upon us lighter'?"

10 And the young men that were grown up with him spake unto him, saying, "Thus shalt thou speak unto this people that spake unto thee, saying, 'Thy father made our yoke heavy, but make thou it lighter unto us;' thus shalt thou say unto them, 'My little finger shall be thicker than my father's loins.

11 And now whereas my father did lade you with a heavy yoke, I will add to your yoke: my father hath chastised you with whips, but I will chastise you with scorpions.'"

12 So Jeroboam and all the people came to Rehoboam the third day, as the king had appointed, saying, "Come to me again the third day."

13 And the king answered the people roughly and forsook the old men's counsel that they gave him,

14 And spake to them after the counsel of the young men, saying, "My father made your yoke heavy, and I will add to your yoke: my father also chastised you with whips, but I will chastise you with scorpions."

15 Wherefore the king hearkened not unto the people; for the cause was from the Lord, that he might perform his saying, which the Lord spake by Ahijah the Shilonite unto Jeroboam the son of Nebat.

16 So when all Israel saw that the king hearkened not unto them, the people answered the king, saying, "What portion have we in David? Neither have we inheritance in the son of Jesse; to your tents, O Israel. Now see to thine own house, David." So Israel departed unto their tents.

17 But as for the children of Israel which dwelt in the cities of Judah, Rehoboam reigned over them.

18 Then King Rehoboam sent Adoram, who was over the tribute; and all Israel stoned him with stones, that he died.

> Therefore King Rehoboam made speed to get him up to his chariot, to flee to Jerusalem.
>
> 19 So Israel rebelled against the house of David unto this day.
>
> 20 And it came to pass, when all Israel heard that Jeroboam was come again, that they sent and called him unto the congregation and made him king over all Israel: there was none that followed the house of David, but the tribe of Judah only.

Tax reformation should be an important election topic every time a nation goes to voting, and tax equality should be enshrined in the laws of a country and not be made an election offer from political parties based on their benevolence. It should rather be etched in the constitutions of the nation, and compliance thereof should be enforceable at law.

If the current tax systems were to be presented before a constitutional court or such human rights courts, it would surely fail the constitutionality test on the basis of being discriminatory, unequal, and unfair. The tax committees fail to be democratic because the issue is limited to a few learned individuals who then embark on a limited consultation process, and often only those who are knowledgeable about tax issues and those who are stakeholders are consulted. The majority are ignored, but they'll be the most affected by the changes in taxation.

Country/ Region	Corporate tax	Individual (maximum)	Payroll tax (usually reduces taxable income)	VAT / GST / Sales
Belgium	34%	64% (max of federal+local) 55%(federal)+ 0%-9% (local)	38%	21% (6% for essential and selected goods)
Finland	20%	61.96% (31.75% national, 16.5-22.5% municipal, 7.71% social security	20.64% (average)	24% 14% (food and fodder), 10% (e.g. accommodation and culture)
Denmark	25% (2014: 24%, 2015:	61.03% (2014)	8% (2014) (included in individual tax)	25%
Aruba	28%	59%		1.5% tax on turnover
Sweden	22%	57%	31%	25% or 12% or 6%

Country/Region	Corporate tax	Individual (maximum)	Payroll tax (usually reduces taxable income)	VAT / GST / Sales
United States	0%-39% (federal) + 0%-12% (state)+ 0%-3% (local)	55.9% (max of federal+state+local) 10%-39.6% (federal)+ 0%-13.3% (state) + 0%-3% (local)	2.9%-15.3% (federal) + 0%-2% (state) + 0%-2% (local)	0%-11.725% (state and local)
Portugal	25%	54%	24%	Normal: 23% Intermediate: 13% Reduced: 6%
Israel	27%	52%	10%-52%	18% on all the products and services (except for vegetables and fruits).
Netherlands	25%/20%	52%		21% (6% for essential and selected goods)
Spain	25%-30%	52%	24%-45% + 37% social security taxes	21% or 10% or 4%

Country/ Region	Corporate tax	Individual (maximum)	Payroll tax (usually reduces taxable income)	VAT / GST / Sales
Austria	25%	50%		20%
Canada	11%-15% (federal) + 0%-16% (provincial)	50% – Surcharge taxes Varies) (15%-29% federal + 5%-21% provincial + $0-$900CDN Health Premium + Surcharge Taxes)	4.95% up to max $2425.50 (CPP) + 1.78% up to max $913.68 (Employment Insurance EI) + varied % of Income Tax (CIP)	5% (federal GST) with exemptions for small-businesses + 0%-10% (PST)
Cuba	30%	50%		2.5% to 20%
Japan	38%	50% (40% national + 10% local)	26%	8% (consumption)
Senegal	25%	50%		20%
Slovenia	16% (2012: 18%, 2013: 17%, 2014: 16%, 2015+: 15%)	50%	0%	22% or 9.5%

Country/ Region	Corporate tax	Individual (maximum)	Payroll tax (usually reduces taxable income)	VAT / GST / Sales
Norway	28% (2014: 27%)	47.8% (2014: 46.8%)	0%–14.1%	25% or 15% (food and drink in shops) or 8% (transportation, cinema, hotel rooms)
Germany	29.8% (average)	48%	41%, 15% for one of the many public health insurances (fixed rate by law), as well as a solidarity tax (depending on income) and a 26% social security tax (retirement + unemployment)	19% or 7% (e.g. food)
Iceland	20%	46%	6%	25.5% or 7%
Australia	30% (28.5% from 2015)	45%,+ 1.5% (Medicare levy)	4.75%–6% (state)	10% GST (0% on essential items)
China	25%	45%		17% with many exceptions

Country/ Region	Corporate tax	Individual (maximum)	Payroll tax (usually reduces taxable income)	VAT / GST / Sales
France	33%	45%	66%	20.0% or 7% or 5.5% or 2.1%
United Kingdom	24% (decrease to 21% in 2014), further decreased to 20% from 1 April 2015	45%	0%-25.8% (National Insurance)	20% Standard Rate; 5% Reduced Rate for home energy and renovations; 0% Zero Rate for life necessities - groceries, water, prescription medications, medical equipment and supplies, public transport, children clothing, books and periodicals.

Country/Region	Corporate tax	Individual (maximum)	Payroll tax (usually reduces taxable income)	VAT / GST / Sales
Italy	31%	43%	39%	22% or 10% or 4% (food, books)
Greece	26% (33% more than 50.000 euro)	42%	44%	23%or 13%
Ireland	25%/12.5%/10%	41%	0%-11%	23% Goods 9%-13.5% Services 0% certain items of food
Chile	0% (the 20% corporate tax rate on distributed profits is deducted from personal income taxes)	40%	10% (AFP private retirement fund) + 2 to 3% (AFP administrative costs) + 7% (healthcare insurance) + 0.6% (unemployment insurance) = up to around 20% of income before taxes (each item has an upper payment limit or ceiling)	19%

Country/ Region	Corporate tax	Individual (maximum)	Payroll tax (usually reduces taxable income)	VAT / GST / Sales
Croatia	20%	40%	37.2% (nationwide), 0–18% (local)	25% (0% on books and some foods)
Gibraltar	10%	40%	N/A	0%
Luxembourg	28%	40% + 12.45% social security charges		15%
South Africa	28%	40%		14%
Taiwan	17%	40%		5%
Morocco	30%	38%		20%
South Korea	22%, 20%, 10%	38% – 3.8%		10%
Argentina	35%	35%		21%
Barbados	25%	35%		17.5% (hotel accommodation 7.5%)
Burundi	35%	35%	N/A	18%
Cyprus	13%	35%	7%	18% (5% or 0% for certain goods)
Gabon	35%	35%	3%	18%

Country/ Region	Corporate tax	Individual (maximum)	Payroll tax (usually reduces taxable income)	VAT / GST / Sales
Iran	25%	35%	35%-15%	1.5-10%
Malta	0%-6.25%	35%		18%
Pakistan	35%	35%		0% or 17% (basic food items)
Sri Lanka	0%-35%	35%		12% or 0%
Thailand	20%	35%	5%-35%	7%
Turkey	20%	35%	40%-35%	18% or 8%
Vietnam	25%	35%		10%
Venezuela	34%/22%/15%	34%		8%-10%/12%

Tax and Tithes

Most preachers will implore their congregants to tithe (tenth) on the gross income rather than on the net income. The theological basis for this is that the increase in income for which one is voluntarily required to tithe on, is the total income accruing to the church member. The tithe system would be easy to apply in a simple agrarian economy where the field's output, the total livestock count and any other increase is easy to number. Determining a tenth of that is easy to almost everyone and it is not a burden of great value to remit the tithe.

The farmer, the merchant or the similar trades are undertaking business by buying inputs and incurring expenses and after a season, they reap the rewards and the increase is computed by subtracting from the total proceeds, the cost of the inputs and expenses that were incurred. However if the worker was to compute their increase in the same way, the preacher, just like our erstwhile governments, would object to such computations of the income. If from the gross salary, a worker would remove the cost of travelling to work, of food consumed, and of accommodation, to name a few, the resultant increase would be a small amount. A tenth of that would be minute and to the chagrin of the preacher, would amount to little.

The taxes already imposed n workers the world over are high enough and for most countries, they average more than 50 per cent of the gross salary or wages. A ten percent tithe on the gross would amount to a grievous burden onto a worker regardless of the quantity involved. It is a matter of great faith for the faithful to return a tenth of their gross income given the amount of deductions and taxes already imposed on their gross income. Giving to Caesar what belongs to Caesar has resulted in the Caesar demanding more and more and at every turn introducing various creative forms of taxes. The little that remains is too meagre to enable a giver to God to give with a free, cheerful and willing heart.

The right to worship their deity in a free and unrestricted manner is therefore under threat for most workers in the world. The preacher should seek to free the workers from an evil tax system that seeks to choke the life out of the religious systems of church finance. Creative and novel ways of wringing money from a sapped membership will not yield much money and even if they were to give their full salaries and wages, that would at most amount to only 45 per cent of their gross. It is in vain to clamour for more tithes and offerings from a working class congregation that is under the curse of the current tax systems. It is a reasonable thing to strive for the freedom of the believers from burning bricks with straw, so that they may go and worship freely in the Promised Land.

VII

Government Finance

Find Us a Virtuous Woman

Proverbs 31:10–31: 10 Who can find a virtuous woman? For her price is far above rubies. 11 The heart of her husband doth safely trust in her, so that he shall have no need of spoil. 12 She will do him good and not evil all the days of her life. 13 She seeketh wool, and flax, and worketh willingly with her hands. 14 She is like the merchants' ships; she bringeth her food from afar. 15 She riseth also while it is yet night, and giveth meat to her household, and a portion to her maidens. 16 She considereth a field, and buyeth it: with the fruit of her hands she planteth a vineyard.

17 She girdeth her loins with strength, and strengtheneth her arms. 18 She perceiveth that her merchandise is good: her candle goeth not out by night. 19 She layeth her hands to the spindle, and her hands hold the distaff. 20 She stretcheth out her hand to the poor; yea, she reacheth forth her hands to the needy. 21 She is not afraid of the snow for her household: for all her household are clothed with scarlet. 22 She maketh herself coverings of tapestry;

her clothing is silk and purple. 23 Her husband is known in the gates, when he sitteth among the elders of the land. 24 She maketh fine linen, and selleth it; and delivereth girdles unto the merchant. 25 Strength and honour are her clothing; and she shall rejoice in time to come. 26 She openeth her mouth with wisdom; and in her tongue is the law of kindness. 27 She looketh well to the ways of her household, and eateth not the bread of idleness. 28 Her children arise up, and call her blessed; her husband also, and he praiseth her. 29 Many daughters have done virtuously, but thou excellest them all. 31 Give her of the fruit of her hands; and let her own works praise her in the gates.

The questions that a government faces are basically the same questions that individuals face and those that households face in the stewardship of their lives. The state is just but a household, a firm, or a company but with a larger application, span, and challenges. The same principles applicable to the household decisions of individuals can be translated to the level of government and applied successfully. Indeed, had the principles of the small man, of the small company, of the household been applied diligently to many a broke government, the results would've been a rosier opposite of the current chaos. The quotation above is about a housewife who runs her household as a perfect economist, and this is what a government should be, a wise housewife running a household perfectly. We shall analyse these in point format for ease of understanding:

Loco parentis

The symbolism of a housewife and her husband and family is rightly applied to a good government. The role of government is to be to its citizens what a parent would be to its children, to work for the best interests of all its citizens and to create wealth and opportunities for all the nation's children. Can a family countenance a situation where the income of the children is taxed at more than half and spent on expensive cars, drinking, and other merrymaking by the parent? Can a family afford a huge amount of parenting, which costs the family a lot to maintain in excess of what they can afford? Should the parent be favouring certain children and not preferring other members of the family, by law, systems, or designs meant to create inequalities that aren't natural?

Loco parentis means that the government has a duty to be a good parent and not violate any of its subjects. The parent will be accountable to the family and be open and transparent to be the pride of her children. In turn the husband and children are glad for the large-heartedness of the virtuous housewife.

It's an often-ignored but important principle of political economy that when dealing with people, a look needs to be made at the relationships established as a result of economic activities. A worker working for a company isn't a mere machine to be used for eight hours a day at a certain speed; rather, it's a child who's been adopted into the company family which should meet the familial needs before the economic considerations. Soldiers will give their lives for a nation which they believe is theirs, but mercenaries will shoot for a dime. Equally a farmer, a tradesman, a builder should all be driven more by the love of their nation family than by personal gain in all their toil. A son works better than a hired worker, and a business partner serves better than a slave. The company is in *loco parentis* to its workers, the government to its nation, and the powerful and rich to those who are weak and poor.

Wool and Flax, Silk and Purple

Government finance is about deciding what to produce and in what proportions from the limited resources and opportunities available, with a fine balance being required between the staple basics and the luxuries. It's often the case that the poor are yearning to be rich, and that on the first instance of having some income they'll rush to adorn themselves with those tokens of luxury that they've yearned for, fine clothes, fancy cars, and other haberdashery which they can get their hand on. They'll be beguiled to incur debt if they can't afford it normally, and their lives will soon be a miserable pretence of affluence. Nations have built their economic systems on this consumerism and have promoted a lifestyle of indulgence of self. The neglect of needful temperance has led to a political economy based on the consumer and individuals throughout most countries in the world; companies and whole nations have sunk into debt roots, trunk and branches, and are literally bankrupt.

Most of the time, children will cry and demand that they be given candy, sweets, and other foods in place of wholesome food. Were a parent to go with their demands all the days of their lives, the children would hardly be well nourished. The coupling of economic decisions of what to produce on uncontrolled consumerism will soon malnourish a nation, and wholesome wealth will elude such a nation.

Fiscal Policy

The government of any country has a role to play in an economy, and it directs the activities, whether in a capitalist economic system or a so-called mixed economy. The government has the power to tax its citizens, and it has expenditures to make in carrying out its governance. The government can influence economic activity in the way and manner in which it raises revenue from its citizens and also in the manner in which, and the persons on whom, it spends the money so collected. A government has to make decisions on both income and expenditure, on how and from whom to collect, and how and on whom to spend the income. These two activities (income and expenditure) can be used to achieve desired economic ends by the government.

Fiscal policy is the use by government of the revenue collection activities (taxation) and expenditure activities (spending) to influence the economic activities and welfare and wealth of its citizens. Fiscal policy is carried out through changes in the level and composition of taxation and government spending in various sectors. Changes in these two variables will affect total economic activity in an economy including demand, and consequently supply, and the amount of savings and investment in an economy. The government, through the fiscal policy, can affect the distribution of income among the economic players.

Lastly, the fiscal policy enables government to influence the allocation of the means of production, resources, and economic opportunities, not only relating to the public sector but even in the private sector. The major instrument of implementing a fiscal policy is the government budget.

Revenue Collection

The collection patens of revenue by the government will show from whom the government is taking and how much the government is taking. Most budgets of nations show the majority of the tax revenue is collected from individuals, and an insignificant amount is collected from other economic players—for example, companies. The amounts collected from individuals are usually so high that half of their annual earnings are dedicated to financing their tax burdens. Companies on the other hand can easily settle their tax obligations from a month's profits in a year.

I've adequately shown in the previous chapter (Chapter 6) on taxation that the tax burden of individuals isn't bearable and is unsustainable, while that of companies isn't only light, but is intentionally made easy by governments through fiscal policy to try and attract investments and to create employment. The effects of these tax incentives are subjective and very debatable, and they don't usually significantly influence the investors' decisions. Secondly, there are taxes that are directly levied on individuals but companies and other players such as the state, are exempted from such taxes e.g., sales tax and value added taxes. The government also taxes individuals and other economic players through the two hidden taxes of inflation (through currency supply policies) and the financing of budget deficits through public borrowing and then monetising the debt. The brunt of these hidden taxes is borne again by the individual taxpayers and always least affects companies and other powerful economic players.

Considering the effects of direct taxation and hidden taxation, one may conclude that currently the fiscal policies of most nations condemn their citizens to lives of slavery in which they work most of their lives to pay taxes and have a few months in which to earn their livings. Tax incidence is grossly unfair, and governments who wish to implement democratic tax systems ought to start by looking at their tax codes and laws.

The second question on revenue collection is, how much should be collected? The current situation is to maximise revenue collection no matter how much pain is caused on the taxpayers. Governments are obsessed with collecting revenue, and the easy targets are the employees who earn wages and salaries. Companies and powerful economic players have the clout to avoid tax or make it difficult for the taxman to tax then. There seems currently to be no limit to how much tax should be collected, and the more is collected the greater the applause for the taxman.

Tax collection should be sustainable and should be influenced by the size of the government and the desired expenditure. The guiding line for the size of government and government expenditure should be the tax base. The size of government should suit the people governed. An oversized government will overwhelm the governed and put them under tax slavery. A government too small for the governed will fail to carry out the expenditure necessary to maintain economic and political order.

The worst ill currently obtained in many nations, particularly developing nations, is a bloated government, the size of which squashes the citizens under its burden, and these can hardly move. A government should be cut to the size of the cloth available. The amount of taxes available should be used to determine the size of government required. The tax base should be limited to a sustainable amount, levied in a fair and justifiable magnitude.

I propose in the discussion on taxation that a tax shouldn't exceed ten per cent of an individual's income. Taxation in a nation should be limited to a tenth of one's increase. Anything higher than a tenth is too much taxation. The government should be of such a size as will fit into that tenth. Anything higher than that is too much government. A good government should live within its means just like everyone else. A government that fails to live within its means should be allowed to die a death that is inevitable and be replaced with one that is sustainable and that lives within its means. Taxpayers should demand and put in place, at their head, a government that they can sustain, that won't enslave them, and that won't tax them into economic wrecks.

Just like any individual should live within his or her means, any government, including the right-sized government, should live within its means. A government that overspends is in effect stealing from its citizens the overspent amount through a debt burden that will have to be financed by more taxation, (direct and hidden, seen and unseen). A government, just like a company or a householder, should be able to live sustainable within its provided means.

Such borrowing to meet particular expenditure as emergency, capital, etc., may be accepted in the short term, but in a period of five to ten years, a government that continuously increases taxes, debts, and size, shouldn't be allowed to continue, because the inevitable end of such a course of action is a debt crisis. Countries that were previously debt free have worked themselves into a debt trap that makes them to be bankrupt and at the point of imploding. The USA debt is a case in point and despite ceilings being imposed by political processes, these ceilings on the debt have recently had to be raised, in order to accommodate more debt. The cases of Greece, Spain and Portugal and even the United Kingdom are all too familiar and it is a miracle that these economies continue to function with such high debt.

Revenue Spending

The revenue collected has to be spent on someone and on something. A government can influence the activities in an economy at this stage through the fiscal policy by determining the recipient of such expenditure. Direct expenditure of issues like capital expenditure (roads, bridges, ports, etc.) normally benefits the major players in an economy. Those engaged by the government in carrying out such projects are usually companies who make good profits out of the transactions. The construction of such infrastructure is usually designed to benefit businesses and companies more than it benefits individuals. The poor only benefit because the free rider can't be eliminated from use. Big business is the main beneficiary. Employment opportunities created by such expenditure are considered insignificant and incidental. The workers in such employment are still subject to slavery wages and slavery taxes, and their lot is hardly improved at the end.

The incidence of most infrastructural government expenditure is on companies and big business. In most government interventions, such as company bailouts and economic stimulus programmes, individuals aren't awarded any stimulus, but companies are offered huge bailouts for their failures to exist within their means. These huge outlays are financed by the poor taxpayer.

An equitable fiscal policy should be one that gives equal tax holidays to all taxpayers. If companies are awarded incentives for setting up in a growth-point area, a similar incentive should be available to the workers of the same area. If a government wishes to bail out a company, it should be done through the souse of the tax and not though arbitrary choices based on fear of the unknown. A bailout shouldn't be handed to a company, particularly one that is profit seeking. It should be on the original taxpayer (through a tax holiday). The money placed back in the hand of these taxpayers should be enough to stimulate economic activity to such an extent that the profit-seeking company will be saved. If it fails to survive, it was destined not to survive.

Currently the tax systems of most countries are such that governments are taxing workers and handing over the money in the guise of stimulus packages and tax breaks to companies who had not paid much tax in the beginning.

If a government in one year was to spend more than it was budgeted to spend, the year in which it spent less, it was expected to refund the tax by way of lower taxes to all who had contributed tax. It can also carry these surpluses to the future and hold a national credit, instead of a national debt. It should be the aid of every government to avoid debt, as one should, and to build a national credit due to spending less than collected, all within a framework of sustainable, fair, and equitable revenue collection and the right size of government.

Distribution of Economic Opportunities

The economic opportunities available to one economic player should be equally available to any other who seeks them. Through the fiscal policy, a government can afford or deny such opportunities. Individuals are often not able to compete against big corporations. When big corporations begin to fail, governments often consider them too big to be allowed to fail and end up bailing them out financially. On the other hand, were an individual to fail or a small start-up business to fail, no government attention would be forthcoming, and the individual or small business's financial situation would die a natural dearth.

The individual is usually denied the means and opportunity to compete with big companies and corporations. Fiscal policy should enable economic players to compete with each other and level the ground to afford the weak a chance at the big time. The incidence of tax and the incidence of fiscal expenditure should be used to carry out a fairer distribution of economic opportunities.

An individual without a credit to history; a company without reputation, a long existence, or a glowing list of customers; a small business without the muscle of a bigger conglomerate; and a poor taxpayer without the influence of a corporate are all usually the victims of a profit-seeking business environment where the forces of supply and demand operate and condemn them as failures. A fiscal policy gives a government an opportunity to address the evils of such a world and should be used to promote such future taxpayers and employers to get on their feet and sustain themselves. A fiscal policy should address rural development, urban squalors, and other ills that deny equal opportunities to other economic players.

Fiscal Incidence

Fiscal incidence is a concept that refers to the combined overall economic impact of both government taxation and expenditures on the real economic income of individuals. While taxation reduces the economic well-being of individuals, government expenditures at least ought to raise their economic well-being. Fiscal incidence is the term for the overall impact of government taxing and spending considered together.

In theory, governments withdraw resources from society in the form of taxation and contribute resources back into society in the form of expenditures. However, the burdens of taxation aren't borne equally by individuals, and the benefits of government expenditures aren't distributed equally throughout society. As a result, the distribution of tax burdens and government expenditure benefits is an important economic question to those concerned with the equity of the fiscal system. When the economic incidence of taxation is combined with the economic incidence of government expenditures, the result is a measure of the overall increase or decrease in welfare that individuals enjoy from the state's taxing and spending policies.

Currently most tax systems allow for very little taxation on companies, and these same companies stand as beneficiaries of better infrastructures, tax holidays, tax incentives, tax exemptions, tax allowances, stimulus packages, and bailouts and stand as the sole beneficiaries of economic opportunities.

On the other hand, individuals are taxed up to their necks and, in return, receive token tax adjustments, no tax exemptions, a measly tax allowance, and no bailouts, stimulus, or allowances that match what companies receive. The current fiscal incidence is glaringly unfair, unequal, and discriminatory.

A fiscal policy should be useful to address the skew that exists and afford equal treatment for each individual or company economic player. For any infrastructure or capital expenditure a company receives a tax allowance to claim the full cost against taxable profits. The costs are exclusive of VAT or sales tax. The individual on the other had isn't allowed any deduction against taxable income if he or she was to purchase a house or a motor vehicle. The cost of the house or vehicle includes VAT or sales tax and is higher than for the company. The individual is least likely to afford such expenditure from his or her overtaxed, slave-wage income. The company, on the other hand, has a reputation, a good credit rating, and the financial muscle to perform such things and will get such opportunities easily. The individual is evidently discriminated in the current set-up of things.

Governments are currently spending their tax revenues on companies and claiming that they're doing so for the benefit of the poor workers who'd be left jobless were the companies to close. Governments are building infrastructures for corporations, roads, and similar infrastructure set-ups in the name of the poor, but it all but benefits the corporations, both in its setting up and in the eventual usage. Corporations and companies receive an incentive for any expenditure that they make. The companies are the most beneficiaries of the government spending, in that besides being awarded the contract to carry out government expenditure, most of the infrastructure that is constructed benefits companies more that individuals.

An example is the infrastructure that was built for the FIFA world cup for 2010 in South Africa and the one for the 2014 version in Brazil. The benefits accruing to a country's majority from hosting a world cup are skewed towards business and government. The stadia, roads and related sporting and transportation and communication infrastructure from the events do not fall to the benefit of the poor and the workers. At their best the benefactors are the businesses who will continue to enjoy the use and availability of the infrastructure after the end of the event. The cost of building the white elephants such as are the stadia, and that of continuing their upkeep and maintenance is borne by the public.

The fiscal policies are at best regressive for most nations as the incidence of tax is on individual taxpayers while the fiscal expenditure incidence is benefiting the companies mostly. The governments are taking the wealth of the poor, underpaid, and overtaxed and putting it into the coffers of the rich, the powerful, and the corporations who least need it.

Government Debt

Governments, like any other legal entities, can take out or give out loans and make financial investments. Government debt is money owed by any level of government. It's also known as public debt or national debt because it's a debt incurred by the government on behalf of the people that it represents, and it's the people or public who are going to pay it off, including the interest thereof. Government debt is a debt incurred indirectly by the taxpayer and will be paid off by the taxpayer. Governments borrow from within the country, usually from companies and other institutions, or can borrow from foreign lenders, such as the International Monetary Fund, the World Bank, or other countries.

Many governments have put their nations in debt, and if they were individuals they would've long been declared bankrupt and would've been red listed, and no one would even consider lending to them or merely trusting them with money. Debt counselling and other remedial actions would've been prescribed to such delinquent behaviour. Surprisingly, the same governments are currently considered by reputable credit-rating agencies to be risk free and to be very creditworthy. Governments are considered able to repay any debts because of the assumed, bottomless ability to tax their people. The effect of such a policy has been spiralling debt and uncontrolled expenditure that has seen several nations drown their people into a quagmire of inescapable debt ruins.

A government that creates debt for its taxpayers is usually too big, not accountable to its taxpayers, or just misinformed about debt. In a democratic political economy, issues that affect the taxpayer such as incurring more debt, increasing taxes, the size of government, and the size of tax should be decided by the people/public, not left to the government to have its own cake, to decide its size, to cut it, and to eat it all by itself.

Stimulus Economics

In its present-day use, stimulus refers to the usually futile attempts to use monetary and fiscal policy to stimulate the economy. The overall motive being to arouse increased consumer spending, which once increased, is hoped to result in moving the economy from a recession or similar situations.

Money is usually pumped into the misfiring economy, and greater budget deficits are encouraged. Heavier government expenditure and greater borrowing are prescribed by proponents for get the economy stimulated. The stimulation is means to waken and jumpstart the economy into creating more demand due to higher consumer confidence, more jobs due to the higher consumption by consumers, more investment in response to the booming economy, and after that, higher taxes for the government due to increased economic activity.

Stimulation

The concept of stimulation is foreign to economics as it's prone to definition and application problems. The biological equivalent is an experimental concept which studies responses to stimuli of the organism under experiment. Economics and political economy aren't lent to empirical experimentation.

What Type of Stimulation?

The experience with stimulus economics has shown that the applied stimuli have not always resulted in the desired effects. Giving banks large amounts of money and tax incentives in the hopes of their lending it out to consumers doesn't often result in such lending, as most of the profit-seeking banks decide to use it for other, less-risky and more rewarding lending. If the expected increased consumerism doesn't materialise, another round of stimulation is usually recommended. The amount of stimulation required or the amount of currency required to get the desired amount of stimulation started is a question not easily answered. Inflation is a definite result of any stimulation by way of increasing the currency supply or running up the public debt. The effects will be felt by the poor majority and rarely by the beneficiaries of the stimulus.

Who to Stimulate?

The target points of the stimuli are difficult to determine, and the decision on the exact place or point to apply the stimulus is one subject to judgemental flaws, depending on the economic system in place. In a capitalist economy, the focus is always on companies creating all economic activity, including creating employment for the grateful employees. The normal practice has been predictably to award the stimulus to the powerful companies and businesses, and a token or nothing to the majority poor.

Stimulation Economics

With the right understanding of what is money and what a currency is, it should be easy to conclude that use of currency (monetary policy) to increase economic activity is an exercise in futility which results in a government secretly taxing the poor, who are vulnerable to inflation, and distributing these revenues to the rich through direct and indirect stimulus. The inflation that results from stimulation activities robs the poor, who aren't recipients of the stimulus, who suffer the effects of inflation, and who will fund the increased public debt by higher future taxes.

Privatising stimulus and nationalising private debts

The current practice in the developed other economies on stimulus is to assist certain industries, particularly financial institutions, and big companies within these industries. The debts of these private companies, which they've accumulated in their private capacities and which are crippling their existences, are suddenly made public debts by the government by such measures as contained in the stimulus packages. The mortgage loans of banks on which consumers are about to default are acquired by the state, and the company is given a stimulus package to start loaning again as it likes. The public is now saddled with the loans, and they'll be financed through taxes.

The stimulus is handed over to private companies to enable them to create employment (and profits for their private benefit), and the public doesn't have access to these profits resulting from stimulus packages. The effects of the stimulus packages are to take more public debt and use the funds raised to finance private wealth. On the other hand, the public is burdened with private debts which the government has now nationalised in trying to save big private companies.

Economic Effects of Stimulation

The application of stimulus in economics isn't only unreasonable, it's not logical. The subject isn't one that allows for such experiments to be carried out as it affects the lives and welfare of people. Placing people into such experiments isn't allowable in a democratic political economy. Where an economy is saddled with public debt, has inflation, and is in a recession, the solution can never be to increase spending or to play around with the currency supply in the economy.

The discussion in this book on taxation and inflation has already shown that a fair and reasonable tax rate would allow economic players to be motivated to work themselves out of debt, out of poverty, and out of unemployment. The stimulus should be focused on individuals and small businesses in an economy so as to encourage individual industry and hard work. The amount of money available in the economy would be greatly increased if governments were to lower their taxes and inflation.

A government, if ever it considered stimulation, should consider the people and players whom it's saddled with the greatest tax burden and award to such a stimulus in the form of reduced taxation. When an economy is in recession, it's informing the players to engage in more activities other than those currently happening. Creating more debt, deficits, and inflation won't take the problem away. Stimulating the economy only postpones those problems, and the issues don't disappear but are fawning for a greater comeback in the near future.

Fiscal Straitjacket and Austerity Measures

The concept of a fiscal straitjacket is an economic principle that requires strict constraints to be harnessed on government in terms of raising revenue and spending, as well as monetary policy, including borrowing. The contemporary term is austerity, and both refer to the dose of measures prescribed on economies that are under debilitating debt, inflation, and kindred economic symptoms.

A government that, over time, raises less than it spends will fall into a debt trap, and a currency crisis is likely to follow, as it tries to spend its way out of debt. The solution that might seem logical is to introduce austerity measures on government expenditure and a straitjacket of what can be performed by government. Austerity measures have usually taken the form of salary cuts for employees, increasing VAT rates, taxing the wealthier at higher tax rates, and reducing pension, health, and other benefits of employees. While this might appear very logical, it needs to be examined in the light of other factors in the economy.

As shown in the discussion on taxes in chapter six, most current tax systems are skewed against the poor and leave the rich largely untaxed. The poor contribute a disproportionately large amount to the tax cake, and the big businesses don't come even close to a fair share of tax contribution. It's always argued in an austerity situation that taxes should be increased, salaries cut and slashed, and government expenditure be reduced. In the current environment, increasing taxes isn't an option as it would debilitate the poor workers who contribute the bulk of government revenue. An increase in taxation coupled with a slashing of the salaries and wages is the best way to suffocate a working class into financial death.

The reduction of government expenditure should only be limited to that type of expenditure that is fruitless and wasteful. The larger part of most government expenditures goes to infrastructure and to social nets, such as welfare benefits, which also to some extent provide some cushion on the poor. Reducing such expenditure will likely further harm the vulnerable. Government is also a significant employer, and any downward tampering with expenditure must not be allowed to result in higher unemployment. Austerity should always be applied equally to companies also, and the unnecessary expenditure that happens between the gross profit and the net profit eliminated.

The governments of the world have been indoctrinated to believe that one needs to give companies and other big businesses as much opportunity, resources, and financing as possible, so that they create employment for the majority of the people, and everyone lives happily ever after. The excessive focus on creating jobs, while noble, is wrong and indicative of the influence and power the corporates and big business have over government policy. The process of achieving such employment creation is also subjective, and makes it worse and tragic. Surely a nation of entrepreneurs is more desirable than a nation of workers, enslaved by a few capitalists.

Conclusions

Government expenditure in austere times shouldn't be limited to the extent that it creates industry within its citizenry. The chief focus of expenditure in straight jacket times should be to provide a social net to those hardest hit by the strait times and mainly to create and support hardworking and industrious entrepreneurs, who will produce real wealth, which will see the economy out of the doldrums. The focus of stimulus and other incentives should be to put money back into the hands that would best use it for the benefit of the economy. Handing out stimulus cake to companies will result in more private profit for very few individuals. Tax incentives for companies for employment creation should be replaced by tax incentives for the majority of the employees who bear the brunt of the tax system every month. Rewarding these with a windfall wouldn't only result in greater consumer-driven expenditure, it would result in greater welfare for a greater part of the population. The savings and capital expenditures that would be the result would lead to a greater numbers of entrepreneurs. Instead of taking over private debt of banks, these workers, if given tax breaks, wouldn't default on their debts and wouldn't they fail to look after themselves, relieving the pressure on the social nets by government.

The issue about the right size of government has already been discussed elsewhere in the book, but suffice to say that a government should be of the proper size for its people, particularly the taxable people. An oversized government will wear down the tax base. Too small a government will fail to provide leadership to the economy. It should be the main objective of government to grow the tax base by creating more entrepreneurs and consequently more jobs. The focus shouldn't be merely on jobs, as jobs aren't determined by government. The development of an industrious nation is something that a government can control. The creation of jobs within a privately owned company is beyond the abilities and ambit of business and shouldn't be attempted at.

In dealing with government finance the economic performance of a government should be measured in terms of the tax base that has been established, though increases entrepreneurs. The ability of the government to contain expenditure and to spend within its means should be chief among the performance indicators. Lastly, the achievements of a government in lowering the gap between the rich and the poor—including whether the overall wealth of the economy, as measured per individual, has increased—should be used to assess the success of a government. A government that achieves higher wealth concentrated in a few individual hands, achieved through worsening other classes of economic players, hasn't been a faithful government.

Government finance shouldn't be aimed at the symptoms of a dysfunctional economy but should attend to the structural causes of the problems. Government debt and inflation are but symptoms of a broken structure. Attempting to address the government debt and the inflation in isolation is a fruitless exercise. The underlying tax and currency structure should be addressed before tackling the effects so as to address the roots of the problems, rather than plucking at the leaves, in the hope of solving it.

VIII

Democratic Political Economy

Instalment Democracy

Participating in an election is a democratic right that, until recent history, has often been denied to other members of society because of their social status. Children aren't allowed to vote because they're considered too young, ignorant, and legally dependant. In some places, women were denied the right to vote for the sole reason of being a woman. Slaves, blacks, oppressed, prisoners, etc., were at various times denied the right to participate in voting (political) because they were considered ignorant, inferior, uncultured, and unfit to participate in such an important process. Most African countries who attained independence from their colonial masters from the 1960s until the 1990s were agitating for a one man (and woman) one vote system, since the imperial governments did not consider natives to be equal to their European decent masters, and could not participate in elections. In the United State, convicts to certain crimes are ineligible to vote in elections. The justification for some of these injustices was that the blacks, slaves or women were not sophisticated enough to be able to participate political processes such as elections

Even when everyone who is eligible to elect leaders is allowed to participate, most democratic nations in the developing and the developed world use a representative system in which leaders are elected once every four, five or six years and during their term s of office they make most decisions on behalf of the electorate without the requirement to consult the public. Waiting for a period of four, five, or six years to vote for someone or a block of leaders who will make decisions for that period might have worked in some time periods, but does it still work in a century of high technological and scientific advances as this age? If national leaders have failed to meet their promises in the first two or three years in office, shall the people suffer them to keep office for the remaining years?

There are some key decisions made annually by governments, including national budgets, which should be subjected to more democratic processes than a five-or-six-year vote. When a citizen votes someone into political office, he or she isn't voting for each of his or her future decisions, neither is he or she giving up his or her freedom of choice. Democracy that is administered in five-year instalments allows for autocracy in the interim. It allows for an autocratic system to be termed a democratic one.

An economic crisis or other economic forces stronger than the electorate are usually at work and will change the package that was promised at election time. The question one may have is whether the electorate is going to be literate on each of the decisions that government has to make in the interim periods. Shall we deny the voter the right to vote because of his or her social standing?

Democracy shouldn't only be limited to the political field in any economic system but should be spread evenly to the corporate sector. Are corporate leaders not dictators in their kingdoms also?

They control armies of workers whom they bid every day to go to and from work, they control swarms of customers, they hold influence with suppliers, they're vocal and given an ear by the government. Democratic political economy should be made applicable to and for the corporate entities so that there's proportional participation in decision-making processes by employees, customers, and other stakeholders, particularly on decisions that affect them.

Political economy is concerned about the economic well-being of a person in the ordinary business of his or her life. It enquires how he or she organises the resources available and how he or she generates and disposes wealth. It's a study of wealth of an individual and of a society and how this affects citizens, individually and as a society.

Inevitably, questions on allocation, creation, and distribution require answers that satisfy all members and players of a society. The allocation question requires answers that address how a society's limited resources and economic opportunities are to be concentrated in particular hands, whether few or many. The question of creation of wealth means that those who create wealth from the means of production to which they have access must determine what and how that wealth is created and how it's preserved for distribution.

Critical in the answer is the requirement to determine what's to be produced and in what quantities, so as to satisfy not only the profit-making requirement, but also the utility question. Optimal production of items that benefit the well-being of society, without overproduction or shortages, should be determined. Distribution requires answers that satisfy all parties wishing to lay their hands on the final wealth cake. The government, the workers, the owners of the means of production and of the resources—they all require being satisfied in a way that enables the entire system to continue in existence and equilibrium.

A failure to answer the first question of allocation results in poverty. Unemployment is the effect of failure to harness all the means of production. Inequalities arise due to failure to distribute correctly between stakeholders.

The history of the people of Africa, and particularly of South Africa, offers a great insight into the fight that is at hand now for the worker against those that oppress him or her. The Freedom Charter, a document that was born out of this historic struggle, is one such document that not only set out the hopes of a people against a political oppressor system, but it contains declarations by a labouring people aspiring to be freed from the economic oppression they faced. A few extracts from the document are considered below with explanations and comparisons of progress.

The People Shall Govern!

> Every man and woman shall have the right to vote for and to stand as a candidate for all bodies which make laws; All people shall be entitled to take part in the administration of the country; The rights of the people shall be the same, regardless of race, colour or sex; All bodies of minority rule, advisory boards, councils and authorities shall be replaced by democratic organs of self-government.

Free People: Not Yet, Uhuru

The working class has, in its entire history, been the one that carries the weight of the business and ruling class. One illustration which was popular in recent history depicting the worker's plight was the Pyramid of the Capitalist System, which depicted at the bottom a burden-laden group of workers who work and feed all above their level. We eat for you, we shoot at you, we fool you, and we rule you were the roles assigned to the increasing levels of power that have the worker under them.

It's interesting that the same depictions can still successfully be used today even in democratic societies. The worker in particular still bears the heaviest weight in creating the economic pie but is allocated the least share, so much as to say they don't have a share at all. The worker, under heavy taxes, debts, inflation, interest rates, and levies, is supporting a system that continually saps his or her reserves and is never satisfied. The worker is reduced to the level of an animal, which is used to till the land by the farmer and never enjoys the benefits. He's a mere tool in the production process, as good as a hammer or chisel, replaceable, dispensable, at the whim of the master.

Labour Unions

Labour unions and workers in general should consider their position in the system and structure of society and utilise their influence for the betterment of society and for the attainment of an improvement of the condition of workers and everyone in particular. The labour unions are in a position of influence in that they lead an influential but oppressed sector of the economy, and their power, just like the power of government, is easily subject to corruption if not properly used.

The lot of labour union activity over time has achieved much inevitable good for the overly oppressed worker. The primary function has been to protect the interests of workers against discrimination and unfair labour practices, assist and lead in negotiation of wage and salary increases, and safeguard the economic security of employees in situations such as layoffs, retrenchment, promotion and transfers.

But have labour unions benefited the worker, as they should have? Is unionism not a way of taming the labourer to be a more manageable beast in the yoke of the capitalist, and in the kraal of the kings of this land? A way to get the brute workers to expend some energy and vent their anger, like a dog barking at a passing car, so that they feel someone has heard and understands their problems, and after that, they're back at their burdens?

The Hebrew children were organised and had representatives while they were in Egyptian captivity. They enjoyed their rights (right to have the tools of work, leave, food, good treatment) and when, as a result of Moses, these were withdrawn, they became angry at Moses for causing the masters to be harsher to them. Unionism might have fallen in the same trap of satisfaction with the status quo, regardless of how bad that state is. It's a cunningly devised way of prolonging the oppression of the workers that is presented as a way of emancipating them. They've sold out to a system and have become a façade of goodness that's but a smoke-screen to hide the true nature of these unions.

Example 3: Landless, unionised, and oppressed

> Exodus 1:8-14 Now there arose up a new king over Egypt, which knew not Joseph. And he said unto his or her people, "Behold, the people of the children of Israel are more and mightier than we.
>
> Come on, let us deal wisely with them; lest they multiply, and it come to pass, that, when there falleth out any war, they join also unto our enemies, and fight against us, and so get them up out of the land."
>
> Therefore they did set over them taskmasters to afflict them with their burdens. And they built for Pharaoh trea sure cities, Pithom and Raamses.
>
> But the more they afflicted them, the more they multiplied and grew. And they were grieved because of the children of Israel. And the Egyptians made the children of Israel to serve with rigour.
>
> And they made their lives bitter with hard bondage, in mortar, and in brick, and in all manner of service in the field; all their service, wherein they made them serve, was with rigour.
>
> Exodus 2:23–25: And it came to pass in process of time, that the king of Egypt died: and the children of Israel sighed

by reason of the bondage, and they cried, and their cry came up unto God by reason of the bondage. And God heard their groaning, and God remembered his with Abraham, with Isaac, and with Jacob. And God looked upon the children of Israel, and God had respect unto them.

Exodus 3:7-8 And the Lord said, "I have surely seen the affliction of my people which are in Egypt, and have heard their cry by reason of their taskmasters; for I know their sorrows; And I am come down to deliver them out of the hand of the Egyptians, and to bring them up out of that land unto a good land and a large, unto a land flowing with milk and honey; unto the place of the Canaanites, and the Hittites, and the Amorites, and the Perizzites, and the Hivites, and the Jebusites."

Exodus 5:1–21: And afterward Moses and Aaron went in, and told Pharaoh, "Thus saith the Lord God of Israel, 'Let my people go, that they may hold a feast unto me in the wilderness.'" And Pharaoh said, "Who is the Lord, that I should obey his voice to let Israel go? I know not the Lord, neither will I let Israel go."

And they said, "The God of the Hebrews hath met with us; let us go, we pray thee, three days' journey into the desert, and sacrifice unto the Lord our God; lest he fall upon us with pestilence, or with the sword."

And the king of Egypt said unto them, "Wherefore do ye, Moses and Aaron, let the people from their works? Get you unto your burdens." And Pharaoh said, "Behold, the people of the land now are many, and ye make them rest from their burdens." And Pharaoh commanded the same day the taskmasters of the people, and their officers, saying, "Ye shall no more give the people straw to make brick, as heretofore: let them go and gather straw for themselves."

And the tale of the bricks, which they did make heretofore, ye shall lay upon them; ye shall not diminish ought thereof, for they be idle; therefore they cry, saying, "Let us go and sacrifice to our God. Let there more work be laid upon the men, that they may labour therein; and let them not regard vain words."

And the taskmasters of the people went out, and their officers, and they spake to the people, saying, "Thus saith Pharaoh, 'I won't give you straw.'

Go ye, get you straw where ye can find it: yet not ought of your work shall be diminished."

So the people were scattered abroad throughout all the land of Egypt to gather stubble instead of straw.

And the taskmasters hasted them, saying, "Fulfil your works, your daily tasks, as when there was straw."

And the officers of the children of Israel, which Pharaoh's taskmasters had set over them, were beaten, and demanded, "Wherefore have ye not fulfilled your task in making brick both yesterday and today, as heretofore?"

Then the officers of the children of Israel came and cried unto Pharaoh, saying, "Wherefore dealest thou thus with thy servants?"

There is no straw given unto thy servants, and they say to us, "Make brick; and, behold, thy servants are beaten, but the fault is in thine own people."

But he said, "Ye are idle, ye are idle, therefore ye say, 'Let us go and do sacrifice to the Lord.'

Go therefore now, and work; for there shall no straw be given you, yet shall ye deliver the tale of bricks."

And the officers of the children of Israel did see that they were in evil case, after it was said, "Ye shall not minish ought from your bricks of your daily task."

And they met Moses and Aaron, who stood in the way, as they came forth from Pharaoh.

And they said unto them, "The Lord look upon you, and judge; because ye have made our savour to be abhorred in the eyes of Pharaoh, and in the eyes of his servants, to put a sword in their hand to slay us."

Shortcomings of Labour Unions

Majoring on Minors

The history of labour has led the unions to consider the employer as the immediate and sole place at which to address the welfare of the employee. All efforts by labour unions have been spent in protecting the employee from the employer. A microeconomic focus has been entrenched in which the individual employee unions engage their different employees or sectors and try as much as possible to address the micro problems affecting the employees in that particular sector or industry.

In this approach the unions have achieved major success on minor issues. The microeconomic focus on small, individual issues makes the unions busy on the small things and has led to the major issues escaping their sight. The focus makes it easy for the unions to be fragmented and divided, and the energies are spent on small issues that rarely address the underlying problems.

Leaving the Major Issues Unattended

The role of government in determining the welfare of employees is largely blurred to unions because historically the unions have had a close relationship with government and the government has been given the role of referee, to address issues between the employee and the employer. However, government is far from being an innocent bystander or an impartial referee. Government is the author of tax legislation that affects the wealth of employees. Governments the world over have given patronage to businesses at the expense of employees in terms of the amounts and rates of taxation. Businesses are hardly taxed, while the employee is taxed to diabolical levels. Government is responsible for monetary policy, fiscal policy, and the effects of inflation and budget deficit that affect the majority employees. Economic opportunities, control over means of production, and a host of other macroeconomic issues are all under the stewardship of government.

Government hasn't been taken to account for its skewed tax policies, neither have the deficit and monetary policies been questioned by unions in the manner and to the extent they ought to have if they're to protect the economic welfare of employees. The powers and elevated status of the company has been allowed to erode the equality of other economic citizens before the law without any voice from labour leaders. A host of other macroeconomic issues which are within the ambit of government have been left unchallenged, because unions have buried their heads in the sand of small, shop-level issues while the plight of workers hasn't been attended to.

Love for Money

Unions have focussed their energies on obtaining more money for their members. Without a correct understanding of what money is and what currency is, it's resulted in an annual standoff for more currency, and this has become a sport in which the unions test the wits and resolve of the employer, and the government plays referee between the two. The salaries of all salary and wage earners are pegged in fixed currency amounts. The government controls the amount of currency and the rate of inflation. The strike season results in increased currency salaries (usually based on inflation rate), and before the end of the year, the purported increase has been eroded by higher price increases, thanks to inflation. Getting more currency at almost the same time doesn't make anyone any better.

Inflation works in such a manner that before the extra currency is even spent, the value (buying power) of the currency has already factored in the increased currency supply in the economy. It's an exercise in futility to clamour for an increase in a currency quantity for salaries and wages, when one doesn't have control over the supply of that currency. The increased salaries are purely inflationary and just like adding paraffin to a fire: it flames quickly and provides short-lived warmth to those around it.

It must surely be a source of sadistic humour for the capitalist and the kings of this world to see a whole group of workers crying for a few more coins of a currency, and once they're awarded the extra percentage, the labourers march back to their workstations and wait for the next strike season. Surely, these masters they giggle in the chambers and congratulate themselves for such a genius way of pacifying the worker. Like a matador, playing and sporting with a bull in a bullfight tauromachia, the kings and capitalists of this land have found a way of amusing themselves.

Turning a Blind Eye
The macroeconomic questions affecting the wealth of the majority of the economic players, such as the size of the government,

the amount of taxation, the incurring of public debt, monetary and fiscal policy (including budgets), and the issues of economic systems and economic structures are macroeconomic issues that labour unions have turned a blind eye to for the major part of their history.

In a democratic political economy the majority should be afforded a chance to determine the amount of tax they shall be levied, and the fairness of such taxation shouldn't be debatable. The monetary and fiscal policies which government embarks upon should be those that don't hard the earnings of the majority workers. A good relationship with government is of utmost benefit to the cause of the oppressed and disadvantaged. However, such a relationship should be used to engage and confront issues affecting the majority, regardless of the inconvenience it may cause to the relationship.

Creating Slaves

Economic policy in most developing countries focuses on developing the skills of the workers and making the workers as efficient as possible. No complementary policy is in place to make these workers employers at some point in time. Once these workers are working for the capitalist, the system is such that it leaves little room for emancipation anyway. The worker is thus condemned to a life of labouring for his or her employer for the rest of the economic life and retires at an old age of want and poverty when he or she receives a meagre pension pegged in currency that quickly vanishes. The same cycle is repeated from generation to generation. There's no choice for the lot of workers to not work and be entrepreneurs. The labour unions and government have not broken the chain of poverty that binds the lot of the people but have sought in policy and practice to perpetuate the slavery of the majority by a cabal.

The history of mankind has shown that whenever a people have been made subjects and servants of a few, or have been condemned to be slaves (paid or unpaid) of another people, that the economic well-being of those subjected has suffered and their economic wealth has perished. The same history has shown that the success of a people and their economic emancipation is directly linked to their political freedom married together with economic freedom. Without access to the means of production and economic opportunities, the course of man has been to hire his or her labour out in a desperate bid to survive.

The Land Shall Be Shared among Those Who Work It!

The issue of land reform can't be overemphasised in terms of its economic significance and its ability to immediately emancipate the lot of the poor. The economic systems currently obtaining in developing nations are such that the land, the majority of it, belongs to the few and rich while the majority is languishing in landlessness and poverty.

Inequalities in or resulting from any form of wealth which was unjustly obtained not only injure those from which it's directly obtained but also injure the economy as long as that injustice continues. Correcting the injustice should be done with sober mind and is to be performed without taking away the fruits of labour from whoever has achieved that wealth through their effort. The economic systems are controlled by the rich, and any policy with which they're not in agreement, won't be allowed and they'll greatly resist it. Any of these economies which insists on implementing a policy such as land reform, is usually subjected to immense pressure and lobbying to the effect that they'll never implement it. Political parties are careful to word their statements and make their manifestos in such a manner so as not to claim land back for free.

The current configuration of land ownership is an inheritance from the colonial days, and that configuration has hardly changed. There are several factors that have frustrated processes like land reformation and restorations.

Democratic Political Economy

It's a principle of political economy that none be made worse off to make another better off. Neither should wealth be obtained by robbing one and bestowing it to another. Land reform shouldn't result in a worse position for individual and for the whole economy. Any form of land reform and restoration must follow such principles for it to be fair and sustainable.

The history of land ownership and appropriation by the colonialists is well documented, and some of the legislation they used to achieve such ends was in most cases only recently repealed. In their pursuit for such legislation they reasoned that the idle native, who had been engaging in subsistence farming, would rather be relegated to a less fertile and smaller place to continue such practices, while the choice land is apportioned to the commercial farmer who would be able to produce many times more than was currently obtaining. The native would also seek for employment created by the commercial farmer, and his overall well-being was considered better off than before. The major beneficiaries of these colonial economics were, however, those in the home country which provided support and blessing for such activities and benefited in many ways than a few from imperialism.

It's interesting to note that, though a minority, most farms are today owned by white families who are the direct descendants of former colonialists. This is particularly the case in developing countries such as South Africa, Namibia, to mention just two examples. This ownership pattern also applies to most of the other spheres of economic resources such as mines, financial houses, and any other notable resource. This trend applies also to the majority of former colonies and former slave nations of the European powers. Be it the Caribbean nations, the Latin American nations, or the Asian Islands, the presence of a rich minority few in the midst of an ever-poor majority is regarded as a normal thing because it's a history-old phenomenon thanks to colonialism.

It's also relevant to note at this point that in relation to slavery, most of these businesses and families who amassed huge fortunes from plantation slavery, when slavery was abolished, were actually compensated by the British government in particular, for the loss of their human property. Britain had no hesitation in compensating these big businesses for the loss caused by the loss of free labour but continue to this day to resist compensation for any of the descendants of the slavery.

By contrast, not a single enslaved man, woman, or child ever received even a penny from the same direction for the soul-breaking toil they endured under thralldom, nor for other accompanying ills of slavery. Nothing for their lives' labour, for the loss of mothers and fathers, children, brothers and sisters, for separation from families, for the pernicious brutality exacted against them, for the violent sexual assaults, nothing even in the shape and size of a mere apology. The First World War resulted in reparations being exacted and extracted from Germany and her allies for the damages caused by the war, European nations had to hold many a treaty, and went to the extent of occupying the resource-rich country, exporting coal and industrial equipment as compensation.

The power configuration of the world hasn't afforded those guilty of slavery, imperialism, and colonialism the grace to recognise the need for an apology, or worse still, compensation. The colonialists are still in the same place and position they were before and have the power to ignore any such calls, through their control of media propaganda, their economic might, and their continuing control of the former colonies. Maybe it's because these ills never ceased in the first place that they find no need for such reparations. The argument put forward is that the reparations will burden the taxpayers of the colonialist countries.

The governments in the developing world have found it politically correct to use the willing buyer–willing seller principle in going about the process of land reform. The government waits for a farmer to decide that he wants to sell his land at market value, and they then buy that farm at that price (using taxpayer money) and use the land for resettlement of landless peasants. The government isn't only limited in the number of farms that are available and suitable for resettlement, but it's limited by the budget available for such purposes as it's restricted by the extent to which it can tax its subjects in order to pay their former masters for the land that was robbed from the majority for no compensation. The principle of willing buyer–willing seller is a capitalist economy principle and can't be used to implement a distribution role, which is a socialist principle requiring sizeable intervention by government. The effect has been a gentle and lackadaisical land reform that, at the current rate, will take many centuries to reach the desired level of economic emancipation.

The powers that be seem to be held in a vice-like grip in an area that is sensitive, and they're under some form of duress and torture not to implement this urgent land reform.

The land reform that occurred in Zimbabwe and the subsequent suffering that attended its people, in the form of inflation, economic hardships, hunger, economic refugee problems, and political upheavals, are pointed as a warning to other developing nations that might flirt with the idea of land reform. The developing world is faced with a mounting need for land reform but is held at ransom by a cabal economic system that threatens to sting the life out of itself if ever such a process of land reform is implemented.

The taxpayers, by the sweat of their brows, have to buy their freedom from the oppressors who took it for nought from them. This policy, while absurd, is the policy that the colonial master countries will listen to. The same masters still control the economies of these countries, and hence the economic policies as well, and won't have any other policy implemented, as it affects their economic interests. The notion that these colonial masters ought to compensate and finance these land purchases isn't even entertained. Hence, we have a situation where the poor are being taxed to fund the purchase of an economic resource which is their own and which was appropriated by usurpation from them.

Restorative justice is a principle in which the offender, or descendants of the offender, participates in the restoration of and in the welfare of the victims. Instead of trying to obtain value and legal exactness from the offenders using legislative and market forces in transactions that are business as usual, restorative justice requires the participation of victims and offenders alike in leading and spearheading the process of restoration.

The legitimacy of current possessors of land may be established in tittle deed and at law, but it fails in the historical analysis. Their tenure is precarious and dependant on the patience of the landless majority and can be rendered useless by a mere change of legislation. Even if property rights are legitimate, they do allow for or don't protect against expropriation. The tittle to the land is threatened by the mere existence of a poor majority who think they have a right to the land owned by a minority.

The sooner these facts are clear in the understanding of the victims and the offenders, the better for everyone, especially the victims, who don't stand to benefit from an antagonistic approach. Were the offenders to lead the process of land reform, and were the victims to be engaged in a way as to make them emancipated, were those who today sabotage the processes of land reform to be at the forefront of advocating for it and reaching out to the victims for a process that won't only preserve the wealth of the current owning minority, but will also afford the not-have minority to generate wealth from their newfound opportunities, then land reform would result in increased wealth for the whole of the people involved. A more secure tenure would be established for those that hold land now, while the land thirst of the majority would be easily satisfied. Leaving land reform to a government is asking for and expecting too much from them. Governments aren't the best institutions to drive a process such as restorative justice, especially where money is involved, as they tend to be less efficient, more rigid, and bureaucratic.

Restorative justice looks at other rights, such as the right to liberty, life, etc., and it compares that to right such as property rights and comes to terms that ensure that a correct balance is struck. It fosters dialogue between victims and offenders and seeks to achieve the highest level of victim satisfaction as well as offender accountability, and economically should result in maximised wealth and welfare for all involved.

One example of restorative justice processes is the Truth and Reconciliation Commission (TRC) in South Africa. The commission was set up in post-apartheid South Africa to try and address the crimes and injustices committed during the apartheid era. The mandate was limited to finding the truth and the victims and perpetrators had an opportunity to come to the truth. Perpetrators would then ask, after giving their testimony, for forgiveness and amnesty from civil or criminal persecution. While it is dubbed as a restorative justice court, it however, failed to achieve the necessary justice and restoration, because it had a trade-off between truth and justice. Restoration and justice were sacrificed and the system was made to lean too much in favour of the perpetrators and the victims were not compensated in any way as a means of restoration. The victims did not feel that justice had been achieved and that restoration in any way, or to the victim's satisfaction, had been done.

Restorative initiatives should be peaceful approaches to problem solving and rights violations, and should seek to engage those who are harmed, and those who did the harm together with the affected communities, etc., in building partnerships and establishing mutual responsibility for such initiatives. It should seek to maximise the wealth and well-being of all involved rather than to engage in adversarial justice processes.

The criminal justice system is based on establishing the exact law that's been broken, who the offender is, and the amount of punishment to be inflicted accordingly. On the other hand, the truth and reconciliation processes that have ever happened only seek the truth and grant pardons for such truth. No restoration, no consulting is made to the victims if they've been redressed; no attention is paid to the grief and harm that might even continue to stalk them for the harm that overtook them. A mere talk show about the truth doesn't completely address the harm the victim and the community have had to bear. It's these shortcomings of these two systems that restorative justice builds on to be offender-and-victim centred and assist both within the community sphere. This means that the offender as well as the victim are engaged in trying to ensure that both justice and restoration are carried out. The offender not only corrected, but are involved in ensuring the victim is satisfied with the outcome. Both the victim and the offender work together to ensure that there is no repeat of the same in future.

The requirement for land reform for the emancipation of the landless is imperative and will be achieved in some way or another.

Are those who currently hold the control and the power over the land wise enough to heed the need for such reform? Should they now stand up and look at ways to initiate the process, assist the cause, and give ideas and advice on how to carry it out, they wouldn't only be held wise but would have shown themselves to be wise. The point of power and riches aren't to engage in the most self-indulgence and gratification, but rather to use that power and riches for the benefit of society—not in giving up the power or the riches, but in using them to uplift the poor and the powerless.

The capitalist mind, however, doesn't think in such fashion as it's based on survival of the fittest, strongest, and biggest. It crushes all competition, exploits the weak, and preys on the vulnerable. So the people have an issue at hand that seeks to spin out of control, which politicians are careful to be politically correct about; however, those in control don't care about the precariousness of their tittle and the decision makers are too scared to bite the bullet. The losers are the poor majority who will still remain landless and have to work the land for those who own it.

Whenever the question of land reform is discussed, the few landlords who currently own vast tracts of land point to the sizes of their operations and to the skills and knowledge required to carry out such grand enterprise, and they point out that no start-up farmer can achieve what they've achieved with the land. They point out that because of this reason, government or anyone else shouldn't ever dare take the land from them and give it to landless non-farmers. They also point out to the few examples of resettled farmers who are struggling to keep up with the demands of farming; they point out these as good examples of the sure failures that will result were land to be taken away from them.

This view isn't only myopic and ill advised, but it speaks of the arrogance of those who hold such a view. It's a historical fact that the farming of colonialism and later periods was heavily supported by government, and the financial institutions and chances of failure were minimal. It's also true that a knowledge and practice of so many years for the farm owners has made them better farmers than the resettled farmers. Shall we expect a perfect farmer of a new, infant farmer who's backed by an imperfect government support and who's ignored by the financial institutions, and most importantly who's closed off from lucrative markets by the established farming cartels? We can expect a child to fail, to make mistakes, because they are young and are bound to make mistakes as they learn about life and soon or latter they will begin to do well. Shall we break their spirits by sneering at them that they're not as good as the white, commercial farmers, or shall we not administer rebukes for mistakes that they should've not committed?

Encouragement should be made and discipline be inflicted, but to refuse to give them land, opportunities, and financial support on the basis that they're not as good as the others is a travesty of justice. A system that doesn't address the risks that threaten its survival adequately will eventually be forced to change, which will be more painful and more disruptive, as it will be carried out in a shorter time and in a less orderly manner, than should the risk have been addressed on time.

Example 4: Land to have and not to have it

> Genesis 47:1–12: 1 Then Joseph came and told Pharaoh, and said, "My father and my brethren, and their flocks, and their herds, and all that they have, are come out of the land of Canaan; and, behold, they're in the land of Goshen."
>
> 2 And he took some of his brethren, even five men, and presented them unto Pharaoh.

3 And Pharaoh said unto his brethren, "What is your occupation?" And they said unto Pharaoh, "Thy servants are shepherds, both we, and also our fathers."

4 They said moreover unto Pharaoh, "For to sojourn in the land are we come; for thy servants have no pasture for their flocks; for the famine is sore in the land of Canaan; now therefore, we pray thee, let thy servants dwell in the land of Goshen."

5 And Pharaoh spake unto Joseph, saying, "Thy father and thy brethren are come unto thee.

6 The land of Egypt is before thee; in the best of the land make thy father and brethren to dwell; in the land of Goshen let them dwell, and if thou knowest any men of activity among them, then make them rulers over my cattle."

11 And Joseph placed his father and his brethren, and gave them a possession in the land of Egypt, in the best of the land, in the land of Rameses, as Pharaoh had commanded.

12 And Joseph nourished his father, and his brethren, and all his father's household, with bread, according to their families.

Genesis 47:27 And Israel dwelt in the land of Egypt, in the country of Goshen; and they had possessions therein, and grew, and multiplied exceedingly.

Exodus 1:6: And Joseph died, and all his brethren, and all that generation.

7 And the children of Israel were fruitful, and increased abundantly, and multiplied, and waxed exceeding mighty; and the land was filled with them.

All Shall Be Equal before the Law!

In the discussion on economic structures in chapter 3 we've shown abundantly that the company stands in a more superior position at law than does an ordinary person. The company was shown to be a sacred cow, a no-go area, with a corporate veil, protecting the owner, beyond which no long arm of the law, nor shareholder, nor worker can reach. The courts, at common law, the government, by statute, and the professionals, by practice, hold the company as more esteemed, as more privileged, and as more important in an economy than an individual.

The tax systems of the present-day world, I've clearly shown in my discussion on taxation, are meant to tax the poor and the workers, while on the other hand the companies, the corporations, and the rich are hardly taxed. The taxation yoke is borne by the poor majority while the few who control the economy aren't taxed to the same extent. The contributions to the national budget revenue, I've shown, is, in the majority of economies, borne by the workers and individuals, through various taxes levied upon them by an unforgiving and unrelenting tax system. Companies, on the other hand, have allowances, tax breaks, favourable rates, and delayed payment and are allowed to deduct all expenses before calculating tax, giving them an unfair, unequal, unjustifiable advantage over the individual.

The economic structures and tax laws being used in the world, particularly the developing world, were handed down to the new nations by their former colonisers, and thanks to these people of great foresight, the worker is still colonised, oppressed, and yoked by the very colonialists which he or she went to war to free him- or herself from. It's not yet, Uhuru.

Poverty, Unemployment, and Crime

> "Overcoming poverty isn't a task of charity; it's an act of justice. Like slavery and apartheid, poverty isn't natural. It's man-made, and it can be overcome and eradicated by the actions of human beings. Sometimes it falls on a generation to be great. *You* can be that great generation. Let your greatness blossom."
> — Nelson Mandela

Creating Unemployment, Poverty, and Crime

In an equal-opportunity political economy society, one's future is determined by one's talents and efforts, and the economy works for every person who's determined to work hard. The systems in place in the current state of affairs are, on the contrary, militating actively for a few and against the majority. The economic system most governments have adopted for their economies is the capitalist, free-market, profit-driven system. It's a system that worships property rights and tramples on any other rights, be they of the majority or minority.

The system uses market forces of supply and demand to decide what to produce, and the same market forces determine who's willing and able to buy and sell goods and services; poor consumers are easily eliminated, and prices are determined as if by an invisible hand. The effect is inevitably to place the means of production in the hands of a very few who control the financial and economic resources. Economic opportunities are only available and accessible to as few hands as possible. These few people are in control of the economic soul, and everyone looks up to and waits upon them for every economic activity. They create production, jobs, and taxable income for the economy.

The role of government in a capitalist economy is an unenviable one, under pressure to create jobs for the majority of its subjects. The economic policies and programmes of government have, as a consequence, been made to give support to the few companies and the rich, who control the means of production and resources, for them to create jobs, wealth, and economic activity. Governments have put up incentive upon another, financial assistance, and every advantage afforded the big businesses in the hope that, in their good time, and they'll get bigger and feel the need to employ additional workers, thereby creating employment for the unemployed.

Governments have ignored the majority of their populations, having focused on a few capitalists, and have played a game of chance in the hope that the money they pump into these corporations through various incentives, will yield some employment.

Unemployment is something that government definitely has control over, and it should ensure that there's as little unemployment as possible. However, trying to create employment through a third party, especially a private business which the government doesn't control and which has different motives and intentions, won't achieve that objective of government. In order to create employment government has to create employers and the enabling environment and support for such new employers.

Secondly, capitalism is located in the major cities and economic hubs, and people are driven by force and by want to go to these cities and towns where they'll seek to obtain a living out of wages. Capitalism has thus tended to create a huge pool of labourers around its centres who are attracted by the opportunities of work that it offers, and the effect has been to create slums and poor neighbourhoods in which there's high unemployment, crime and other vices, and general poverty.

Unemployment in a capitalist system is rooted in the fact that there are limited or no available resources for the majority of the people to employ as they're concentrated in a few hands. Resources such as land and capital are placed in the control of market forces, and the government's role is to minimise its intervention and influence to allow these forces to create wealth, employment, and other desirable economic activity.

Capitalism by its nature isn't designed to ensure full or 100-percent employment at any time in the economy. Capitalism is based on concentrating people in a single or a few places. It's also built around concentrating resources in a few hands. Capitalism is meant to have the labour as dependent upon the system as possible by making them labourers and consumers reliant on the wages they receive. The profit motive of the capitalist doesn't give room for employee emancipation or development other than is necessary for the worker to carry out his or her duties or servitude more efficiently.

Because of the withdrawal of any other means of production from their grasp and being left with no other survival channel other than seeking employment from the capitalist, everyone who seeks to survive will head to the towns and cities to look for work. The effect is a crowded labour market where a large number aren't employed.

The capitalist sets up his or her business such that the worker earns his or her wage and hands it right back to the capitalist by buying items like rent, transport, and food from the same capitalist. In towns and cities, the worker is paid just enough to make him or her totally dependent on the employer. The employer controls almost every facet of the employee's life. There's no alternative for the employee to employment. The employee doesn't have enough spare time to engage in any other trade. The capitalist controls almost all trade that one can engage in. It would be inefficient to compete against the capitalist. The capitalist controls the transport, the market, and the finance and will hardly allow competition. The capitalist won't buy from small, upcoming traders, but he buys from fellow capitalists. Unemployment in the capitalist system is worsened by the fact that the doors to engage in alternative trades, other than wage labour, are closed, and the capitalist has got the keys in his or her pocket. The only competition to labour is machinery, and these the capitalist uses to eliminate labour and to maintain unemployment. The capitalist has the labourers enslaved to him or her by a total dependence and doesn't entertain any competition to price them from him- or herself. The capitalist uses his or her might to snuff it out in the budding those who manage to venture into any trade that might compete against the capitalist.

Democratic Political Economy

> "When a man is denied the right to live the life he believes in, he has no choice but to become an outlaw."
> — Nelson Mandela

The effect of the current system is to choke and retard growth of any form from the poor and the working class. The poverty and want that obtains in the squalor towns and cities is extreme and continuous. In contrast, the poor are occasionally exposed to a more affluent and luxurious-looking life in the not-so-far, low-density areas where the rich and affluent live, and the poor behold the items of luxury the rich flaunt frequently such as cars, houses, among others. The contrast is glaring and growing every day, and soon crime sets in as the only form of emancipation for the poor. Justification for such isn't easy to come by for those in dire poverty, and given that little hope exists for their exit from their current circumstances, they may choose to become outlaws. They consider it better to enjoy the fruits of crime for a season and suffer the effects than to suffer the condemnation of poverty for a lifetime.

I've already discussed how a system that creates extremes of poverty and riches is bound to fail as it sets itself in a destructive mode. The rich fight the poor off their riches. Crime and violence exists in greater proportion in those countries where there are the greatest disparities between the rich and the poor.

It's prudent for the rich in a society to work for the emancipation of the very poor. The best policing and security systems won't address the system problems of poverty and crime. Fighting crime (just like any other vice) should be linked to the root causes; crime is a symptom of a system that isn't functioning properly. Attending to the symptoms is an exercise in futility which will exhaust the system and worsen its entire functionality. Plugging the floodgates of crime requires attending to the problem that breeds crime.

The system has deprived the poor town dwellers the right to land and any other means of production; they're denied economic opportunities and are denied a choice of life. Poverty reign is at such a force that theirs is a fight and constant struggle for survival. The solutions lie in what has been denied these victims of a system that created them. Land, economic opportunities, an education, financial opportunities, etc., have been kept away from the reach of the poor, and the effect is a sure harvest of the seeds of want long sown.

IX

The Reformation

World Serve the Queen

The Reformation—a period generally regarded as officially starting in October 1517 by the publication, nailed on a door, of a list of the ninety-five theses by Martin Luther—had forerunners who had spoken and agitated about the need for such reform. The men and women who began the Reformation were honest and looking for the truth about salvation, in the midst of what was taught and practised at the time, which they weren't satisfied would guarantee their salvation.

The Reformation, while mainly a religious event, was a precursor to and indeed was the cause of a change of the political and economic set-up of the day. The church had civil powers, was the richest among a growingly poor majority, was taxing and requiring several payments from the people, and was the major player in whatever affected the welfare of the people.

In the period that followed the Reformation, new forms of nations were established and new forms of governments were constituted. The economic systems that spawned from the Reformation were predominantly free-market economies premised on the dislike of any central authority control on the daily activities and transactions and on economic resources. The type of political systems formed also ranged towards a semi-democratic political system in which the people were in one way or the other emancipated and afforded a say in the choice of leaders through voting and representation. Although absolute kings and queens and their kingdoms remained, the Reformation allowed them to have a say in the religious, legal, and economic choices of their subjects, a privilege which had been a prerogative of one central authority before the Reformation. In particular, the system of tribute, tax, and selling of indulgencies, with all the money going to the church in Rome, was ended by the Reformation, and a system that was impoverishing the rest of Europe was done away with.

One of the most intriguing results of the Reformation was the birth of the British Empire and its great influence on the rest of the world history that followed. The severance of ties with the church in Rome enabled the empire to have enough resources available for its merchants and other men of commerce to grow and expend the bounds and influence of the British Empire. The church had previously controlled the hugely agrarian land in the European continent, and with the Reformation, land was restored to the separate nations to be used for their interests under their various monarchies.

This empire began to influence much of the world through trade, colonisation, industry, and many other spheres, so much so that the English language became to be considered the world language and with that its laws, economics, and political culture was spread wherever it expanded. The slave trade, the industrial revolution, and the triangular trade between Europe, Africa, and the Americas all were largely controlled and greatly influenced by the British Empire. Thus the imperial support of the capitalists operating these trades and those championing the industrial revolution ensured that the world political economy had a visible British imprint. The British were in charge of the world political economy, and the political economy in turn served the British.

One by-product of the post-Reformation political system was the rise of special interest groups and lobbies. Money affords the bearer to wield political influence and the right to be heard. Capitalists emerging from the slave trade and the industrial revolution determined the type of government and the policies to be followed, and these were forced onto the majority by means necessary. One such example was the end of slavery, championed by the British not because of a sudden, newfound love and sympathy for the slave, but because it no longer suited the political economy of the day. It was no longer in the economic interest of the British Empire for the slave trade to continue as it was configured, so a moral cause for its abolition was sought to turn the tide against the pro-slave lobby.

The current political economics of the world are no different, and the foundation thereof was laid during the birth of capitalism. Such capitalism was and continues to be imperialist in nature, serving the interests of the king or queen and designed to channel all benefits to his kingdom or her queendom. The slavery, exploitation, and subjection characteristics are still present. The design to have all benefits channelled to the ruler's coffers and give all control and say to the ruler as well as the total dependence of the subjects to the mercies of the ruler are all present in their raw state. The world powers today are using a system of government designed mainly by the British and similar empires, for the benefit of the majesty and control of the territories and meant to channel all resources and benefits from throughout her vast empire to the step of her majestic throne. The rulers of the former colonies have not only upheld the queen's policies, but they continue to hold their people under the king or queen's rule by enforcing their economic policies, systems, and structures. These governments are surely oppressing their citizens for the empire's sake.

World serve our gracious Queen
Long live our noble Queen
World serve the Queen
Send her victorious
Happy and glorious
Long to reign over us
World serve the Queen

All lords and kings arise
Scatter her enemies
And make them fall
Confound their politics
Frustrate their knavish tricks
On Thee our hopes we fix
Queen save us all

Thy choicest gifts in store
On her be pleased to pour
Long may she reign
May she defend our laws
And ever give us cause
To sing with heart and voice
World serve the Queen

Not in this land alone
But be God's mercies known
From shore to shore

Lord make the nations see
That men should brothers be
And form one family
The wide world over

From every latent foe
From the assassins blow
God save the Queen
O'er her thine arm extend
For Britain's sake defend
Our mother, prince, and friend
God save the Queen

Freedom Again

"Though no longer a slave, he's in a thraldom grievous and intolerable, compelled to work for whatever his employer is pleased to pay him, swindled out of his hard earnings by money orders redeemed in stores, compelled to pay the price of an acre of ground for its use during a single year, to pay four times more than a fair price for a pound of bacon and to be kept upon the narrowest margin between life and starvation..."

—Life and Times of Frederick Douglass

The question of the poor and of the lower classes of the world hasn't been dealt with from the point of these folks who the rich and powerful look at with amused contempt and pity, but no thinking has been frankly done to establish the reason for the plight of the majority.

When in the bondage of slavery the slave worshipped freedom as divine and considered it the pinnacle and end of all his struggles. The African took to war and gave his life in liberation wars to free his people and declared the victory day a national holiday in which to always remember the past struggles. Freedom was sought as the end to all slavery, all prejudice, all problems, and all injustices.

Slavery ended by a ceremonial declaration, colonialism disappeared with the raising of new colourful flags, and apartheid was announced worldwide as dead. A few score years down the line, and the free slave is still groping for freedom just like those who were ululating for the end of colonialism are still longing for freedom. There's no freedom among the free; they're not free in freedom. Voting and democracy weren't the freedom envisaged by the poor and oppressed and they've to shout again the old cry for freedom.

The road to emancipation of the slave and the oppressed has been made a long and winding narrow path that should involve education, employment, enlightenment, and urbanisation, and refinement and a change of culture from one's own, to that of the rich and powerful. The poor are to work their way up through such means as would not reach fulfilment even in a lifetime. To emancipate a negro or an African under colonialism, we're told that we need to educate them first and train them in the skills and trades that will enable them to get employed. The education is substandard, the work is slavery dressed in a work suit, and the remuneration a pittance. They race on foot against those on horseback. The oppressor is way ahead as they've had headway of many years.

In theory, education is good, making one civilised, reasonable, and acceptable, but it's actually slow, it eliminates the weak and the poor. Turning the uneducated into learned workers is OK, but it falls short of bliss. Giving the poor alms, donations, and aid isn't only insulting and humiliating, it makes them disabled. Bliss is when the former slave and the poor are made capable and competitive, put on the path to success to make out their own paths to salvation.

It's always a matter of time before the freedom of the oppressed will become an urgent requirement. It's not a sustainable system that involves one oppressing the other, and before time, signs will begin to show that the oppressive system isn't working. The negative results of the system will soon begin to outweigh the benefits to the oppressor. The oppressor will seek to extend the status quo by means of his or her power and experience. The changes required to a failing system are inevitable, and the choice is between a timely correction and a belated forced adjustment. Colonialism, apartheid, and slavery were all profitable for a while but became toxic not only to the victims, but also to the masters, and while some sought to hold on to them, they soon let go one way or the other. It's a wise choice to prefer the least painful way out of a system that's outlived its benefits. The liberation of the majority from an oppressing minority is a risky delivery which requires a dedicated midwife.

The oppressor has on his side all the resources, machinery, and might that can be mustered by someone in a power position, and at stake are his economic interests. The colonised, enslaved, and the worker have nothing on their side other than the need to survive. Poor, ignorant, and inexperienced, the oppressed have to be freed from the claws of a cunning captor. Like a cat toying with mice, the captor has the advantage and will mercilessly mesmerise the victim to his or her demise.

The saviour of the people isn't found in a single individual with messianic status who will bring them deliverance on a platter, neither is it to be found in the liberation war hero who indeed laid his or her life for the masses and risked his or her being for the children of the nation. It's not out of the gun barrel that it will emerge, and we won't find it in a revolution of the Bolshevik sort. The enemy uses the ignorance of the masses to oppress them and the blindness of the myopic to be ahead of them. He or she uses the mind to control the native into his or her ways, to bridle the native in the harness, and to trick the native into serving the enemy.

Economic Interests

Are the oppressed to look to their oppressors for a saviour, seeing the oppressor is powerful, experienced, and knows what is best for the oppressed? Or are they to seek a saviour among their lot, blind leaders to lead them to the Promised Land?

Colonialism was mostly overthrown by liberation wars, fought by poorly armed guerrilla fighters who were willing to die at the hands of the more advanced armies of the colonialists. The colonialists were protecting their economic interests, and it was only at the assurance of the safety of such interests that they yielded their political powers. They pointed to the lack of experience in power as the reason the oppressed weren't able to be in that position.

Those who supported slavery were quick to point out that allowing the slave to go free wouldn't only affect their own economic interest, but would also affect the welfare of everyone else as things produced by free slave labour would increase in price. They also argued that the slave is better off a slave than as free, as slavery offered him or her a chance to have something to occupy his or her time and assures the slave of food and shelter. Left alone, ignorant, and without any trade skill, they argue, the slave would be unemployed and worse off.

Their gruel by right

The worker is entitled to their salaries and wages. At least ninety percent of their salaries and wages, after income tax, after inflation, after property taxes, tolls, sales taxes, and all other taxes.

A worker is entitled to their salary by right and without it being subjected to deductions by the government which amount to more than ten percent.

The right to equality at law, at tax, at opportunities and at power. Every citizen, whether corporate or incorporate, should be allowed an equal standing at all laws, including business laws, tax laws and civil laws, and an equal chance of success and opportunities. The right to a fair tax system that does not widen the gap between the rich and the poor.

A right to economic and legal structures that work in their favour and that are fair and just in their operation. The right to participate in the choice of such systems and the right to be consulted when they are changed in ways that will affect the wealth of the worker.

The right to sound money and to a stable currency. The worker should be remunerated in a currency that they have faith in and that will not be manipulated in some ways to diminish the value thereof. The employment agreements should be denominated in a manner that preserves the salary against inflation, against currency value loss, and deliberate weakening of the currency through printing of money and other such shenanigans.

The right to a properly sized government in line with the ten percent tax maximum. No government should impose themselves in a greater financial burden than the fair and reasonable taxes can sustain. The size of government should be as the taxes can afford and nothing more. A government that overspends should look for funding elsewhere and in ways that do not erode the wealth of the citizens.

The poor should not be discriminated against in matters of interest rates, credit allocation, and risk profiling. Setting interest rates in discriminatory fashion and on subjective basis should not be practiced. The charging of higher interest rates to perceived riskier people and lower rates to less riskier people is blatant discrimination and should be banned from civilised societies.

Every person born to a nation has a right to the wealth thereof by birth. The land, the opportunities, the employment available therein is by right belonging to all citizens. No few individuals should seek by law, by power or other means to deprive others of these. Every effort should be made to ensure that the citizens enjoy in the greatest and fairest measure such benefits in their lifetime.

Matigari

Ngugi wa Thiong'o's *Matigari*, (Heinmann 1989), is a political story written in parable form, of a former liberation war fighter who returns to his land (an unnamed African country) ready to lay down his weapons and "trade them for the belt of peace." Matigari, emerging from the forest long after the war has ended, buries his war gun at the foot of a tree and goes in search of the fruits of the victory. To his chagrin, he finds that despite gaining independence, his people are still dispossessed and being exploited by their corrupt leaders that houses are still in the hands of the Europeans and their native equivalent, and that at the black factory workers are still at the mercy of foreign investors. The masses are fed with propaganda and imbued with foreign influences in every facet of life. Matigari then has to contend not only with the former oppressors but also with the new oppressors in the form of sell-outs who are now in the trappings of power and using it to oppress their own people while they seek applause from their puppet masters. The government is led by former war comrades of Matigari who've since sold out the masses for political interests and business interests, manifested through corruption, bribery, and respecting businesses ahead of the people.

In *Matigari*, the saviour disappears without anyone knowing what happened to him, whether he's dead or alive, or where he is. He dies, or does he? He's killed, or is he? Where is the one seeking for truth and justice? What is the point of the saviour disappearing among the people and the bushes before delivering the people? Did Ngugi wa Thiong'o miss the plot? Are we hopeless, without a saviour? Whom are we to follow then, and who shall show us the way? A great orator maybe, a leader, a hero who will think for us and speak for us against our oppressors, someone who cares about us and who has our interest at heart.

Matigari need not be dead, unless he be dead in us. Who is Matigari? He is the slave that seeks freedom, the worker hoping for emancipation, and the poor man embittered by broken promises of salvation. A bull yoked to the plough longing for the freedom of the open green fields, or a herd boy draped in fine clothes and shoes, longing for the countryside and the wild fruits. Where is Matigari? Son of the Soil slaving it out in the concrete jungle, caged in an economic zoo.

Redemption Songs

Voices, loud and quiet, distant and near, have started to question the democracy, the freedom, and the liberty that have failed to deliver on promises. One has to look at the songs, poetry, and literature of the oppressed and of the colonised to hear these voices. There are the "House of Hunger," "God's Bits of Wood," "Waiting for the Rain," and "The Grass is Singing," and the singer has been crying, "Not Yet, Uhuru."

The economic systems of the world are outdated and are unfairly skewed and favoured towards the powerful and the rich. The economic structures are no better, and the money systems work to exploit the poor. Inflation takes away silently the value out of the currencies, and high taxation is set by the government upon the people as a goblin over the cursed and sucks the lifeblood out of the workers and everyone else. Governments spin debts of astronomical amounts upon the population, and they spend most of the tax revenue on helping established businesses and ensuring concentration of resources, opportunities, and financial power in a few hands and on the other side poverty, unemployment, and exploitation of the majority. The government leaders have turned the hope of freedom into a satire of *Animal Farm* proportions, and there's no Matigari in sight. What shall you do?

Redemption Song

(Writer: Bob Marley, from the album Uprising (Label: Island/Tuff Gong. Producers: Bob Marley/Chris Blackwell)
Old pirates, yes, they rob I,
Sold I to the merchant ships,
Minutes after they took I
From the bottomless pit.
But my hand was made strong
By the hand of the Almighty.
We forward in this generation
Triumphantly.
Won't you help to sing
These songs of freedom?
'Cause all I ever have:
Redemption songs,
Redemption songs.

Emancipate yourselves from mental slavery.
None but ourselves can free our minds.
Have no fear for atomic energy,
'Cause none of them can stop the time.
How long shall they kill our prophets,

While we stand aside and look? Ooh!
Some say it's just a part of it,
We've got to fulfil the book.

Won't you help to sing
These songs of freedom?
'Cause all I ever have:
Redemption songs,
Redemption songs,
Redemption songs.

Emancipate yourselves from mental slavery.
None but ourselves can free our minds.
Wo! Have no fear for atomic energy,
'Cause none of them-a can-a stop-a the time.
How long shall they kill our prophets,
While we stand aside and look?
Yes, some say it's just a part of it,
We've got to fulfil the book.

Won't you help to sing
These songs of freedom?
'Cause all I ever had:
Redemption songs,
All I ever had,
Redemption songs,
These songs of freedom,
Songs of freedom.